To
Kathy

Contents

Preface

This book explores all the major features of modern FORTRAN in a non-technical, easy-to-understand manner.

The author assumes the student has had no previous exposure to data processing or to a programming language. Avoiding areas that involve an in-depth knowledge of mathematics or of other scientific subjects, the book concentrates on the language itself. Hundreds of examples and worked-out programs are given that illustrate the principles discussed. While simple, the examples and exercises are educational and provide a foundation upon which a student can build when required to solve problems in the classroom or in industry.

While the book demands little knowledge in the area of mathematics and science, it is desirable that the student have, at least, a slight familiarization with algebra and trigonometry.

The text is suitable for a one or two-semester course in programming in junior college or in freshman courses in four-year schools. The book is also suitable for use by those who must learn FORTRAN on their own without an instructor.

The author wishes to express appreciation to Mrs. Freda A. Allen for her skillful work in the preparation of the manuscript. To my wife, Katie Worth, goes an extra measure of appreciation for her valuable assistance.

Thomas Worth

Non-Technical FORTRAN

CHAPTER 1

Introduction

HISTORY

A computer is a remarkable machine that has the ability to process data with almost incredible speed and accuracy. Consider, for example, the fact that a computer can perform in *one second* the work that would require a clerk *several years* to duplicate. The clerk would have to work day and night during this time without a break. Equally impressive is the fact that the work of the computer would almost surely be error-free while that of the clerk would be riddled with errors.

Still, a computer is not a magical device. It has no intelligence, no imagination, no intuition. The work that it does with such fantastic speed and accuracy has to be planned ahead of time by a human. In short, a computer can do nothing on its own. A human is the guiding force behind the spectacular feats that a computer appears to accomplish.

Humans must have a means by which they may communicate with a computer. They may not speak to it since computers have no ears; they may not give it handwritten notes since computers have no eyes. True, experiments have been made in these two areas. Some day computers may be able to see, hear and understand, but that day is still far into the future.

How then, may a person tell a computer what it is to do to solve a problem? There are two common methods. The older of the two methods requires a person to punch computer-understandable instructions upon data processing cards. These cards are fed to a computer in such a way that the machine mechanically or optically senses the positions of the holes and thus understands what is punched. The newer of the two methods allows computers and humans to communicate via terminals that look like typewriters. Ordinary telephone lines connect these terminals with computers. In this text, we will discuss both methods of communicating with a computer. The former method, using punched cards, is called "batch"; the latter, using terminals, is called "timesharing".

Today, whether people use a computer in the batch mode or in the timesharing mode, they must use a language which is understandable to the computer. Over the years, many computer languages have been developed for this purpose. The most widely used of these languages are COBOL, PL/I, ALGOL, BASIC, and FORTRAN. Each of these languages has its advantages and disadvantages. For example, COBOL is an ideal language for use in business data processing, PL/I is a flexible language for both business and scientific data processing, ALGOL is the favorite of many for scientific work, and BASIC is an easy-to-learn and easy-to-use, but somewhat limited language, for general purposes.

FORTRAN's forte is its flexibility and universality for scientific problems. It is the oldest of the languages mentioned above and perhaps the best known wherever computing is done.

FORTRAN had its beginning in 1955. With IBM's support, a group of computer users developed the specifications for a new language which was to assist relatively inexperienced persons in planning solutions to mathematical, scientific, and general data processing problems. The name FORTRAN was given to the new language, the name being derived from the beginning letters of the words <u>For</u>mula <u>Tran</u>slator.

FORTRAN was designed to accept English words in special ways. Some of those English words were (and still are) READ, PRINT, IF, GO TO, DIMENSION, DO, CONTINUE, STOP, FORMAT. The original FORTRAN vocabulary had less than two dozen words.

When FORTRAN was first invented, it was simply called FORTRAN. Later, as it was improved, the language became known as FORTRAN I, FORTRAN II, and finally as FORTRAN IV. A FORTRAN V has been under development for some years but has not yet been released.

FORTRAN has always been designed to be "upwards compatible". This means that a machine that understands a later version of FORTRAN should be able to process a program written in an earlier version. This objective has not always been accomplished completely, but has been achieved to a major degree. The inverse property is not available. That is, a FORTRAN IV program cannot be processed by a computer that understands only FORTRAN I or FORTRAN II.

Nowadays, most general-purpose computers being built and sold, do understand FORTRAN IV. In fact, many FORTRAN's offer extentions which go beyond the specifications of FORTRAN IV. Purchasers of computer systems demand these modern FORTRAN's with extensions. The term FORTRAN IV, itself, is disappearing. Modern FORTRAN systems are simply named FORTRAN, and that is the term we'll use in this text.

BATCH

We said earlier that there are two methods for using a computer. The two methods (modes) are "batch" and "timesharing". In batch mode, this is the sequence of events:

Step 1 - Problem Awareness

The user becomes aware of a problem. He or she gives the problem thorough consideration to determine whether it is a candidate for computer solution.

If not, the person employs whatever other method is most appropriate.

Step 2 - Problem Becomes Candidate For Computer Solution

The user comes to the conclusion that a computer can be used to solve the problem. This person has at least a rough idea of how the computer is to be employed.

Step 3 - Flowcharting

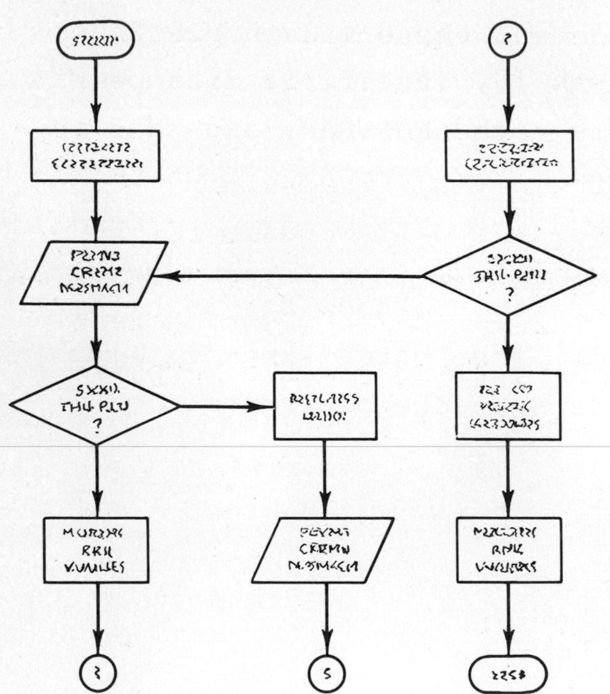

The user begins developing a flowchart to aid in the problem solution. We'll have more to say about flowcharts later.

Step 4 - FORTRAN Programming

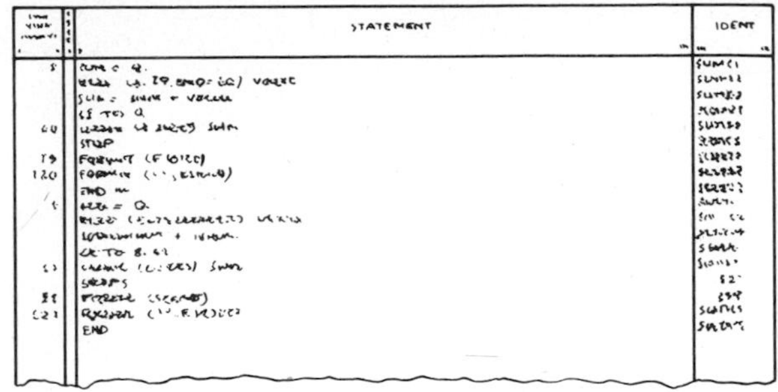

The user writes instructions in the FORTRAN language upon a FORTRAN coding form. The process of writing FORTRAN instructions is called "programming". The coded instructions become a FORTRAN "program". The person who writes a program is called a "programmer".

Step 5 - Source Deck is Punched

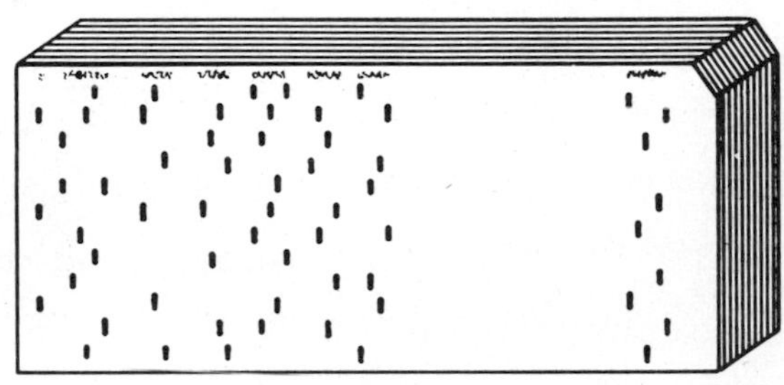

The FORTRAN coding form is delivered to a keypunch operator. The keypunch operator punches a data processing (Hollerith) card for every line coded upon the FORTRAN coding form. The keypunch operator uses a machine which looks like an overgrown typewriter. The machine is called a "keypunch" or "card data recorder". The deck of cards which results from the keypunch operation is called the "source deck". The program punched upon the source deck is called the "source program".

Step 6 - Input Data is Prepared

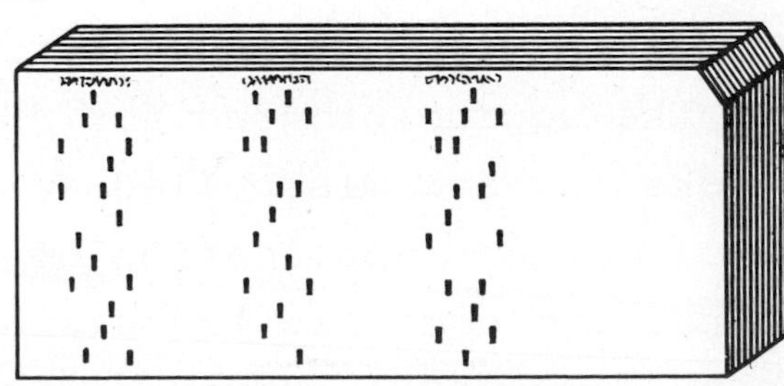

The programmer must provide input data for the source program. Often, though not always, input data is punched upon data processing cards. The programmer punches those cards or has a keypunch operator punch them.

Step 7 - Job Control Language (JCL) Cards are Prepared

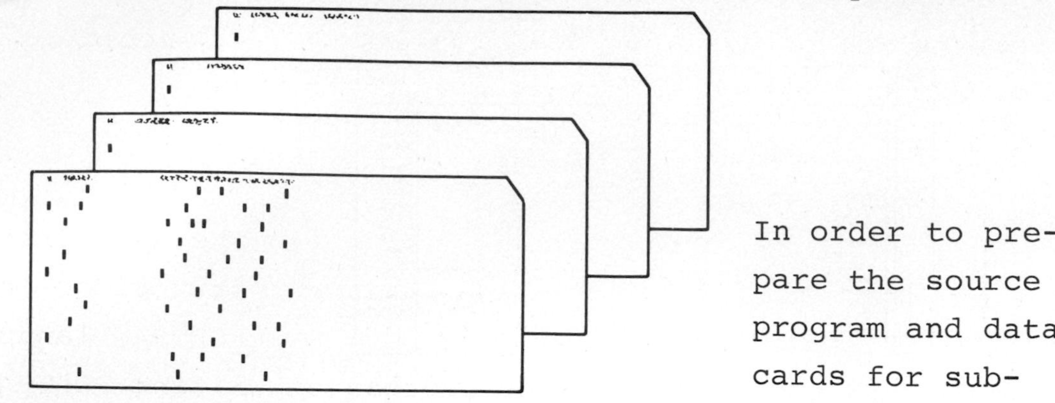

In order to prepare the source program and data cards for submission to the computer, the user must punch a few more cards called Job Control Language (JCL) cards. These cards are not FORTRAN language cards but cards required by the computer being used. JCL cards enable a user to communicate directly with the computer. Certain facts that the computer needs to know, such as the user's name and address, the charge number, the name of the programming language, etc., must be given before a job can be processed. The combined deck of source cards, data cards and JCL cards may now be submitted to the computer.

Step 8 - Compilation

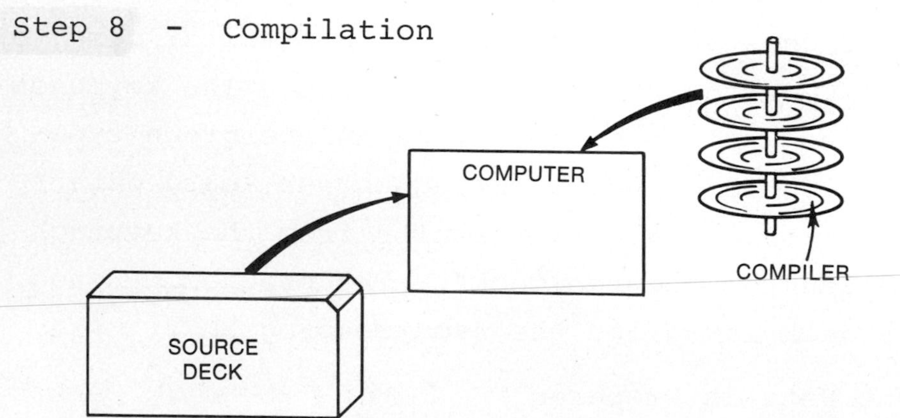

The combined decks from Step 7 are submitted to the computer for a process called "compilation". During this process, the computer checks the source program for *obvious* errors. All the computer looks for are misspelled words, incorrect punctuation, and the incorrect application of FORTRAN rules. If no errors are found, the computer translates (converts) FORTRAN instructions to computer language. Computer language consists of only two characters, zeroes and ones.

If errors are found, the processing of the program ends

promptly. The programmer receives a report that tells what errors were detected. The programmer must correct those errors and make another attempt to compile.

Step 9 - Execution

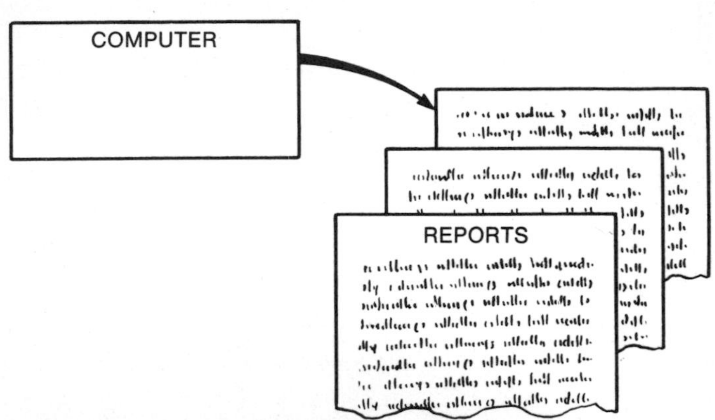

If no errors are detected during compilation, the computer begins to solve the original problem. Answers are generated for the programmer's inspection.

Step 10 - Debugging

Before accepting computer results, the programmer must check the reasonableness of the answers given by the computer. The process of ferreting out errors and correcting them is called "debugging". The programmer may have given the computer instructions which were accepted by the computer because they were *technically* correct, but which were *logically* incorrect. Only a thorough, thoughtful study of the computer results can convince the programmer that the results should be accepted.

Step 11 - Documentation

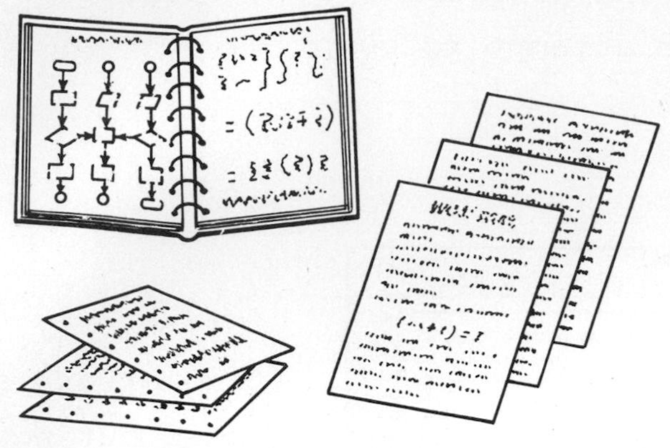

The programmer should not consider a job complete until he or she has documented the job completely in a formal or informal report. The report should include the equations that were used, the flowcharts, the FORTRAN coding, and all the other details that will enable another person, at some later date, to understand how the problem was solved. There will undoubtedly be a day in the future when someone will need to have this information. If it is not available, much difficulty may arise in trying to reconstruct how the problem was originally solved.

BATCH SUMMARY

While the eleven steps involved in batch processing may, at first, sound complex, the steps are not difficult to follow. Once mastered, a programmer will proceed through the eleven steps without giving them a second thought.

TIMESHARING

In the timesharing mode a programmer follows these steps:

Step 1 - Dialing up

The programmer picks up an ordinary phone and dials the computer's telephone number. Hearing a high-pitched tone through the receiver, the user knows that he or she is connected to the distant computer.

Step 2 - Becoming connected

The user places the receiver in a special "cradle" located upon a typewriter-like terminal. The receiver is snapped firmly into place.

Step 3 - Entering the program

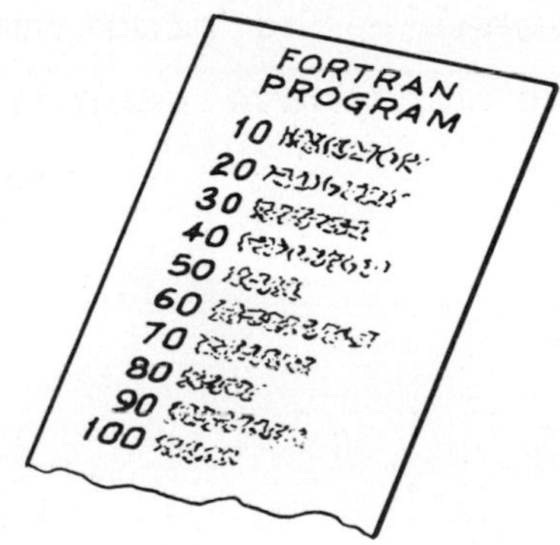

The distant computer and the programmer begin a "conversation". In this communication, the computer validates the user, then permits the person to type (or enter through paper tape) a FORTRAN program. (Later in this text, full details will be given concerning how this task is actually accomplished.) The programmer then directs the computer to execute (run) the program.

Step 4 - Debugging

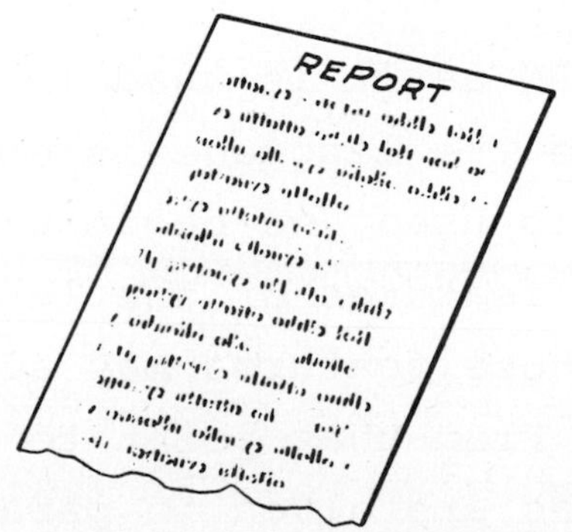

The computer gives the required output by typing it upon the user's terminal. The user may then inspect those results. If satisfied, the user may disconnect (hang up the phone) or go to Step 5.

If the user wants to make changes, he or she enters those changes and requests another execution. This procedure may continue for as long as the user wishes.

Step 5 - Saving a program

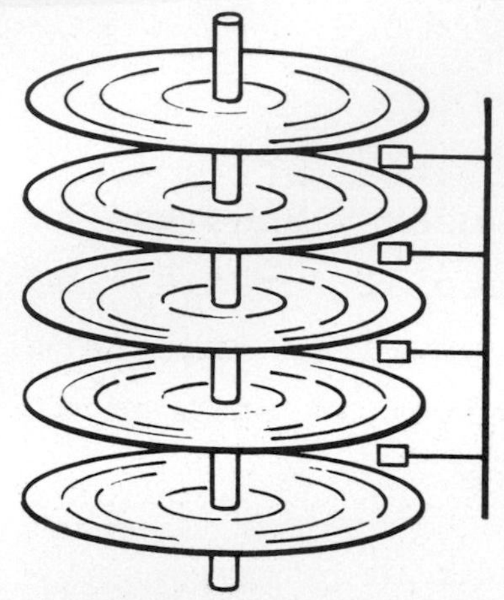

The user may request the computer to save the program at the computer site. This is done so that the user may retrieve the program at a later time. This step is optional - the programmer may not want to save the program once results have been obtained.

Step 6 - Documentation

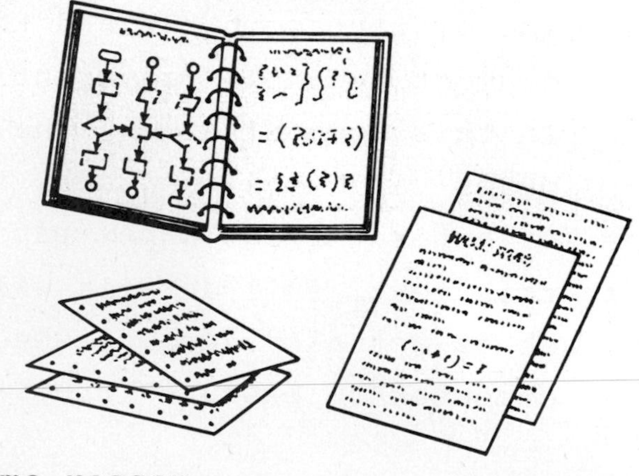

The user documents the job in the same way that a batch programmer performs the task, and for the same reason.

PLAN OF THIS BOOK

In this book, we present FORTRAN as it is used in both the batch and timesharing modes. Since the language is essentially the same regardless of which mode is used, we begin with the batch mode. Then, when sufficient features of the language have been discussed, we show how those features may also be employed in the timesharing mode. From that point to the end of the text, discussions of features are given in parallel for both batch and timesharing modes.

EXERCISES AND PROBLEMS

1. Give two differences between the way a human solves a complex mathematical problem and the way that a computer accomplishes the task.
2. What are the two modes that persons may use in communicating with a computer?
3. What does the term "upwards compatible" mean?
4. In what year was FORTRAN invented?
5. How many steps are there in the development of a "batch" FORTRAN program?
6. How many steps are there in the development of a "timesharing" FORTRAN program?
7. According to this text, is there a great difference between batch and timesharing FORTRAN?
8. What is a FORTRAN program?
9. What is a "source" deck?
10. What are JCL cards?
11. What is meant by the term "compilation"?
12. Why is the documentation of a program important?
13. What is meant by the term "debugging"?
14. Why might a programmer wish to save a program developed while operating in the timesharing mode?
15. A typical computer requires ten microseconds (10/1,000,000 of a second) to do a multiplication problem like this one.

$$\begin{array}{r} 89645394 \\ \times \underline{46305365} \end{array}$$

    If it takes a human ten minutes to work out the same problem, how many times faster is a computer over the human?

CHAPTER 2

Getting Started

STATEMENTS

In the batch mode, FORTRAN programs are written in the form of "statements". A statement is an instruction to the computer. Some representative statements are

```
      P=(R+S) * (T-V)
      IF (W-(A*B)/D) 9,4,17
      READ (5,18,END=40) L,K,F
      WRITE (6,20) DEL,QUAN
   25 FORMAT (1X,3F10.2)
```

The above statements are not to be construed as a portion of any actual program. They are independent statements presented here merely to give an idea of what FORTRAN statements look like. You should not be concerned if you do not understand what they mean. You aren't expected to understand them at this time.

FORTRAN statements are written upon a form called a FORTRAN coding form. Figure 2-1 shows an *actual* FORTRAN program written upon a coding form. Though the program is simple, it is one which, if presented to a computer for execution, would actually run.

FORTRAN forms are divided into columns - 80 columns across. Make sure that you place only one FORTRAN character per column. (In FORTRAN, the space is also considered a character.) When you code letters of the alphabet, use capitals.

You are not expected to understand at this time what the example program does. (For the curious, we might say that the program sums the values punched upon a deck of data cards.)

STATEMENT NUMBER (1–5)	CONT (6)	STATEMENT (7–72)	IDENT (73–80)
		SUM = 0.	SUMS1
8		READ (5,79,END=60) VALUE	SUMS2
		SUM = SUM + VALUE	SUMS3
		GØ TØ 8	SUMS4
60		WRITE (6,120) SUM	SUMS5
		STØP	SUMS6
79		FØRMAT (F10.0)	SUMS7
120		FØRMAT (' ',F12.2)	SUMS8
		END	SUMS9

Figure 2-1

Do study, though, the organization of the program. Each line written upon the coding form is called a "statement". There are nine statements in the program. Each statement represents an instruction to the computer. Observe that statements begin at column 7. They may actually begin anywhere to the right of column 7, but column 7 is the normal starting position. *Do not go past column 72 when you code FORTRAN statements.*

STATEMENT NUMBERS

Some statements include statement numbers. These numbers are arbitrarily selected by programmers and do not have to be in any particular sequence. The fact that statement numbers do not have to be in any particular sequence, may come as a surprise. The reason is that statement numbers are not used to sequence statements but merely to identify certain ones; to act as labels for them. Any conveniently-selected statement numbers will serve this purpose but, of course, for the sake of neatness and regularity, statement numbers should be selected so that they are coded in increasing sequence.

The smallest statement number that may be used is "1" and the largest is "99999". Every statement *may* be given a statement number should the programmer care to provide it; however, in actual practice, only a relatively few statements actually require them. As we go along, we'll show which statements *must* have statement numbers and which need not. When statement numbers are given, they may appear on the coding form *anywhere* between columns 1 and 5. In a program there must not be any duplicate statement numbers.

Spacing within statements is flexible. This means that you may place as many blanks between statement elements as you please. Extra blanks will be ignored. You can code statements neatly in whatever manner pleases you. In Figure 2-2, for example, statement 8 is interpreted by the computer in exactly the same way regardless of how it is written.

STATEMENT NUMBER (1–5)	CONT (6)	STATEMENT (7–72)	IDENT (73–80)
8		READ (5,9,END=60) VALUE	
8		READ (5,9, END=60) VALUE	
8		READ(5,9,END=60)VALUE	

Figure 2-2

In FORTRAN programming, there are only a few situations where spacing must be provided in a rigorous manner. These instances involve only certain kinds of FORMAT statements. We'll discuss these rigorous spacing requirements when we discuss FORMAT's. For the present, feel free to write FORTRAN statements and statement numbers neatly in whatever form pleases you.

CONTINUATION FIELD

If a statement cannot be written entirely on one line, the continuation column in the FORTRAN coding form is used to indicate that a statement is to be continued. In this text, very few statements are so long that they have to be continued. Later in the text there are examples of how continuations are indicated.

IDENTIFICATION

There are eight columns on the FORTRAN coding form (73-80) that may be used for any identification purpose that the programmer wishes to employ. "Identification" may be the name of the program, the programmer's name, or possibly the programmer's location. Also, sequence numbers may be given in the identification field. The identification field is not used to a great extent by programmers and we will not emphasize it in this text.

FORTRAN CHARACTERS

When you write FORTRAN statements, keep in mind that keypunch operators are not mind readers. They can't distinguish between l's and I's, zeroes and oh's, 5's and S's, 2's and Z's, etc., unless you write these characters clearly and unambiguously. Usually, keypunch operators do not understand FORTRAN so they will not be able to interpret what you intend when the formation of your characters is not clear.

In Figure 2-3 you can see all the characters that may be used in FORTRAN. Try to write your statements using the forms illustrated.

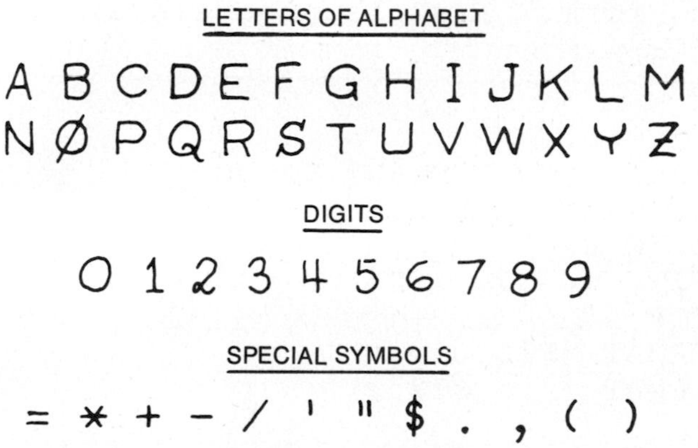

LETTERS OF ALPHABET

A B C D E F G H I J K L M
N Ø P Q R S T U V W X Y Z

DIGITS

0 1 2 3 4 5 6 7 8 9

SPECIAL SYMBOLS

= * + - / ' " $. , ( )

Figure 2-3

The space (blank) is also considered a FORTRAN character. Normally, blanks are ignored by FORTRAN but there are times when the presence or absence of blanks in a statement is important. If one or more blanks are important in the way that a statement is written, we'll indicate individual blanks by the small letter "b" with a slash through it.

Here's an example:

```
30  FORMAT (11HƀENDƀOFƀJOB)
```

When we write an example in the way shown above, it will be clear that it doesn't matter how many blanks there are between "30" and "FORMAT" or between "FORMAT" and "(11H.......)" but that it *is* important how the blanks are positioned within the parentheses.

To illustrate how an output line is printed, we give the illustration shown in Figure 2-4.

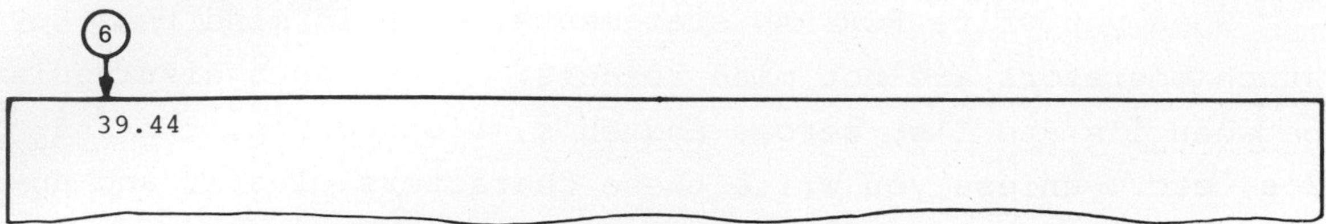

Figure 2-4

The illustration shows that the "3" appears at print position 6 on the output paper.

In this text, we give many examples of how complete programs or portions of programs are written. We usually do not show the coding form. Example programs are often shown this way:

```
      SUM = 0.
    8 READ (5,79,END=60) VALUE
      SUM = SUM + VALUE
      GO TO 8
   60 WRITE (6,120) SUM
      STOP
   79 FORMAT (F10.0)
  120 FORMAT (' ',F12.2)
      END
```

You should assume that statements begin in column 7 and that statement numbers lie between columns 1 and 5. Where the slashed small letter "b" is *not* shown, you may assume that spacing within the example statements is not important.

As an example of how a FORTRAN statement is punched upon a source card, consider the FORTRAN statement:

```
   23 READ (5,8,END=50) A,B,C
```

Written upon a coding form, the statement appears as shown in Figure 2-5 on the following page.

STATE-MENT NUMBER 1 5	CONT 6	STATEMENT 7 72	IDENT 73 80
		other FORTRAN statements	
23		READ(5,8,END=50)A,B,C	

Figure 2-5

Punched upon a card, the statement appears as shown in Figure 2-6.

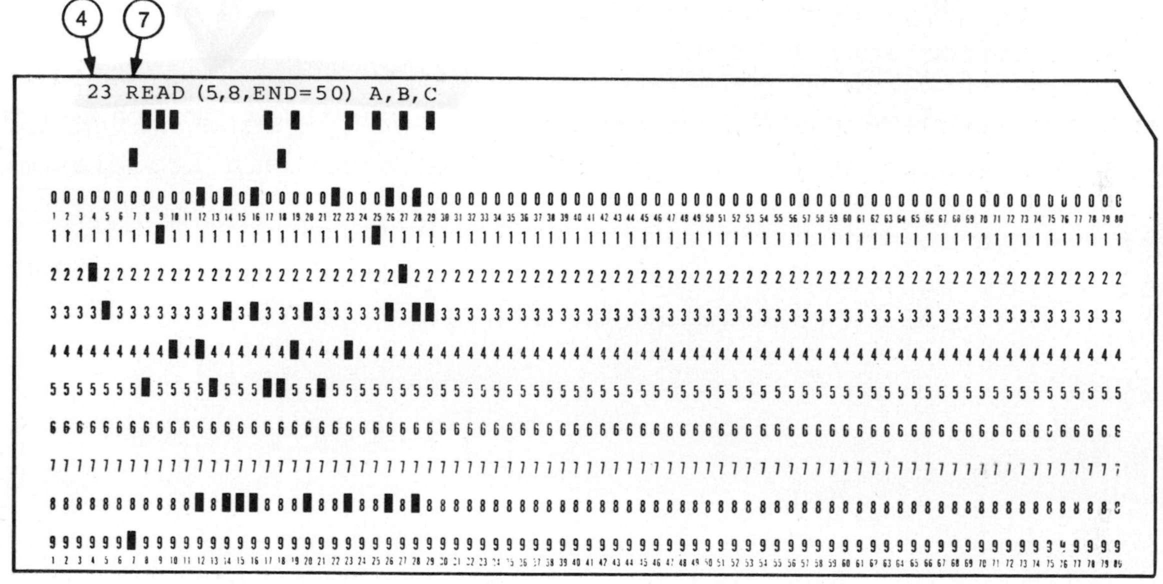

Figure 2-6

The characters on the card are punched in exactly the same columns that they appear on the coding form.

EXERCISES AND PROBLEMS

1. What is a FORTRAN "statement"?

2. Fill in the blank: FORTRAN statements may be written between columns 7 and 72, inclusive.

3. What is the smallest statement number you may use in a FORTRAN program? The largest? 1 9999

4. May there be duplicate statement numbers in a FORTRAN program? NO

5. Do statement numbers have to be in numerically increasing sequence in a FORTRAN program?

6. Is it permissible to give statement numbers to all FORTRAN statements?

7. What general comment can you give concerning spacing within FORTRAN statements?

8. For what purpose may the "identification" field be used in a FORTRAN coding form?

9. A FORTRAN program consists of 200 coded statements. How many punched cards would you expect to find in the corresponding source deck?

10. When coding a FORTRAN program, why should a programmer take extra care in distinguishing between certain troublesome characters?

CHAPTER 3

The ASSIGNMENT Statement

THE BASIC DATA PROCESSING CYCLE

Many data processing problems, whether they be business or scientific, are solved using a standard technique. The technique involves the employment of these steps in a computer program:

1. Obtain some data from within the program or from an external source such as magnetic tape or punched cards.

2. Process the data by altering its form or by performing required calculations.

3. Provide some output such as a paycheck, a line printed upon a report or some information recorded on an external medium such as magnetic tape.

The three steps of the procedure are then repeated over and over until there are no more data available in the data source.

Pictorially, the procedure can be illustrated as shown in Figure 3-1 on the following page.

The illustration gives an example of a "flowchart". A flowchart is a pictorial plan which shows how a problem is to be solved. The flowchart may be very general as the one shown on the following page, or it may be minutely detailed. In a later chapter, we will discuss the preparation of flowcharts in much more detail.

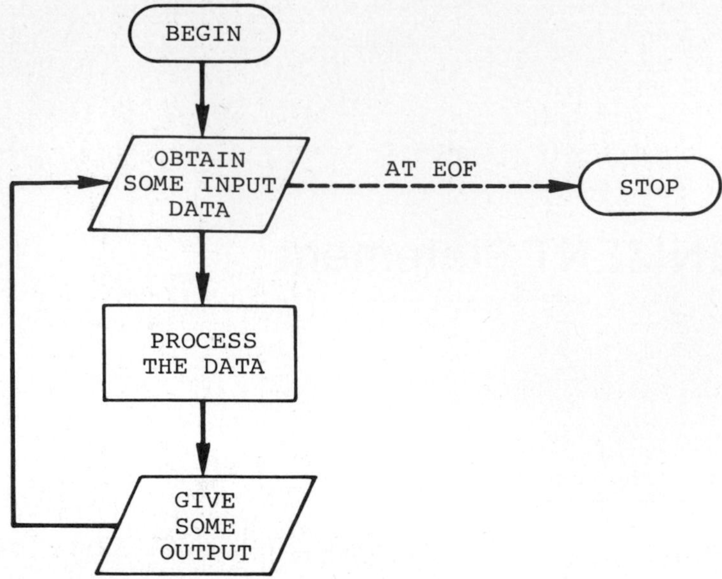

Figure 3-1

In the flowchart shown above, the code EOF means "end of file". When the source of the data being processed becomes exhausted, it is said that there is an "end of file". At-end-of-file times many data processing problems are considered complete and the computer program giving the problem solution ceases executing.

In this chapter, we concern ourselves with Step 1 of the basic data processing cycle, specifically the portion of Step 1 which refers to the obtaining of data from *within* the program itself.

THE ASSIGNMENT STATEMENT

Data may be built right into a FORTRAN program by the use of "assignment statements". Here are some examples of assignment statements:

```
F = (A+GAR)/3.7
DEL = 43.78
QDC = -3.3
TEMR = TEMR+AVAL
```

An assignment statement is a FORTRAN statement which has three parts. Study the first assignment statement shown above. It has these three parts:

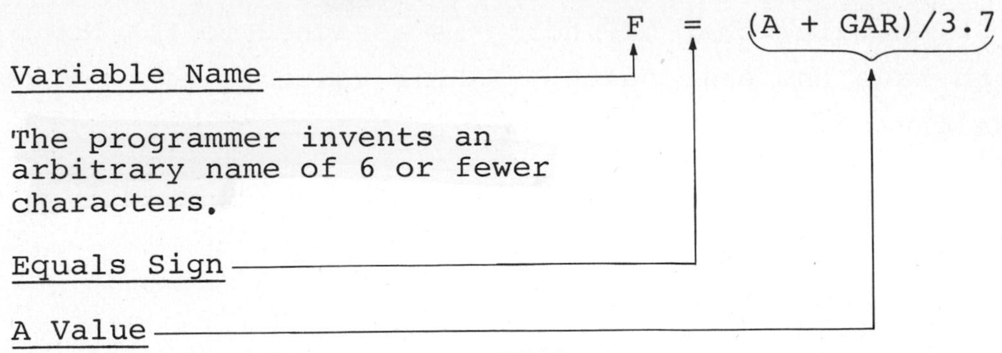
F = (A + GAR)/3.7
Variable Name
The programmer invents an arbitrary name of 6 or fewer characters.
Equals Sign
A Value

A value is given to the right of the equals sign.

The value that is shown at the right of the equals sign may be a number such as "3.5" or "-3.249"; it may be a variable name such as "XL" or "SIM"; or it may be an expression such as "(W+X)*(W-A)" or "B*B".

An assignment statement is referred to as such because the value shown on the right hand side of the equals sign is given to (assigned to) the name shown on the left hand side of the equals sign.

Assignment statements may or may not have statement numbers depending upon the logic behind how the statement is being used. The above example statement does not have a statement number.

A programmer tells the computer about a value that he or she wishes to use by writing an assignment statement. Suppose, for example, the program is to use a depreciation rate of 12½%. To define this rate into a program, the programmer may give this statement:

```
DEPRAT = .125
```

The value ".125" is assigned to the variable name "DEPRAT". That name will continue to hold the value ".125" for the duration of the program or until the program changes the value in a planned way.

An assignment statement may assign to a name the value that another name holds. Example:

```
F = GRP
```

The value that GRP holds is assigned to F. Now F and GRP both have the same value. (GRP's value is not changed by the assignment.)

The result of a computation may be assigned to a name. Example:

```
HHM = DEG - .035 * P
```

The result of the calculation "DEG - .035 * P" is assigned to HHM. (The minus sign indicates subtraction and the asterisk indicates multiplication.) It is to be understood, of course, that when the computer actually executes this statement, the names DEG and P will previously have been given actual numeric values.

A name in a program is called a "variable name" because a programmer may assign any value he or she pleases to such a name. The programmer may have the program change the value whenever it is necessary to do so. The name that a person gives to a value should reflect or hint at what the value represents. For example, the name "DEPRAT" reminds a user of the words "depreciation rate"; the name "AREA" reminds the user that some area is being represented; the name "VOLSPH" suggests that the volume of a sphere is being represented.

When you invent a variable name, you may use up to six characters to represent some value. (Some FORTRAN systems permit only five characters, others permit up to 8.) Those six characters may be letters of the alphabet and digits. The beginning character of a variable name *must always* be a letter of the alphabet. These next variable names are correctly formed.

```
RADIUS
T
A2B4
D98765
JACK
```

These variable names are incorrect.

```
5L                  Begins with a digit.
F-FILE              Includes an illegal character (-).
```

INTERVALS Too many characters.

After values have been assigned to variable names, those values may be referred to by their names and used in various parts of a program. Example:

```
    PI=3.14159
    RADIUS=2.5
    AREA=PI*RADIUS*RADIUS
    CIRCUM=2.0*PI*RADIUS
    VOLUME=(4./3.)*PI*RADIUS**3
    WRITE=(6,20)RADIUS,AREA,CIRCUM,VOLUME
20  FORMAT (1X,4F15.2)
    STOP
    END
```

In this program, "PI" is assigned the value "3.14159" and that value is used three times to compute "AREA", "CIRCUM", and "VOLUME". The variable "RADIUS" is assigned the value "2.5" and that value is used several times in various computations. When the program prints the values of "RADIUS", "AREA", "CIRCUM", and "VOLUME", the actual values printed will be "2.50", "19.63", "15.71", and "65.45".

The example program illustrates the 3-step data processing cycle as follows:

Step 1. Values are assigned to "PI" and "RADIUS".

Step 2. Values are computed for "AREA", "CIRCUM", and "VOLUME".

Step 3. Results are printed.

The procedure terminates after one cycle since there are no further input values for the program to use.

You should not be concerned if you don't understand all the statements in the above program. We have not yet discussed FORMAT's, WRITE, etc. We will do so soon.

AN EDUCATIONAL PROGRAM

Here is a program which a programmer would never actually write since its construction is poor. But, poorly constructed or not, the program is educational. Study it closely:

```
      F=6.7
      TP=3.72
      X5=-9.
      P=F+TP
      WRITE (6,3)F,TP,X5,P
    3 FORMAT (1X,4F10.2)
      X5=-4.
      T=X5+F
      F=F+1.2
      B=F+X5
      WRITE (6,88)F,TP,X5,P,T,B
   88 FORMAT (1X,6F10.2)
      T=F+5.3
      STOP
      END
```

The computer obeys the instructions within this program *in the same order* that they are given. That is, the computer first assigns "6.7" to "F", then "3.72" to "TP", etc. The process continues until the computer encounters the STOP statement. Execution of the program then terminates.

Let's follow the program step by step. The program first assigns "6.7" to "F". The computer selects any convenient cell and calls it "F". It places the value "6.7" in that cell. We might imagine that memory cell to have the appearance shown in Figure 3-2.

6.7
F

Figure 3-2

The program then assigns "3.72" to "TP". There are now two memory cells involved. See Figure 3-3.

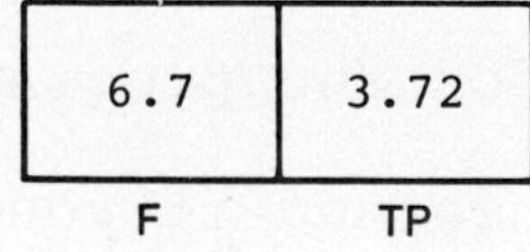

Figure 3-3

The computer then assigns "-9." to "X5". "X5" is a third memory cell. See Figure 3-4.

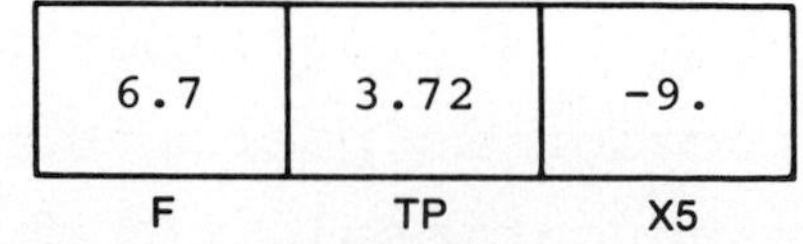

Figure 3-4

The computer then adds the contents of "F" and "TP" and assigns the result to "P". See Figure 3-5.

6.7	3.72	-9.	10.42
F	TP	X5	P

Figure 3-5

The program then prints these four values. Printing does not destroy or change the values in memory. They are still available for further work.

Whenever the computer is given a WRITE command, it prints whatever values were last assigned to the given names. The device used is a high-speed printer attached to the computer system.

The program then assigns "-4." to "X5". This action *destroys* the value previously assigned to "X5". The new value takes its place. See Figure 3-6.

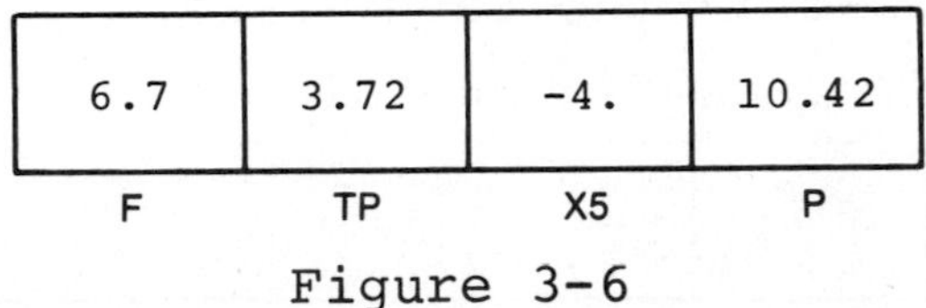

Figure 3-6

The computer then calculates a value for "T". The result is given by the sum of "X5" and "F". Since the current values of "X5" and "F" are "-4." and "6.7", respectively, the program assigns "2.7" to "T". Note carefully that the computer does not concern itself with the fact that "X5" once held the value "-9.". It is the *current* value of a variable that the computer uses when making a calculation or when printing an answer.

Memory now appears as shown in Figure 3-7.

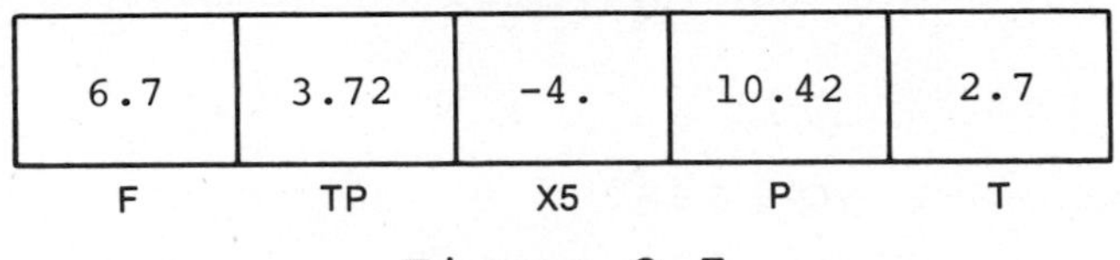

Figure 3-7

The computer then computes "F". To do this, the computer adds "1.2" to the current value of "F" (6.7) and assigns the result *back* to "F". See Figure 3-8 on the following page.

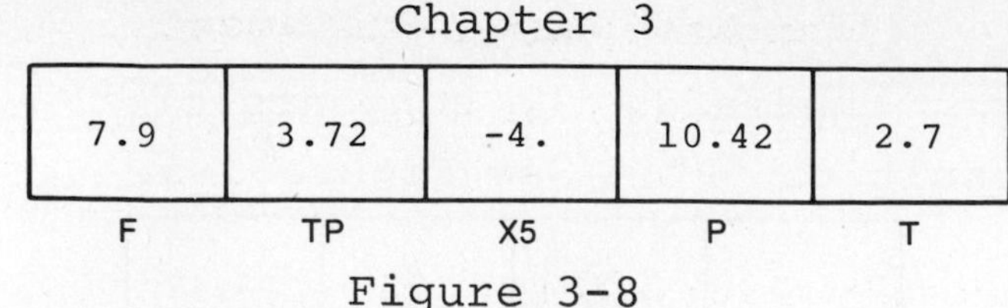

Figure 3-8

In the next command, the computer is directed to add "F" and "X5". Since "F" currently holds the value "7.9", that value is added to "X5". The result "3.9" is therefore assigned to "B". See Figure 3-9.

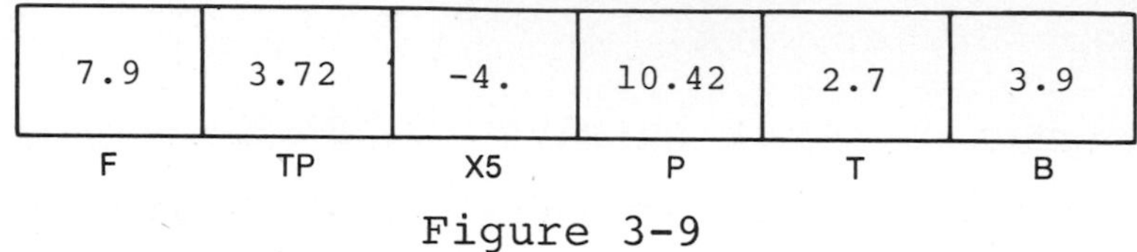

Figure 3-9

These are the values which are printed in response to the second WRITE statement.

The program makes one last calculation. It adds "5.3" to "F" and assigns the result to "T". Since "F" currently holds the value "7.9", this is the value used. The result, "13.2" is assigned to "T". See Figure 3-10.

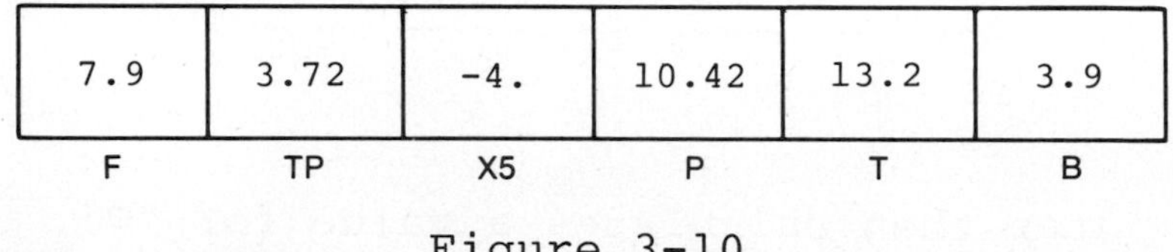

Figure 3-10

These values are not printed since the program stops when it encounters the STOP statement.

As you followed this program step by step, you saw that the program never worried about something it had done in the past. It always concerned itself with the immediate task to be performed and nothing else. If an earlier result is ever to be adjusted because the value assigned to a variable has changed, that value has to be reassigned with a new assignment statement.

Observe that when you assign a number to a variable name, the number must never include an imbedded comma. Examples:

```
LAMBDA = 84763456
INT = -162788
CONST = -.063948
PI = 3.14159
```

If numbers are negative, minus signs are placed at the left of each number.

TYPES OF VALUES AND VARIABLES

In FORTRAN, there are six different types or kinds of values which may be used. These are "real", "integer", "double precision", "complex", "logical" and "character" values. In this chapter, we will discuss only the real and integer types. In later chapters we will discuss the other four types.

A real value is a number which includes an imbedded decimal point. Some examples of real values are:

```
18.6
 9.7
-7.6
14.0
-8.
```

Integer values are numbers which do not have decimal points. Some examples are:

```
384
-77
 14
 -7
```

The maximum sizes that these numbers may have depend upon the computers upon which the FORTRAN programs are to be run. Such real numbers as "924.763", "-827.97", and "-.00034786" are acceptable on most machines without any problem, and such integer numbers as "347834501", and "-200062613" are also acceptable. We'll say more about maximums later but, for now, do not concern yourself with whether numbers you'll need for assigned problems in this book can be expressed. You may assume that they can.

Real values are usually assigned to real variable names. A real variable name is one that begins with any letter within the range "A" through "H" and "O" through "Z". Some systems permit the dollar sign ($) as one of the characters in the real set.

These names are all permissible real variable names:

X
VOLUME
A3PW
HENRY
PHI
THETA
RADIAN
D3377

These names are not permissible for the reasons given:

453X7	A real name must begin with a letter of the alphabet from "A" through "H" or from "O" through "Z".
JIM	A real name must begin with a letter of the alphabet from "A" through "H" or from "O" through "Z". (JIM is an integer name.)
SILICON	A name may have a maximum of six characters. (Some systems permit eight.)
PAY-RT	Variable names may include only letters of the alphabet and/or digits.

Integer values are usually assigned to "integer" variable names. Integer variable names are formed in the same way as real names except that the beginning letter of the name must be a letter from "I" through "N", inclusive. (Memory aid: Observe that "I" and "N" are the first two letters of the word "integer".)

These integer names are correct:

I
MAXVAL
MINVAL
J9436

These integer names are not correct:

PI	An integer name must begin with a letter of the alphabet ranging from "I" through "N". (PI is a real variable name.)
33K	An integer name must begin with a letter of the alphabet ranging from "I" through "N".

INTERVAL	An integer name may consist of a maximum of six characters. (Some systems permit eight.)
KNT-PG	Integer names may include only letters of the alphabet and/or digits.

In writing assignment statements, one *usually* assigns an integer value to an integer name or a real value to a real name. Like this:

```
WPM = 36.7
PGSIZE = 11.5
JSIZE = 18
MIN = -366
```

It is not wrong, though, to assign an integer value to a real variable name or a real value to an integer name. In the former instance, the computer appends a decimal point to the stored number; in the latter example, the computer truncates (chops off) the fractional part of the number. Example:

```
W = 66
```

The computer stores the value "66." in the memory cell "W".

```
KIM = 26.7
```

The computer stores the value "26" in the memory cell "KIM". The computer *does not round* to "27".

```
L3 = 26.3
```

The computer stores the value "26" in the memory cell "L3".

```
NTIME = RK + 3.6
```

If RK's value is "7.3", the computer first computes 7.3 + 3.6 (10.9), then assigns "10" to "NTIME".

Rounding can be "forced" by having the computer add ".5" to a calculation. Thus,

```
M = X + .5
```

assigns "8" to "M" if X's value is "8.3"; it assigns "9" to "M" if X's value is "8.5".

EXPRESSION

An expression is a group of two or more variable names or values connected with arithmetic operators. Some expressions are:

```
P + Q - 3.6

(D-TM) / RPM

(A*B) * (A+B)

J - L * NL + 18
```

An expression is called a "real expression" if all the values or names in it are real. It is called an "integer expression" if all the values or names in it are integer. Thus, "P+Q-3.6" is a real expression; "J-L*NL+18" is an integer expression.

Some computers do not permit mixing variable types in expressions. Hence, the statement

```
P = (R - K + 3.6) / 4
```

is illegal since the expression contains real and integer values and names. The computer will not accept the statement. Today, a growing number of computers do accept mixed expressions. The expression above would automatically be changed to a real one. You should assume that your computer accepts mixed expressions unless you learn otherwise.

If your computer does accept mixed expressions, there's a risk that the result you receive may be an unexpected one. Example:

```
T = A + K/5
```

What value does "T" get if "A" holds the value "9.4" and "K" holds the value 21? You might expect "13.6". Actually, the computer performs the "K/5" calculation in integer mode giving the *integer* result, "4". The value assigned to "T" is, therefore, "13.4".

The rule is this: "When two integers are given in a divide operation, the result is always an integer value." If either or both of the values are changed to real numbers, the computed result is a real one.

If at all possible, you should avoid mixing modes in an expression. At the very least, you should make sure that two integers are not involved in a divide operation. If you change "5" to "5." in the example on the previous page, the computer will give the correct answer.

To test your knowledge of integer and real values, study this next program, then predict what the values of A, B, KC, ID, JD, E, F, and G will be.

```
          A  = 2.8
          B  = 1.9
          KC = A+B
          ID = A+B+.2
          JD = A
          E  = 17-3
          F  = 2.6+5/2
          G  = 2.6+5/2.
          WRITE (6,20) A,B, KC, ID,JD,E,F,G
      20  FORMAT (1X,2F10.1,3I10,3F10.1)
          STOP
          END
```

The computer will print these values:

```
A         2.8
B         1.9
KC        4
ID        4
JD        2
E         14.0
F         4.6
G         5.1
```

You still don't know what FORMAT's are all about, but you don't need to know anything about FORMAT's in order to answer the above question.

We also acknowledge that you haven't been exposed to calculations involving "+", "-", "/", and "*" yet but we're sure you can guess that "+" means "add"; "-" means "subtract"; "/" means "divide" and "*" means "multiply".

EXERCISES AND PROBLEMS

1. Name the three steps that are included in the basic data processing cycle.

2. What is an assignment statement? Give an example.

3. What are the three parts of an assignment statement?

4. What is a "variable name"? How many characters may a variable name consist of?

5. What three forms may a value take on at the right of the equals sign in an assignment statement?

6. In the statement

```
W = 9.4
```

what is the value assigned to W?

7. In the statement

```
M = JC8
```

what is the value assigned to M?

8. In the statement

```
KIM = KIM + 5
```

what is the value assigned to KIM?

9. In the statement

```
CIR = 2. * 3.14159 * R
```

what is the value assigned to CIR?

10. What is incorrect with the statement shown below?

```
X + Y = 3.5 - Z
```

11. What is incorrect with the statement shown below?

```
A + B = C
```

12. What are the six types of variable names and values that may be used in FORTRAN?

13. What is a real value? Give an example.

14. What is an integer value? Give an example.

15. Real names begin with what letters of the alphabet? Give an example.

16. Integer names begin with what letters of the alphabet? Give an example.

17. What is incorrect with these real variable names?

```
EXTENSION
9X
R-FIX
L34567
```

18. What is incorrect with these integer variable names?

```
HENRY
INDIANA
NEW-55
6LEVEL
```

19. Is it all right to assign an integer value to a real name or vice versa? Explain.

20. What is an expression? Give an example.

21. Study this program:

```
      N = 26
      K = 13
      J = 6
      K = 4
      J = 3
      N = K + 2
      WRITE (6,4) N,K,J
    4 FORMAT (1X,3I10)
      STOP
      END
```

What values will the computer give for N, K, and J?

22. Study this program:

```
      X = 6
      J = 25.3
      K = 25.6
      WRITE (6,5) X,J,K
    5 FORMAT (1X,F10.1,2I10)
      STOP
      END
```

What values will the computer give for X, J, and K?

CHAPTER 4

The READ Statement

ASSIGNMENTS

We said earlier that the basic data processing cycle consists basically of three steps. In Step 1, some input data is obtained; in Step 2, the input data is processed; and in Step 3, some information is printed - perhaps a line of a report.

In the last chapter, we concerned ourselves with Step 1. This is the step where some input data is provided for the program to process. We saw that one way to provide input data is by the use of the assignment statement. The assignment statement causes a real or integer numeric value to be stored in a memory cell. That memory cell has a real or integer name.

As examples,

```
PRINC = 3650.50
```

assigns the real value "3650.50" to the real name PRINC, and

```
LEVY = -367
```

assigns the integer value "-367" to the integer name LEVY.

Assigning input values to variable names has its disadvantages. It is, for example, a rather tedious method. You need to code as many assignments statements as there are values to be assigned. A more convenient way to store numeric values into named memory cells is by use of the READ statement.

A JOB SETUP

In order to understand how the READ statement works, it is

necessary to review a program setup. Figure 4-1 shows a program ready to be submitted to a computer.

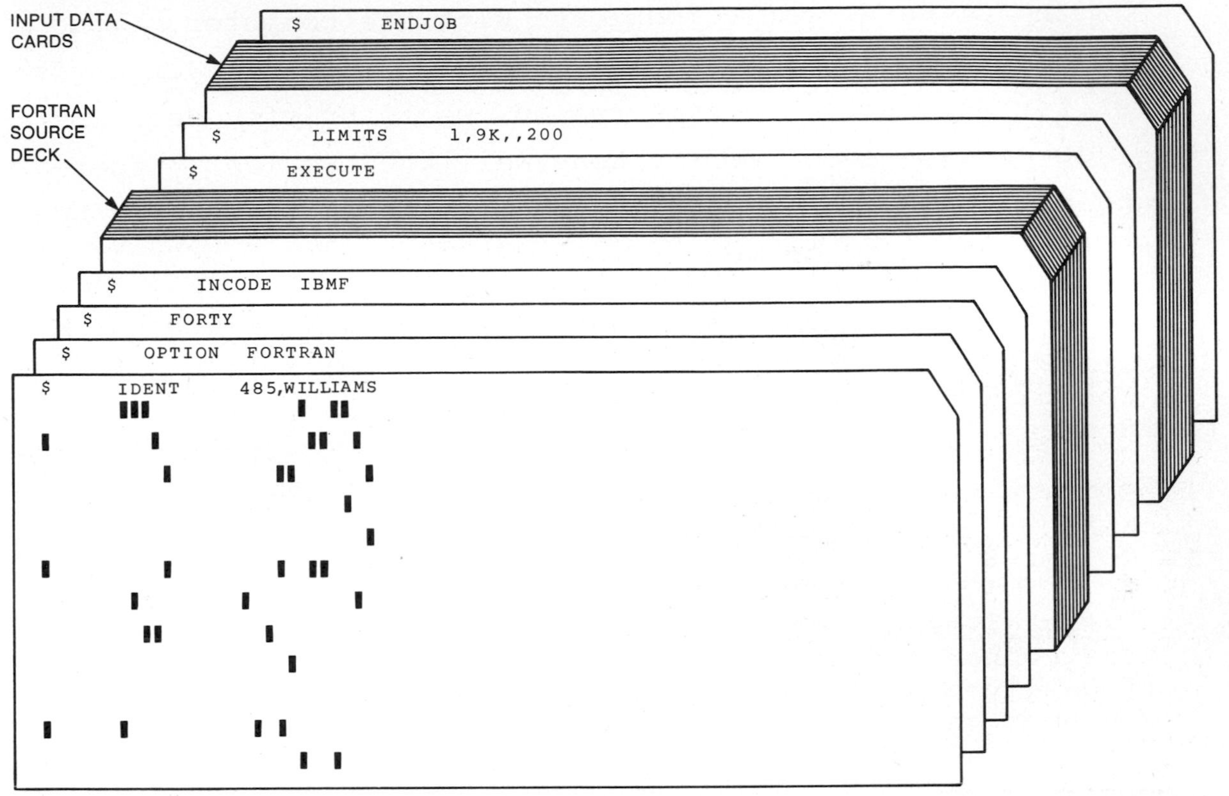

Figure 4-1

There are three categories of cards in the program setup. First is the FORTRAN source program. It is punched upon a deck of Hollerith cards forming a source deck. Find the source deck. Second, the input data cards constitute the data deck. Note the position of the data cards. Third, the interspersed cards showing a dollar sign ($) in column 1 of each card are called "control" cards or "job control language" (JCL) cards. Observe how they are intermingled within the program setup.

A full discussion of JCL cards is not appropriate here since it is not actually a FORTRAN topic. These types of cards vary from computer to computer. Since the programs in this text were prepared for a Honeywell 6000 Series Computer, the JCL cards shown apply to that machine. Should the computer at your site be an IBM 370, a CDC 7800, a UNIVAC 1110, or some other machine, you would need to learn how to punch the JCL cards required for your machine. Your instructor or project leader will assist you in this task.

With JCL cards you communicate with the computer. You give it certain facts it needs to know. Since all JCL cards exist for basically the same reason, we'll briefly describe the JCL cards needed for the Honeywell 6000 Series. Understanding those cards will help you understand the theory behind the ones used on your machine.

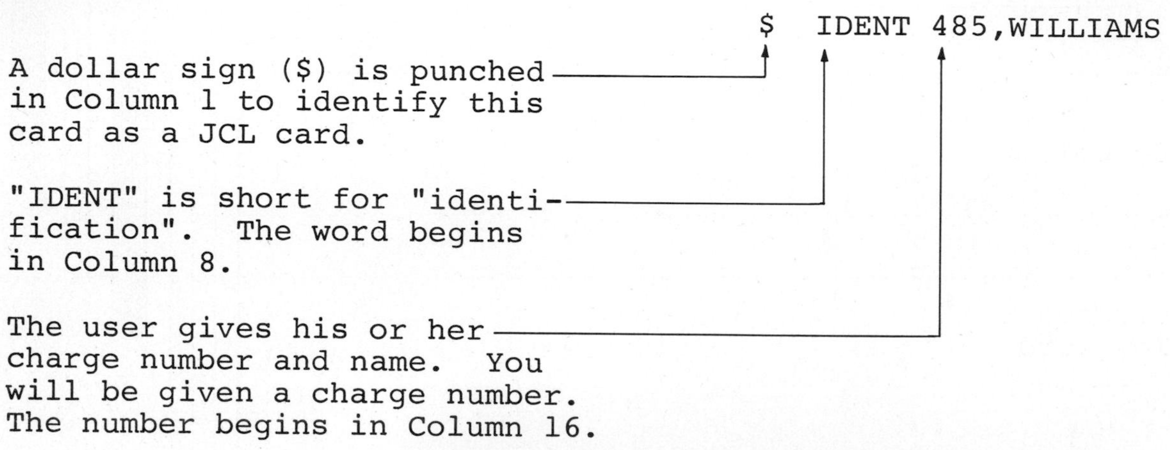

$ IDENT 485,WILLIAMS
A dollar sign ($) is punched in Column 1 to identify this card as a JCL card.
"IDENT" is short for "identification". The word begins in Column 8.
The user gives his or her charge number and name. You will be given a charge number. The number begins in Column 16.

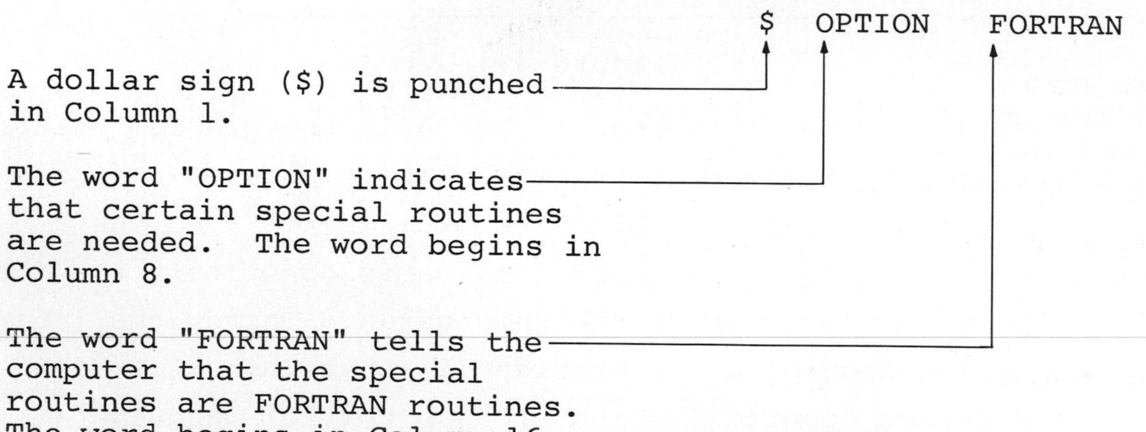

$ OPTION FORTRAN
A dollar sign ($) is punched in Column 1.
The word "OPTION" indicates that certain special routines are needed. The word begins in Column 8.
The word "FORTRAN" tells the computer that the special routines are FORTRAN routines. The word begins in Column 16.

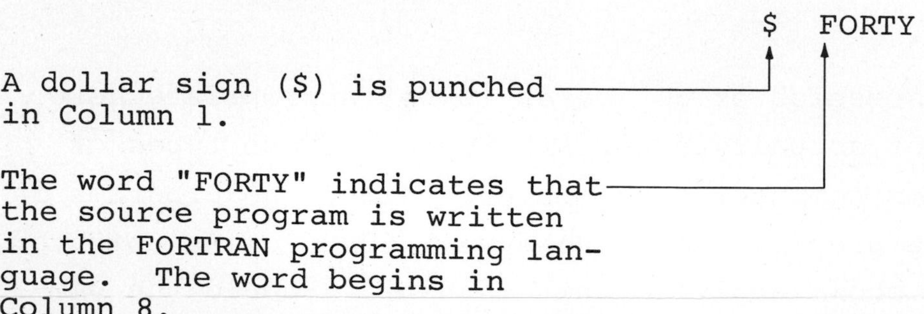

$ FORTY
A dollar sign ($) is punched in Column 1.
The word "FORTY" indicates that the source program is written in the FORTRAN programming language. The word begins in Column 8.

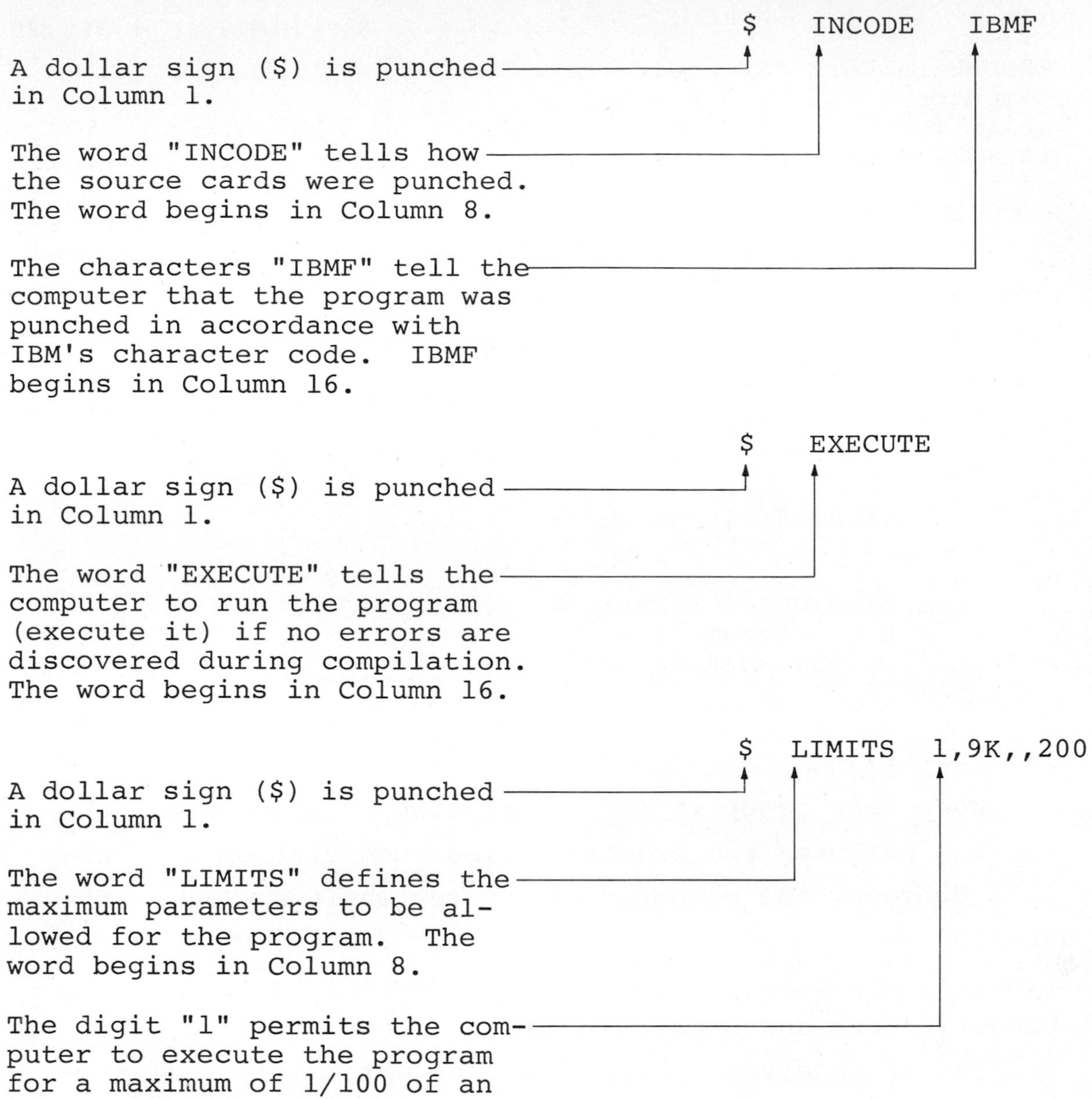
$ INCODE IBMF
A dollar sign ($) is punched in Column 1.
The word "INCODE" tells how the source cards were punched. The word begins in Column 8.
The characters "IBMF" tell the computer that the program was punched in accordance with IBM's character code. IBMF begins in Column 16.
$ EXECUTE
A dollar sign ($) is punched in Column 1.
The word "EXECUTE" tells the computer to run the program (execute it) if no errors are discovered during compilation. The word begins in Column 16.
$ LIMITS 1,9K,,200
A dollar sign ($) is punched in Column 1.
The word "LIMITS" defines the maximum parameters to be allowed for the program. The word begins in Column 8.
The digit "1" permits the computer to execute the program for a maximum of 1/100 of an hour. This is plenty of time for a simple program.

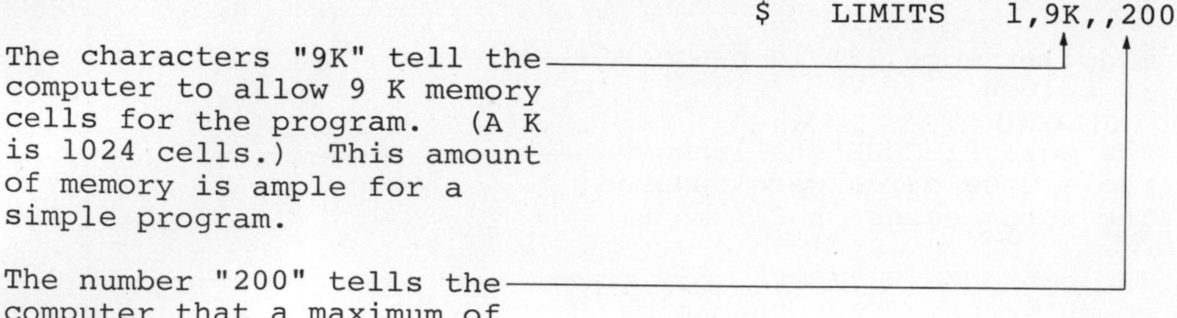

$ LIMITS 1,9K,,200
The characters "9K" tell the computer to allow 9 K memory cells for the program. (A K is 1024 cells.) This amount of memory is ample for a simple program.
The number "200" tells the computer that a maximum of 200 lines are to be printed.

The parameters shown here begin in Column 16.

$ ENDJOB

A dollar sign ($) is punched in Column 1.

The word "ENDJOB" separates one person's program from another's. The word begins in Column 8.

PROCEDURE

When this setup is first submitted to a computer, the machine performs the process called "compilation". During this process, the computer checks for obvious errors (mis-spelled FORTRAN words, improper punctuation, etc.). Finding none, it converts the FORTRAN instructions to computer language (zeroes and ones). If the computer finds errors, the programmer receives a report telling which errors were detected. The programmer must correct errors by discarding incorrect source deck cards and replacing them with correct cards. The programmer then presents the program to the computer for another attempt at compilation.

If, and only if, the compilation attempt is successful, the program goes into execution. The computer obeys the instructions that were originally punched in the source deck and which now exist in the computer's memory in machine-language form.

Any input data cards that the program requires are now obtained, card by card, from the deck of data cards. The

FORTRAN instruction, in machine-language form, which calls for the "reading" of these cards is the READ instruction.

THE READ INSTRUCTION

A programmer may write a READ instruction in a variety of ways. Here are some.

```
      READ (5,9) X,Y,J
300   READ (5,20,END=30) L,D,X,F
      READ 35,FF, LF, SK
```

Any of these READ statements may be preceded by a statement number should the logic of the program require it.

A SAMPLE PROGRAM USING READ

```
      READ (5,17) GL
17    FORMAT (F10.0)
      H = GL*GL
      WRITE (6,24) GL,H
24    FORMAT (1X,2F10.1)
      STOP
      END
```

This program obtains a data value from a punched card. It assigns that value to "GL". Then the program multiplies GL by GL and assigns the result to H. Finally, the program prints the value of GL and H and stops executing.

A READ statement always obtains the next available card from the data deck. In the example given above, there is no real data "deck" since the "deck" consists of only one card. Future examples show more conventional data decks.

You have probably observed that the above program contains two FORMAT statements; the first is identified with the statement number "17", and the second, with statement number "24". The first FORMAT is associated with the READ statement and the second with the WRITE statement.

Examine the READ statement. It looks like this:

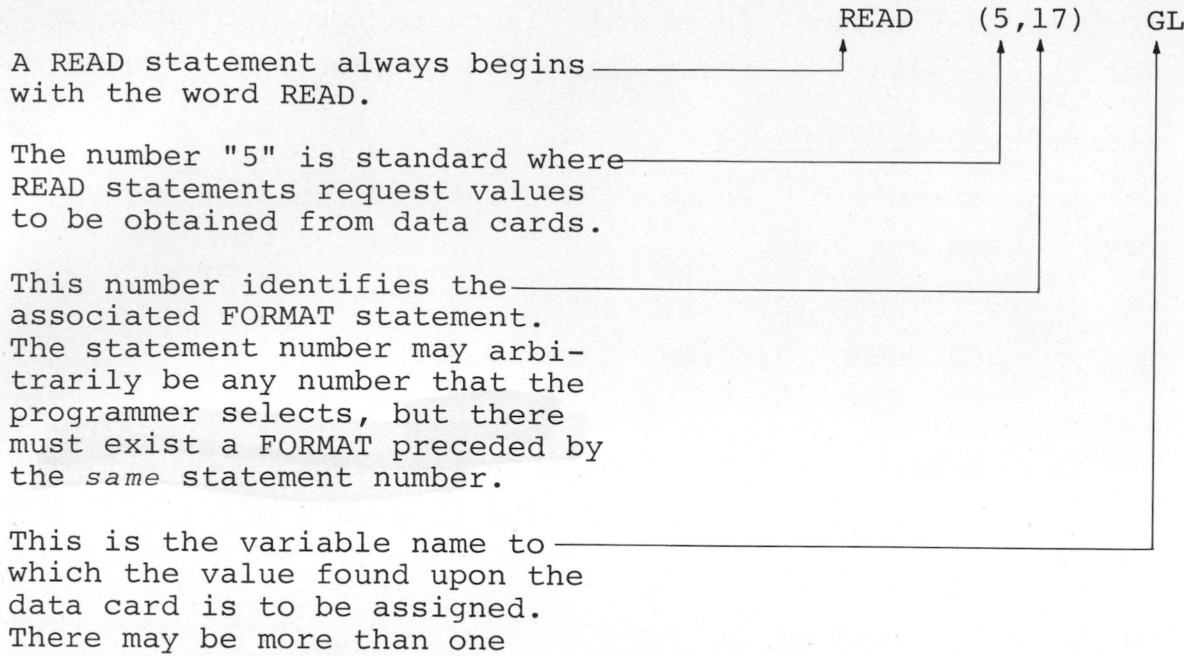

READ (5,17) GL
A READ statement always begins with the word READ.
The number "5" is standard where READ statements request values to be obtained from data cards.
This number identifies the associated FORMAT statement. The statement number may arbitrarily be any number that the programmer selects, but there must exist a FORMAT preceded by the *same* statement number.
This is the variable name to which the value found upon the data card is to be assigned. There may be more than one variable name here.

THE FORMAT STATEMENT

A FORMAT statement tells *where* on a data card the value to be assigned is located. Let's look at the FORMAT statement referenced above:

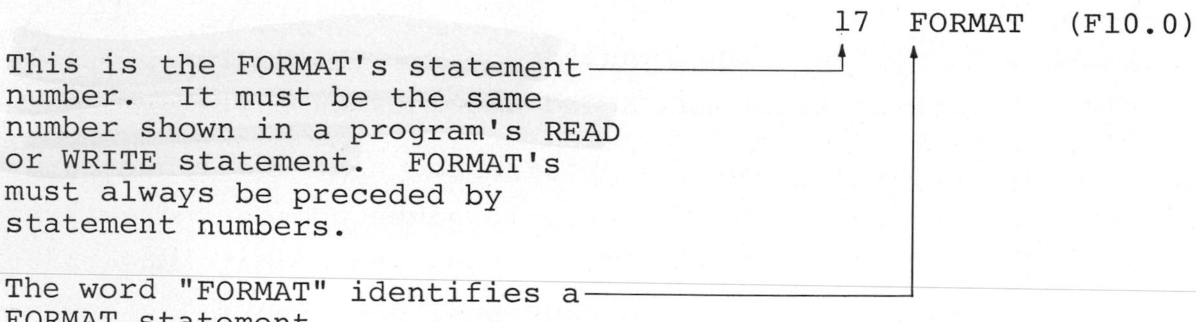

17 FORMAT (F10.0)
This is the FORMAT's statement number. It must be the same number shown in a program's READ or WRITE statement. FORMAT's must always be preceded by statement numbers.
The word "FORMAT" identifies a FORMAT statement.

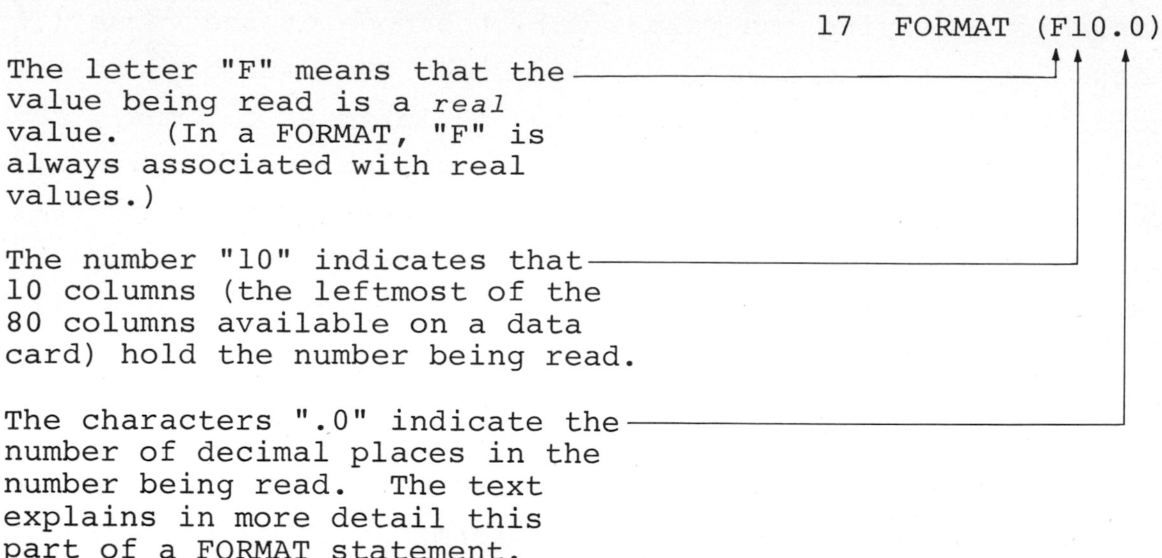

17 FORMAT (F10.0)
The letter "F" means that the value being read is a *real* value. (In a FORMAT, "F" is always associated with real values.)
The number "10" indicates that 10 columns (the leftmost of the 80 columns available on a data card) hold the number being read.
The characters ".0" indicate the number of decimal places in the number being read. The text explains in more detail this part of a FORMAT statement.

A DATA CARD

Now let's examine the data card which might be used in this example. See Figure 4-2.

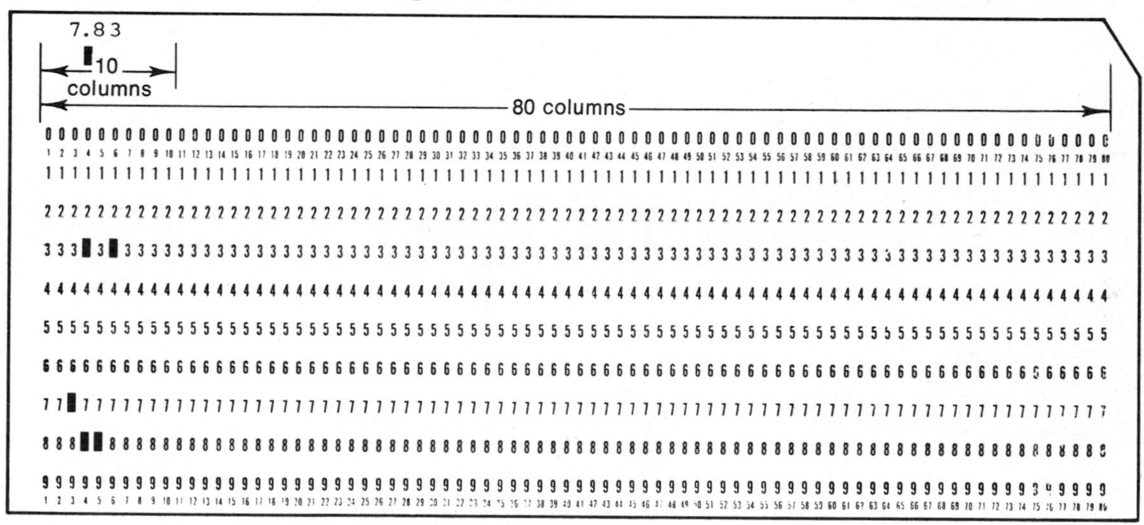

Figure 4-2

When the READ statement is executed, the program scans the card and assigns the value it finds, "7.83", to GL. The program continues from that point.

The READ and FORMAT statements of the sample program act as teammates. The associated statements are:

```
      READ (5,17) GL
   17 FORMAT (F10.0)
```

The two statements define the source where the value is to be obtained ("5" means card data deck), the name of the variable receiving the value (GL), the mode of the value ("F" means "real"), the number of columns on the data card that hold the value ("10" refers to the 10 leftmost columns), and the number of decimal places (".0" means no decimal places, but this part of a FORMAT statement is overridden if the value punched on the data card includes an actual punched decimal point. The value punched upon the sample data card *does* include a decimal point; therefore, "7.83" is assigned to GL, not "7.0". We'll have more on this ".0" topic later.)

STOP

The STOP statement causes the termination of the execution phase of a program. The STOP statement is often placed just ahead of the END statement, but it can be found anywhere in a program. Example:

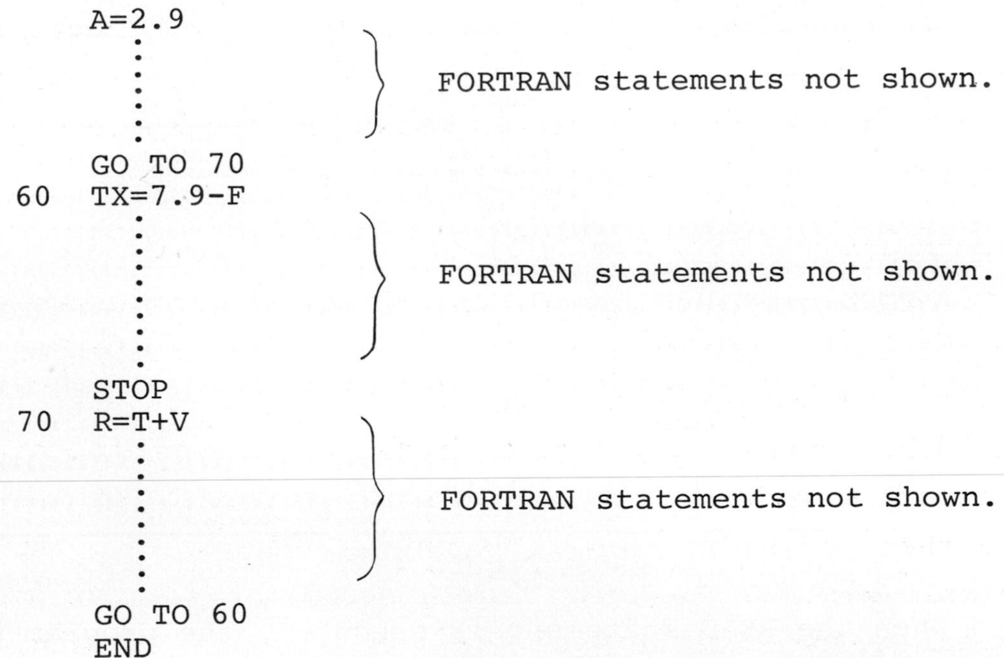

A=2.9
FORTRAN statements not shown.
GO TO 70
60 TX=7.9-F
FORTRAN statements not shown.
STOP
70 R=T+V
FORTRAN statements not shown.
GO TO 60
END

Observe that the program jumps from point to point as it executes. Finally, the STOP statement causes a termination of the execution.

There may be more than one STOP statement in a program. The program will stop whenever it encounters *any* STOP statement. Example:

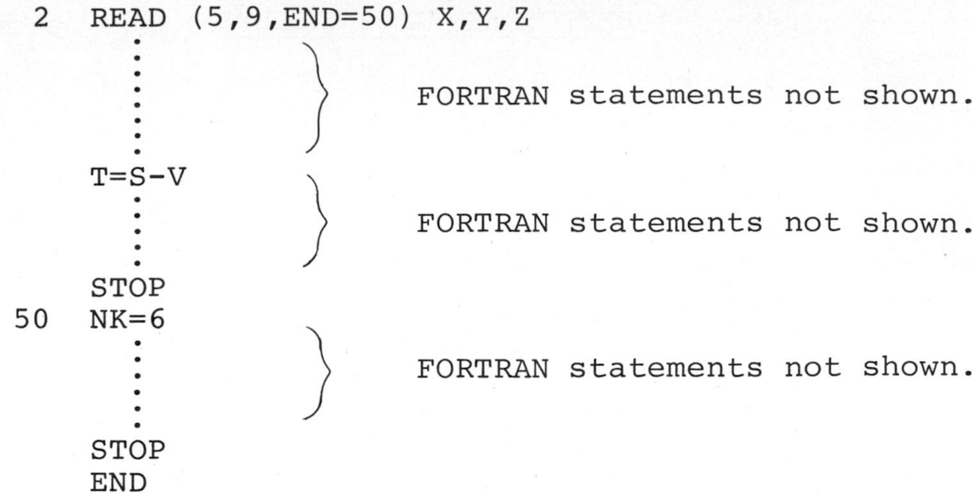

```
 2  READ (5,9,END=50) X,Y,Z
    .
    .     }   FORTRAN statements not shown.
    .
    T=S-V
    .     }   FORTRAN statements not shown.
    .
    STOP
50  NK=6
    .
    .     }   FORTRAN statements not shown.
    .
    STOP
    END
```

As the program executes, it may encounter the first STOP statement shown. If so, the program terminates there. Or, it may execute in such a way that it encounters the second STOP statement. If so, the program terminates there.

Remember, more than one STOP statement can legitimately be given in a program but only one END statement may be given. The END statement must always appear at the end of the FORTRAN program.

DISTINCTION BETWEEN STOP AND END

A STOP statement causes the termination of a program's execution; an END statement causes the termination of the compilation process. You'll recall that programs must be compiled before they can be executed. The END statement tells the compiler that there are no more statements in the program and that, therefore, compilation must terminate. There must be only one END statement in a program and it must physically appear as the last card of the source deck. If program execution begins, the STOP statement, when encountered, causes it to terminate. Since there may be a number of legitimate ways that program execution may terminate in any given program, there may be more than one STOP statement in the program. There must be at least one STOP statement in a program.

STOP= CALL EXIT

EXERCISES AND PROBLEMS

1. Why is the READ statement useful in providing data to a program?

2. What is the function provided by JCL cards?

3. What is accomplished during the process of compilation? Give two products resulting from the process.

4. Why is a FORMAT statement given in association with a READ statement?

5. In the statement

```
   88  READ (5,39) P, N, T
```

   what does the number "5" designate?

6. Refer to Question 5. What does the number "39" designate?

7. In the FORMAT

```
   39  FORMAT (F10.0)
```

   What does the "F" designate?

8. How many END statements may you give in a FORTRAN program? How many STOP statements?

9. What is the distinction between the STOP and END statements?

10. Are FORMAT's associated with WRITE statements as well as READ statements?

11. Is it true that FORMAT's must always have a leading statement number?

12. Study these statements:

```
       READ (5,18) R
   18  FORMAT (F20.0)
```

   Where would you expect to find the value for R punched upon a data processing card?

13. Study these statements:

```
       READ (5,23) T
   23  FORMAT (F10.0)
```

If the number punched upon the card, within columns 1 and 10, inclusive, is "5.86", what value will the computer assign to T?

14. Is the statement given below correct?

```
READ (5,24) DX, IG, ED
```

15. Refer to Question 14. How many numbers would you expect to find punched upon the corresponding data card?

CHAPTER 5

More About READ and FORMAT Statement

READING REAL VALUES

In the last chapter, we saw that a READ statement can be used to obtain input data values from punched cards. Once those values have been obtained, the FORTRAN program will continue with the processing of the data.

A READ statement references a FORMAT statement. That statement tells *where* on the data cards the input values have been punched.

Consider these two statements:

```
      READ (5,95) DEL,HYP,PROD
 95   FORMAT (3F10.0)
```

The FORMAT could have been written

```
 95   FORMAT (F10.0,F10.0,F10.0)
```

Both ways give exactly equivalent FORMAT's. In the former example, the "3" ahead of "F10.0" indicates that "F10.0" is to be used three times. The former method is easier to use since it requires less coding effort.

The READ statement shows that three values are to be obtained from a data card and are to be assigned to variables DEL, HYP, and PROD. These are all real values.

The data card which is to be read might look like the one shown in Figure 5-1 on the following page.

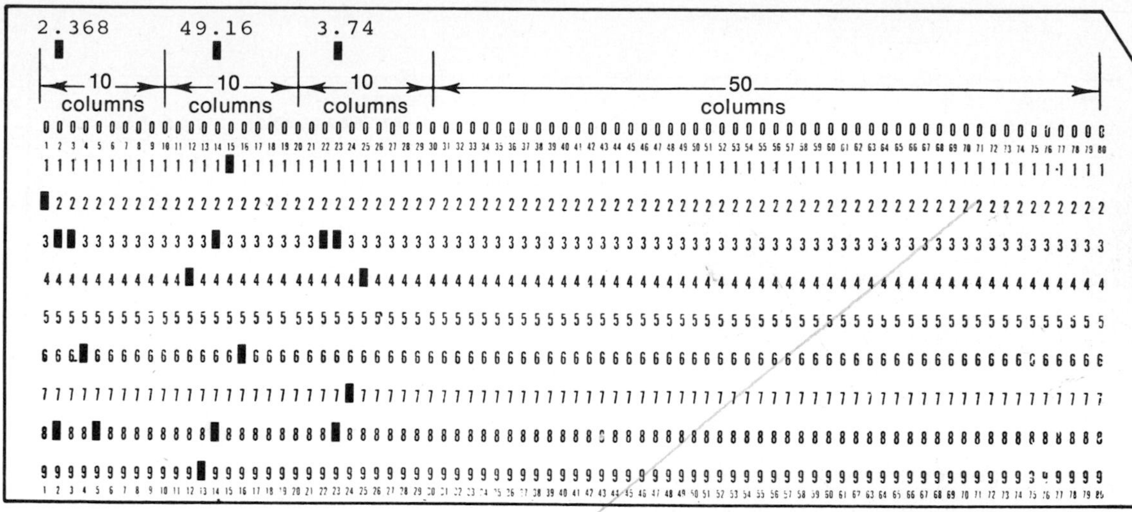

Figure 5-1

The value punched within the leftmost 10 columns of the card (2.368) is assigned to DEL; the value punched within the next 10 columns (49.16) is assigned to HYP; and the value punched within the next 10 columns (3.74) is assigned to PROD.

It is important to observe that the FORMAT matches the punched data. That FORMAT shows that the value to be assigned to DEL, is to be obtained according to F10.0; that the value to be assigned to HYP, is also to be obtained according to F10.0; and, finally, that the value to be assigned to PROD, is to be obtained according to F10.0.

When the values punched on the data card being read actually include decimal points, the ".0" parts of FORMAT's have no meaning. They are overridden and the *actual* values punched are the values assigned. (Even when overridden, ".0" must be coded.)

Real values are sometimes punched *without* decimal points. See Figure 5-2 on the following page.

Now, when these values are read, the corresponding FORMAT must show where the decimal points are assumed to be located. Consequently, a FORMAT must be designed which gives this information. Here is a FORMAT that is designed for the card shown on the following page.

```
83 FORMAT (F10.3,2F10.2)
```

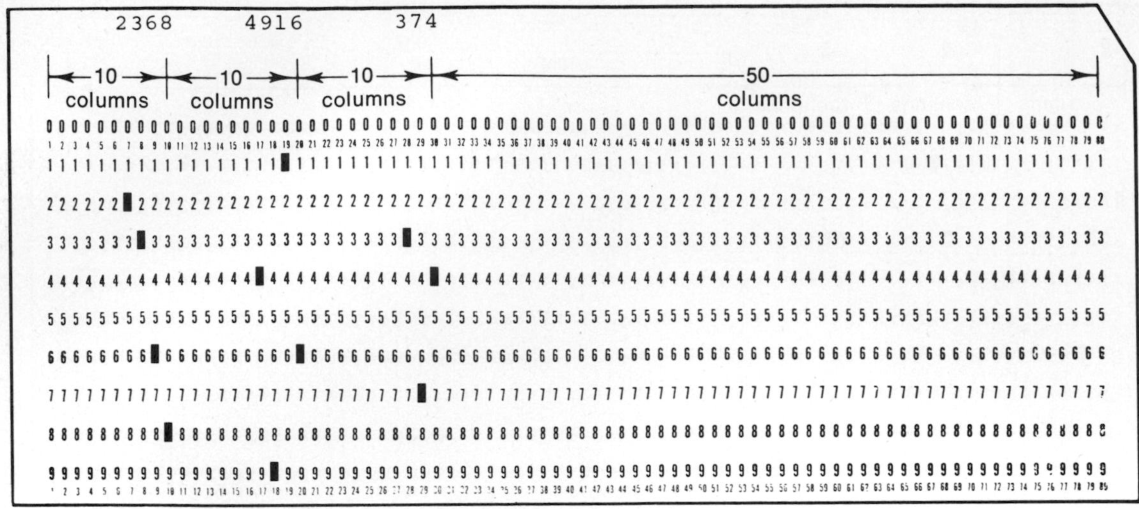

Figure 5-2

This FORMAT could be written in an equivalent way like this:

```
      83  FORMAT (F10.3,F10.2,F10.2)
```

The FORMAT's show that the first value is punched within the leftmost 10 columns of the card and that the value has three decimal places. When the value "2368" is read, it is stored in the computer's memory as "2.368". The next value is punched within the next 10 columns of the card. It is assumed to have two decimal places. The value read is "4916" but it is stored in memory as "49.16". The third value is punched within the next 10 columns. It, too, is assumed to have two decimal places. The value read is "374" but it is stored as "3.74".

An important observation is this: When a punched real value actually includes a decimal point, the value may be punched *anywhere* within the column positions (field) reserved for the number. When a punched real value does not include a decimal point, that value *must be right adjusted*. The term "right adjusted" means that a value must be punched at the extreme right of the field reserved for it.

READING INTEGER VALUES

Integer values may also be obtained from cards. Here are two statements which obtain values of JX, JY, and JZ from a data card:

```
          READ (5,18) JX,JY,JZ
       18 FORMAT (I8,I6,I10)
```

Figure 5-3 shows a data card which could be the object of the two statements given above.

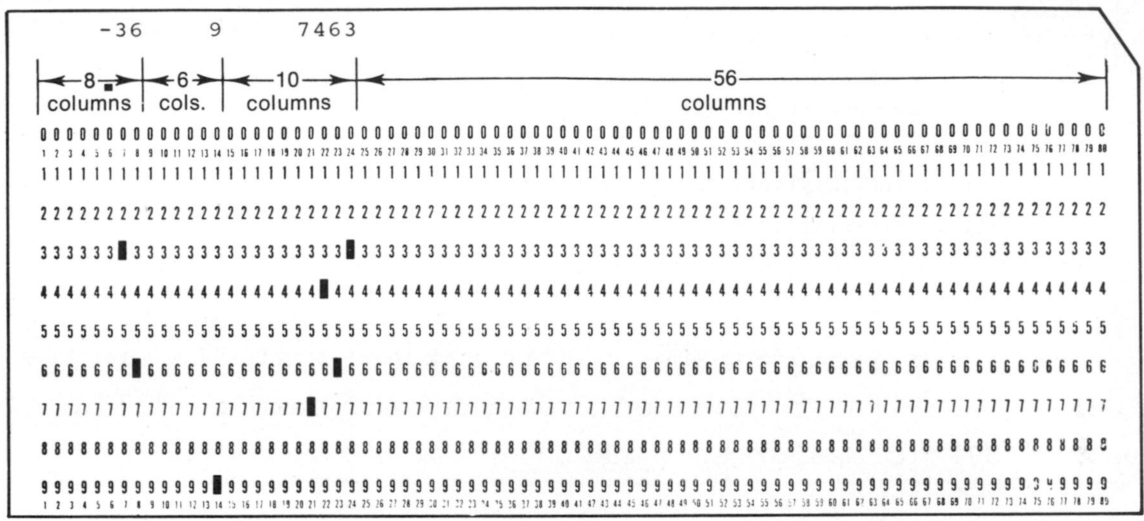

Figure 5-3

JX, JY, and JZ are integer names. The FORMAT shows "I" within parentheses rather than "F". The letter "I" indicates that integer values are to be read; the letter "F" indicates that real values are to be read.

The FORMAT shows that 8 columns are reserved for the first field; 6 columns are reserved for the second field; and 10 columns are reserved for the third field. Since the three fields are reserved for integer values, the FORMAT makes no reference to decimal places.

Integer values *must always* be right adjusted in the fields reserved for them. In the example, "-36" is assigned to JX, "9" is assigned to JY, and "7463" is assigned to JZ.

A READ statement may be used to obtain both real and integer values punched on data cards. Here is an example:

```
          READ (5,8) KP,D7,E,NUM
        8 FORMAT (I5,F8.0,F10.0,I8)
```

Figure 5-4 shows a data card that might be associated with the two statements shown above.

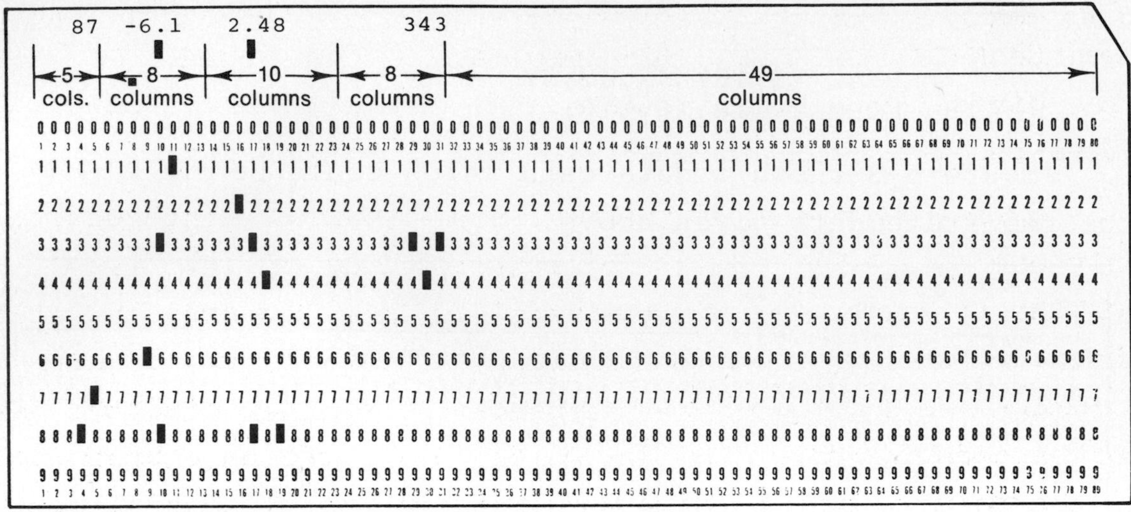

Figure 5-4

KP is an integer name. It is matched with "I5" in the FORMAT. The value obtained from the data card is "87". The value "87" is assigned to KP.

D7 is a real name. It is matched with "F8.0" in the FORMAT. The value obtained from the data card is "-6.1". The value "-6.1" is assigned to D7.

E is also a real name. It is matched with "F10.0" in the FORMAT. The value obtained from the data card is "2.48". The value "2.48" is assigned to E.

NUM is another integer name. It is matched with "I8" in the FORMAT. The value obtained from the data card is "343". The value "343" is assigned to NUM.

Observe that real and integer names must have matching real and integer portions in the FORMAT statement.

An entire program that contains the above statements could be this one:

```
      READ (5,8) KP,D7,E,NUM
    8 FORMAT (I5,F8.0,F10.0,I8)
      KAPPA = KP*NUM
      QUE = D7+E
      WRITE (6,20) KAPPA,KP,NUM
   20 FORMAT (1X,3I10)
      WRITE (6,15) QUE,D7,E
   15 FORMAT (1X,3F10.1)
      STOP
      END
```

This program reads four numeric values, then uses them to compute KAPPA and QUE. Two lines are then printed. The first line gives the values of KAPPA, KP, and NUM. The second line gives the values of QUE, D7, and E.

In this simple illustration, there are few statements and only one data card. Few programs are this simple. Many FORTRAN programs contain hundreds, if not thousands, of statements. There may also be thousands of data cards. The *order* in which the READ statement (or statements) are executed must correspond with the order in which data cards have been placed in the card reader. It is the programmer's responsibility to make sure that data cards are stacked in the proper sequence.

SIMPLIFIED READ

A simplified form of READ is available. It looks like this:

```
READ 8,KP,D7,E,NUM
```

In the statement, "8" is the FORMAT number. The names KP, D7, E, and NUM are names representing values to be read. Observe the differences, especially in punctuation, between this form of READ and the more general form

```
READ (5,8) KP,D7,E,NUM
```

In this text, we will emphasize the latter form since it is the more general and flexible form.

EXERCISES AND PROBLEMS

1. Study the statement that follows.

   ```
   95  FORMAT (3F8.0)
   ```

   How many fields does the FORMAT define?

2. Refer to Question 1. Is the statement shown there equivalent to the one given below?

   ```
   95  FORMAT (F8.0,F8.0,F8.0)
   ```

3. Study these statements:

```
      READ (5,8) PT, MK, ND
    8 FORMAT (3I10)
```

Does the FORMAT correctly match the READ statement?

4. Must real numbers punched upon data cards always have imbedded decimal points?

5. Study the following statements

```
      READ (5,17) A,B,C
   17 FORMAT (3F10.2)
```

What is the effect of ".2" in the FORMAT if the values of A, B, and C include imbedded decimal points?

6. Refer to Question 5. What is the effect of ".2" in the FORMAT if the values of A, B, and C do not include imbedded decimal points?

7. What does the code letter "I" given within FORMAT's indicate?

8. In a FORMAT may you give both the code letters "F" and "I"?

9. In a READ statement, may you show the reading of both real and integer values?

10. Study these statements:

```
      READ (5,14) I,J,K,L,M,N
   14 FORMAT (6I10)
```

How many columns of the data card are used to represent integer values?

11. What does the term "right adjusted" mean?

12. Study this READ statement:

```
      READ (5,18) D,L,F
```

Rewrite the statement in "simplified" form.

13. Study the following statement:

```
   37 FORMAT (F10.0,2I10,F10.0,4I10)
```

How many values would you expect to see punched upon the corresponding data card?

14. Study the following statement:

```
49  FORMAT (3F8.0,2I6,7I3,2F10.0)
```

How many values would you expect to see punched upon the corresponding data card?

15. Study the following statement:

```
57  FORMAT (80I1)
```

How many values would you expect to see punched upon the corresponding data card?

16. What is wrong with this format designed for reading a data card?

```
 3  FORMAT (3F15.0,5I10)
```

CHAPTER 6

The WRITE Statement

A REVIEW OF THE BASIC DATA PROCESSING CYCLE

The basic data processing cycle involves three steps. We have seen that those steps are:

1. Obtaining input data values
2. Processing those values.
3. Printing output.

In previous chapters, we concentrated upon Step 1. We saw that input data may be obtained by assignment statements such as

```
PL = 49.836
```

or by READ statements such as

```
READ (5,19) CP,FRN,K
```

We still have Steps 2 and 3 to discuss. We'll delay a discussion of Step 2 for a later chapter. All we'll say about Step 2 now is that "processing" often, but not exclusively, involves the performance of calculations.

Step 3, the step we explore in this chapter, involves the printing of results.

PRINTING ANSWERS

To print results, the WRITE statement is used. Here are some examples of WRITE statements:

```
WRITE (6,3) W,L,FR
WRITE (6,21) KR3,LR3,ND6,JE4
```

PRINTER OUTPUT PAPER

The output paper used by the high-speed printer attached to a computer is folded "accordion style". It appears as shown in Figure 6-1.

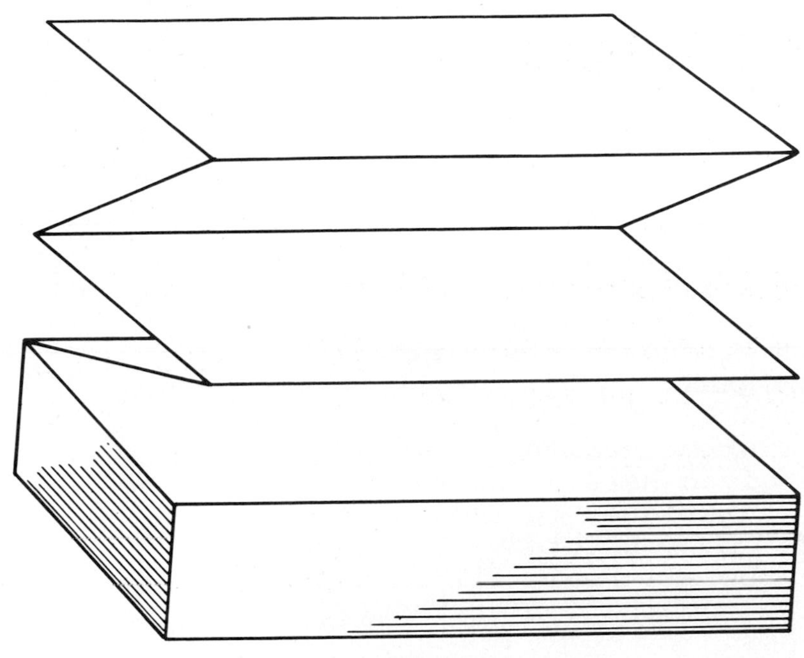

Figure 6-1

Each sheet is 14½" wide and 11" deep. It has a capacity of 132 printed characters across the page. As many as 66 lines of information may be printed on a single sheet.

The printer prints from page to page continuously. The WRITE statement causes printing to take place.

Just as READ statements are always teamed with FORMAT's, so also are WRITE statements. Within parentheses of a WRITE statement, there are two numbers; the leftmost is "6" and means "printer", the rightmost refers to a FORMAT statement. In

```
WRITE (6,3) W,L,FR
```

the "6" means "printer" and the "3" references the FORMAT identified with that statement number. The FORMAT tells *where* on the output paper the values of W, L, and FR are to print.

Using the WRITE statement shown above, we define on the following page the various elements of a WRITE statement:

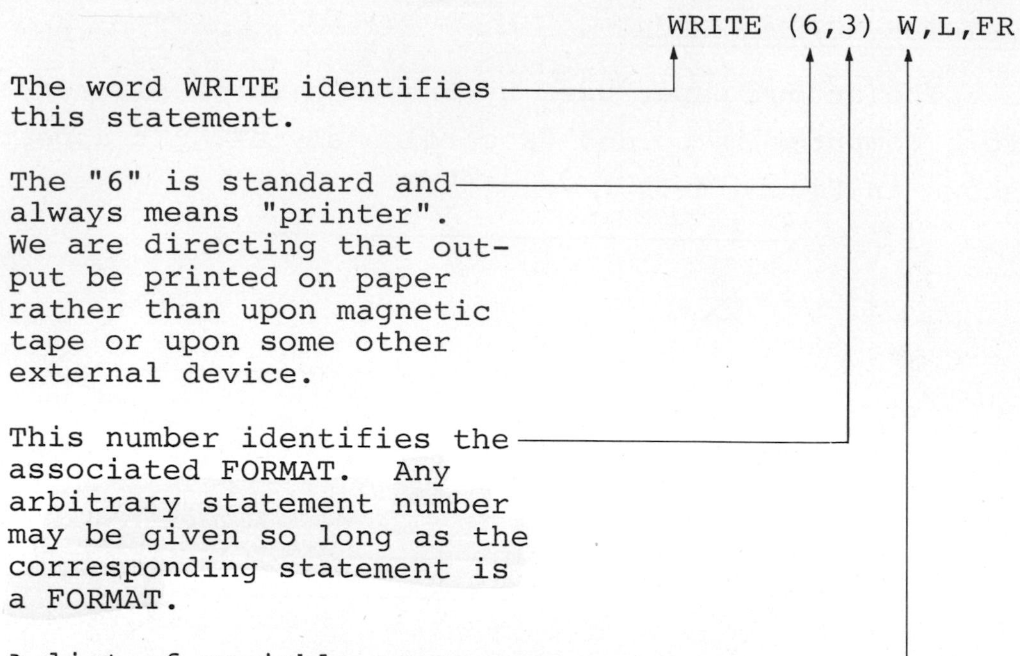

WRITE (6,3) W,L,FR
The word WRITE identifies this statement.
The "6" is standard and always means "printer". We are directing that output be printed on paper rather than upon magnetic tape or upon some other external device.
This number identifies the associated FORMAT. Any arbitrary statement number may be given so long as the corresponding statement is a FORMAT.
A list of variable names may be given here. The values last assigned to those names are to be printed. The names may be all real, all integer, or a combination of the two types.
Statement numbers may or may not be included with WRITE statements depending upon the logic involved.

OUTPUT FORMATS

A FORMAT that could be used with the illustrated WRITE statement might be:

```
3  FORMAT (1X,F8.1,I9,F12.2)
```

When the program executes the WRITE statement, it uses the various parts of the FORMAT to tell it how and where to print the values of W, L, and FR.

Observe that there are four parts in the FORMAT separated by commas. The leftmost part, "1X", tells the printer to print the line "normally". We'll explain what "normally" means later in this chapter. Please accept the code on faith for now.

The second part of the FORMAT, "F8.1", tells the printer

to print the value that W holds, using eight column positions on the output page, and giving that value *rounded* to one decimal place. Observe that W is a real name and that the "F" in "F8.1" designates a real value. The "8" in "F8.1" tells how many print positions are to be used on the answer paper, and the "1" in "F8.1" gives the number of decimal places. If the value last assigned to W was "3.846", the value printed is "3.8"; if the value last assigned to W was "3.853", the value printed is "3.9".

The third part of the FORMAT, "I9", tells where the value last assigned to L is to print. The name L is an integer name; the letter "I" in the FORMAT designates an integer value. The "9" in "I9" tells the computer to use 9 print positions to print the integer value last assigned to L.

Finally, the fourth part of the FORMAT, "F12.2", tells where to print the real value last assigned to FR. The computer will use 12 print positions and print the value rounded to two decimal places.

After the WRITE statement has been executed, the printed line could appear as shown in Figure 6-2.

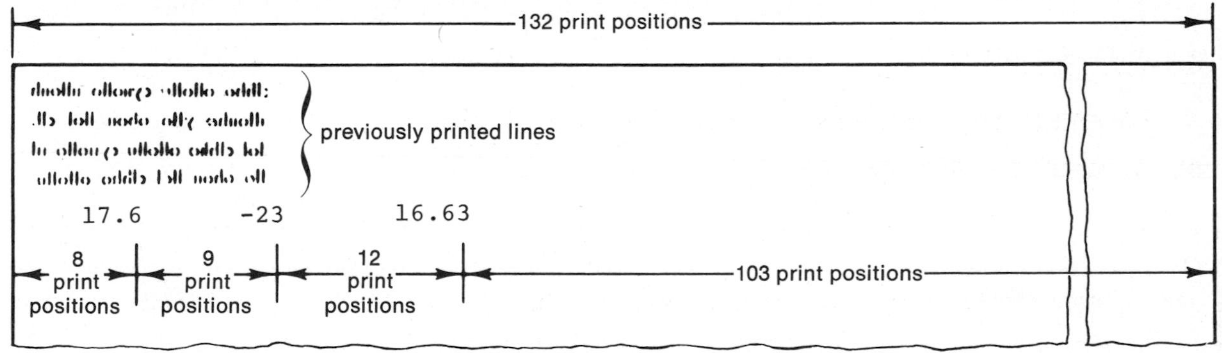

Figure 6-2

Observe that the three values are printed right adjusted in the fields reserved. The value last assigned to W is printed in the leftmost 8 print positions of the paper. Four print positions are actually used; therefore, there are four blanks ahead of "17.6".

The value last assigned to L is printed in the *next* 9 print positions. Three print positions are actually used;

therefore, there are six blanks ahead of "-23".

The value last assigned to FR is printed in the *next* 12 print positions. Five print positions are actually used; therefore, there are seven blanks ahead of "16.63".

Since 29 print positions are actually used, the 103 remaining positions of the line are left blank.

On some computers, the maximum length of a print line is not 132 characters but 136, 144, 120, or even 72. The length used in this example is fairly typical.

PRINTING MESSAGES

A program will often be required to print a heading or a message of some sort. Suppose we want the computer to print "THERE IS ERROR IN DATA". We can employ a WRITE and FORMAT set this way:

```
      WRITE (6,26)
  26  FORMAT (1X,'THERE IS ERROR IN DATA')
```

Observe that there are no variable names given in the WRITE statement. We are not asking the computer to print the values last assigned to any variables; we are asking it to print a *literal message*. That message is given in the corresponding FORMAT.

As in the previous example, the code "1X" means "normal printing". Figure 6-3 shows what the print line looks like.

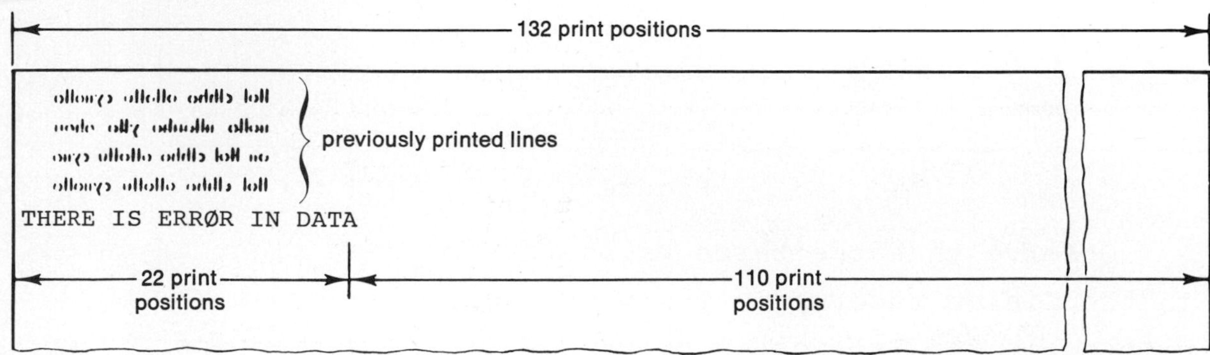

Figure 6-3

The message has 22 characters. It therefore prints between columns 1 and 22, inclusive, upon the output paper. The remaining 110 positions of the paper are left blank.

Suppose you need to print a message which gives the word "COST" beginning at print position 30, the word "IDENTIFICATION" beginning at print position 80, and the words "FINAL DISPOSITION" beginning at print position 110. You can provide a WRITE and FORMAT set that looks like this:

```
     WRITE (6,47)
47   FORMAT (1X,29X,'COST',46X,'IDENTIFICATION',
    *16X,'FINAL DISPOSITION')
    ↑
    └──── This is continuation code
```

In the FORMAT the code 1X means "normal printing", the codes "29X", "46X", and "16X" provide *blanks* on the print line. Figure 6-4 shows the printed line.

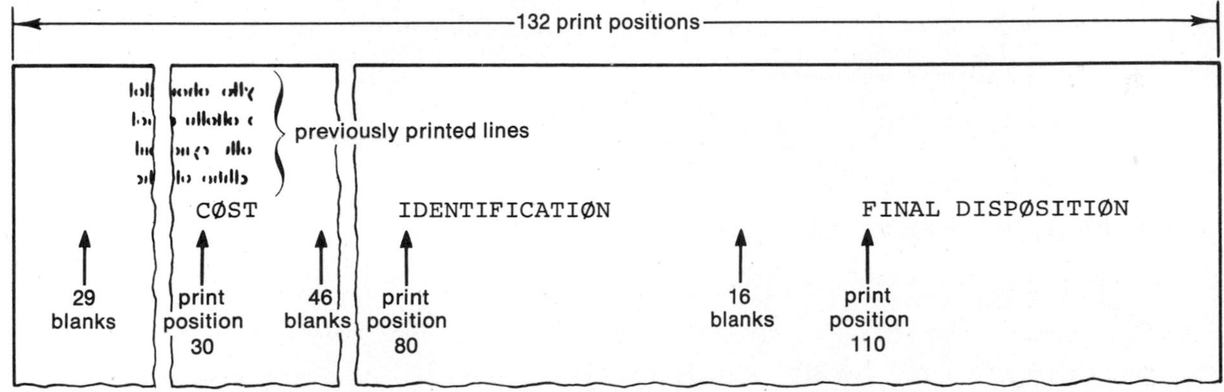

Figure 6-4

The FORMAT has seven parts. The meanings of those parts are:

PART	FUNCTION
1X	Provides "normal printing".
29X	Gives 29 blanks ahead of the word "COST".
'COST'	The word "COST" is printed.
46X	Gives 46 blanks ahead of the word "IDENTIFICATION".
'IDENTIFICATION'	The word "IDENTIFICATION" is printed.
16X	Gives 16 blanks ahead of the words "FINAL DISPOSITION".
'FINAL DISPOSITION'	The words "FINAL DISPOSITION" are printed

In a FORMAT, the letter X preceded by a number tells how many blanks are to be provided in a print line.

CONTINUATIONS OF STATEMENTS

Did you notice that the FORMAT statement was so long it had to be continued? The continuation column on the FORTRAN coding form is used to give continuation codes. See Figure

STATEMENT NUMBER (1–5)	CONT (6)	STATEMENT (7–72)	IDENT (73–80)
		other FORTRAN statements	
		WRITE (6, 47)	
47		FØRMAT (1X, 29X, 'CØST', 46X, 'IDENTIFICATIØN',	
	*	16X, 'FINAL DISPØSITIØN')	

Figure 6-5

In the coding form, column 6 is reserved for a continuation indicator. When a statement must be continued on a second, third, fourth, or additional coding line, an asterisk (or any other character except zero) indicates that the statement is to be continued. When showing continuations, you may use the same character throughout a program, or you may use different ones, such as "1", "2", "3", "A", "B", "C", etc.

Figure 6-6 shows some ways that statements may be continued.

STATEMENT NUMBER (1–5)	CONT (6)	STATEMENT (7–72)	IDENT (73–80)
		D = E + F	
	1	- G + H	
		K = L - N +	
	1	M - I	
	2	+ J	
		F = X + Y	
	*	- Z + R	
	*	+ S + T	

Figure 6-6

Normally, one continues a statement when he or she approaches column 72 and finds that there are not enough column positions remaining on the line to finish the statement. It is not necessary to go all the way to column 72. The continuation may be made at any convenient point.

The coding form on the previous page gives the statements

```
D = E + F - G + H
K = L - N + M - I + J
F = X + Y - Z + R + S + T
```

There was plenty of room to write each of these statements in full upon a coding line, but we elected to continue them simply to show how column 6 could be used.

Portions of FORMAT's may call for the printing of literal messages while other portions may call for the printing of values. Consider this example:

```
      WRITE (6,23) B,K
   23 FORMAT (1X,'VALUE OF B=',F6.1,' VALUE OF K=',I5)
```

Suppose the value of B (in memory) is "9.67" and the value of K is "87". Figure 6-7 shows the line that is printed.

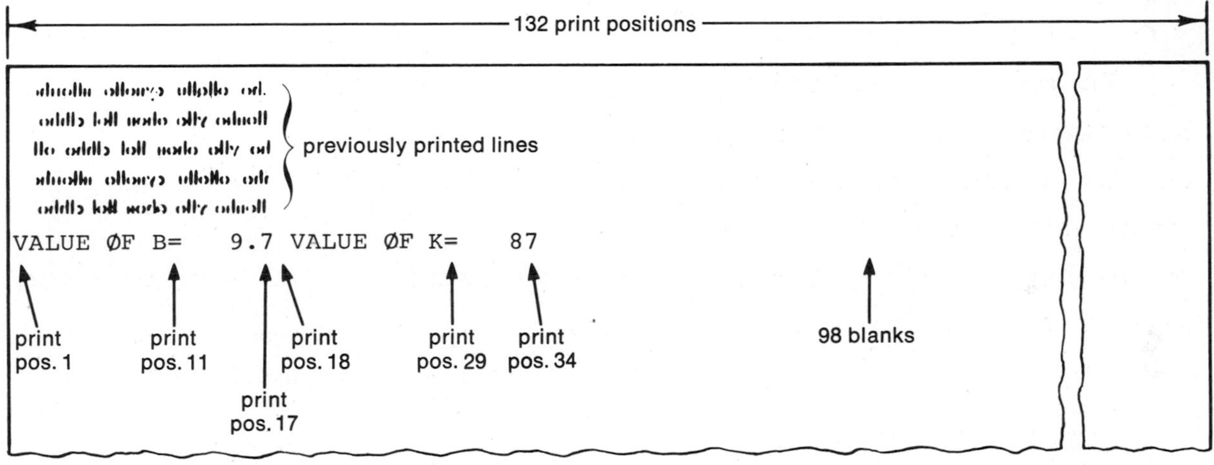

Figure 6-7

The FORMAT calls for normal printing (1X). It also directs the printing of "VALUE OF B=" beginning at column 1 and extending through column 11.

Then the variable "B" shown in the WRITE statement is matched with "F6.1" in the FORMAT and B's value is printed. There are three blanks ahead of the "9".

The literal message " VALUE OF K=" is then printed. The message includes a blank ahead of "V" since the FORMAT clearly shows a blank there. The message begins at print position 18 and extends through print position 29. The blank was provided ahead of the "V" so that the printed line would be easier to read.

Finally, the portion of the FORMAT that reads "I5" is matched with the value of "K". K's value is printed preceded by three blanks.

HEADINGS

Sometimes a literal message is to be printed at the top of the output page. The printing code given at the beginning of the FORMAT should now be the digit "1" preceded and followed by a single quote mark. Example:

```
      WRITE (6,22)
   22 FORMAT ('1',50X,'COST REPORT')
```

This FORMAT has three parts. The meanings of those parts are:

PART	FUNCTION
'1'	The line being printed is directed to appear *at the top* of the next available printer page.
50X	The line is to have blanks from print positions 1 through 50. (There are to be 50 blanks.)
'COST REPORT'	The heading "COST REPORT" is to print beginning at print position 51.

Figure 6-8 shows the printed line

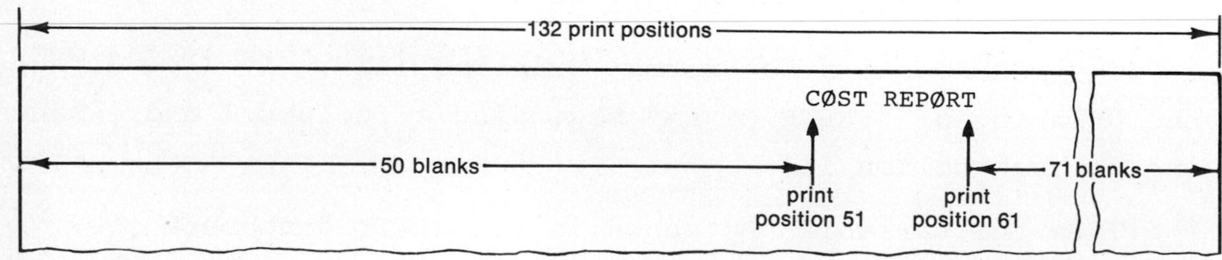

Figure 6-8

PRINTER CODES

You are now familiar with two printer codes. They are

```
1X
'1'
```

The first printer code (1X) tells the printer to print the

requested line on the next available line of the output paper. For example, if 20 lines have already been printed on the output paper, and the computer encounters these statements:

```
      WRITE (6,18)G
   18 FORMAT (1X,F10.2)
```

the printer will print the value of G on the 21st line. The value will be printed right adjusted within print positions 1 through 10 and will be rounded to two decimal places.

The next code ('1') tells the printer to print the requested line at the top of the next available page. For example, if 20 lines have been printed on a page and the program encounters these statements:

```
      WRITE (6,7)
    7 FORMAT ('1','FINAL RESULTS')
```

the printer will advance to the top of the next page and print "FINAL RESULTS" beginning at print position 1.

If you wish to do so, you may always give the printer code "1X" in an alternate way as shown in the example below:

```
      WRITE (6,33)W
   33 FORMAT (' ',F10.2)
```

There are two single quote marks with a single blank between them. The FORMAT shown is equivalent to

```
   33 FORMAT (1X,F10.2)
```

There are two other printer codes which you may sometimes want to use in FORMAT's. They are:

```
      '0' and '+'
```

The former (zero) causes a blank line to be printed *ahead* of the requested line. That is, the printer double spaces before printing. Example:

```
      WRITE (6,7)M
    7 FORMAT ('0',I8)
```

The latter code (plus) causes the requested line to print *on top of* the previously printed line. (Admittedly, this feature may not be too useful.) Example:

```
      WRITE (6,30)
   30 FORMAT ('+','THIS LINE IS SUPERIMPOSED ON ANOTHER')
```

The table that follows shows the four codes that you may select from when giving an output FORMAT statement:

CODE	FUNCTION
1X, ' ', or 1Hب	The requested line prints upon the next available line of the output paper. (ب means "blank")
'1', or 1H1	The requested line prints at the top of the next page.
'0', or 1H0	The requested line prints *after* the computer has given one blank line ahead of this one.
'+', or 1H+	The requested line prints on top of the line that was last printed.

USE OF H IN FORMATS

Instead of using single quotes surrounding literal messages in FORMAT's, a person may optionally count the characters in the message, then place that count ahead of the letter H. For example, the statement

```
   19 FORMAT (1X,10HEND OF JOB)
```

is equivalent to

```
   19 FORMAT (1X,'END OF JOB')
```

Observe that there are ten characters in the message "END OF JOB". The characters "10H" inform the program of this fact, then the ten characters themselves are given.

Here are additional sets of FORMAT's that are equivalent:

```
   33 FORMAT (1X,5HALPHA,20X,4HBETA)
   33 FORMAT (1X,'ALPHA',20X,'BETA')

   77 FORMAT (1H ,F10.2)
   77 FORMAT (' ',F10.2)
   77 FORMAT (1X,F10.2)
```

You'll probably find that using single quotes exclusively is more convenient than counting characters. However, a few FORTRAN systems do not allow the use of single quotes and you'll have to use the "H". We recommend that you use "H" only if you have to.

USE OF SLASHES

Slashes (/) may be used in FORMAT's to cause line "slewing" (printer advancement) before or after a line has been printed.

```
      WRITE (6,27)PR
   27 FORMAT (1X,F10.2//)
```

The two slashes cause the printer to advance two lines *after* the value of "PR" has been printed. This causes one blank line to be printed on the output paper. The rule to remember is that when slashes appear at the end of FORMAT's, the printer provides one less blank line than the number of slashes shown (four slashes give 3 blank lines; three slashes, two blank lines, etc.).

A question might arise as to what this next FORMAT accomplishes:

```
      WRITE (6,27)PR
   27 FORMAT (1X,F10.2/)
```

One slash provides *no* blank lines after the value of PR is printed. ~~You get exactly the same results as if you had written~~

```
      WRITE (6,27)PR
   27 FORMAT (1X,F10.2)
```

Slashes provided in the middle of a FORMAT call for line slews. For example, if you give this set of statements:

```
      WRITE (6,24)
   24 FORMAT ('1',20X,'AAAAA'/1X,20X,'BBBBB')
```

the printer will print *two* lines. The printer will print "AAAAA" at the top of a page beginning at print position 21. Then, it will print "BBBBB" on the *next line*, also beginning at print position 21. The code "1X" in the FORMAT is the printer control code of the second line.

If there had been two slashes instead of one in the FORMAT, the printer would have given one blank line between "AAAAA" and "BBBBB".

Consider now this example:

```
      WRITE (6,19)R,S,T
   19 FORMAT (1X,F10.1//1X,F10.1///1X,F10.1)
```

The printer will print the value of R on the next available line. Then it will skip a line and print the value of S on the next available line. Finally, the printer will skip two lines and print the value of T on the next available line. Figure 6-9 shows the output.

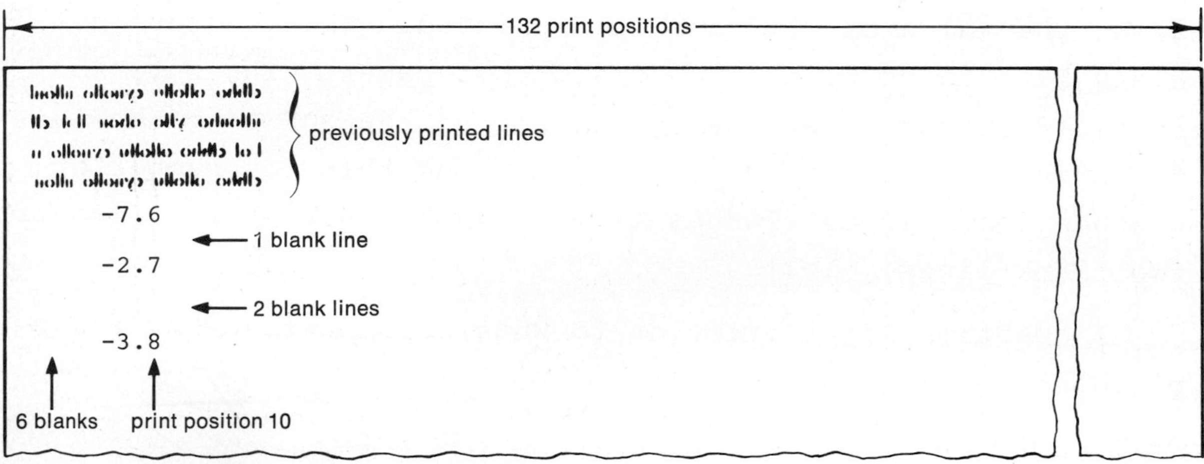

Figure 6-9

If the slash is at the beginning of a FORMAT, the printer will advance the printer *before* the requested line is printed. Example:

```
      WRITE (6,9)P
    9 FORMAT (/,1X,F8.1)
```

The printer will advance an additional line position from where it was located after the last line was printed. This slew has the effect of giving a blank line *ahead* of the line being printed. If there had been two slashes instead of one, the printer would have provided two blank lines. When slashes come at the beginning of a FORMAT, therefore, the printer will give as many blank lines as there are slashes.

Now that we understand how to obtain output, the meaning of this next program should be clear.

```
      WRITE (6,4)
4     FORMAT ('1',50X,'YEAR TO  DATE'/1X,51X,'COST REPORT'//)
      WRITE (6,5)
5     FORMAT (1X,40X,'ITEMS',15X,'DOLLARS'//)
      READ (5,7) NUM,AMT
7     FORMAT (I10,F10.0)
      WRITE (6,9) NUM,AMT
9     FORMAT (1X,I43,14X,F10.2)
      WRITE (6,10)
10    FORMAT (/,1X,'END OF REPORT')
      STOP
      END
```

Figure 6-10 shows the output that might be given.

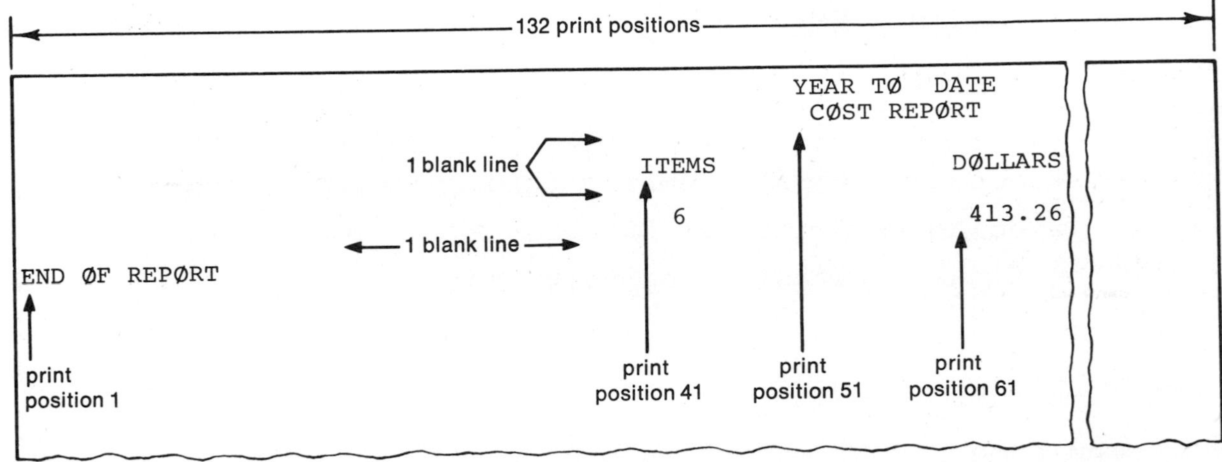

Figure 6-10

SIMPLIFIED PRINT

A simplified form of the WRITE statement is this:

```
PRINT 9,NUM,AMT
```

In the statement, 9 represents the FORMAT, and the names NUM and AMT represent values to be printed.

Observe the difference between the above statement and the more general form

```
WRITE (6,9) NUM,AMT
```

The word PRINT is used instead of WRITE. The punctuation is also different.

In this text, we will emphasize the WRITE form since it is the more general and flexible.

FORMAT LOCATIONS

FORMAT's may be located anywhere in a program so long as

they are ahead of the END statement. Since the computer examines a program thoroughly during compilation, it has no difficulty knowing what a FORMAT says when one is referenced. The last program example shows five FORMAT statements. The program would have worked exactly the same if all FORMAT's had been grouped either at the beginning of the program or at the end, just ahead of the END statement.

SKIPPING COLUMNS ON DATA CARDS

When reading cards, columns may be skipped by the use of "X" in FORMAT's. Example:

```
      READ (5,9)P,Y
    9 FORMAT (10X,F10.0,10X,F10.0)
```

The computer skips columns 1 through 10, picks up the value for P in columns 11 through 20, then skips columns 21 through 30, then finally picks up the value for Y in column 31 through 40.

MULTIPLE USES OF FORMATS

The same FORMAT may be used by several READ's, or several WRITE's, if those READ and WRITE statements find them acceptable. Any FORMAT may be used by either READ or WRITE statements. Thus, if required, the FORMAT

```
   80 FORMAT (1X,F10.2)
```

may be used several times by both READ and WRITE statements. If used for reading, the code "1X" causes the first column of the data card to be skipped.

REPEATED USE OF FORMATS

A FORMAT will be used over and over until the required number of values has been read or written. If a FORMAT contains more defined fields than required, the extra parts of the FORMAT will be ignored. Example:

```
      WRITE (6,9) A,B
    9 FORMAT ('1',F8.2,F6.1,F9.3)
      WRITE (6,10) X,Y,Z
   10 FORMAT (' ',F10.2)
```

The values of A and B will be printed according to "F8.2" (for A) and "F6.1" (for B) in FORMAT 9. The "F9.3" part of the FORMAT will be ignored.

Then, the values of X, Y, and Z will be printed according to the "F10.2" part of FORMAT 10. Since three values are to be printed, FORMAT 10 will be used three times. The computer prints four lines. The values printed appear as shown in Figure 6-11.

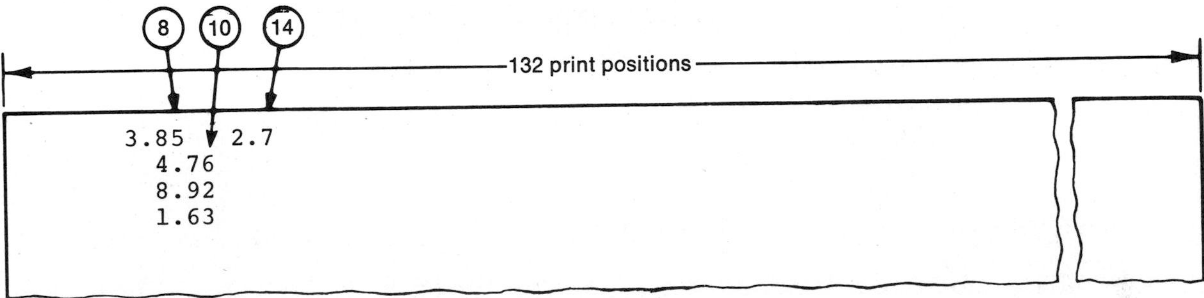

Figure 6-11

Where READ's are concerned, the principle is the same. Portions of FORMAT's are ignored or repeated as shown above. Cards are involved, though, rather than printed lines.

EXERCISES AND PROBLEMS

1. In a WRITE statement, what is the meaning of the "6" given within parentheses?
2. What number besides "6" would you expect to find within parentheses in a WRITE statement?
3. What is the purpose of the FORMAT statement that is associated with a WRITE statement?
4. May a FORMAT statement be used by more than one WRITE statement?
5. May a FORMAT statement be used by both READ *and* WRITE statements within a single program?
6. How many different printer control characters may you show in FORMAT statements? Identify them and give their meanings.

7. What is the purpose of slashes given in FORMAT statements?

8. What code letter of the alphabet is associated with real values in FORMAT statements?

9. What code letter of the alphabet is associated with integer values in FORMAT statements?

10. What does the code letter "X" in FORMAT statements accomplish?

11. May the list of variable names given in a WRITE statement include both real and integer names?

12. What is the capacity of a page of computer output paper? Give the capacity in number of characters per line and in number of lines per page.

13. What characters may you use in column 6 of the FORTRAN coding form when you wish to show statement continuations?

14. If B's value is "9.268", what will the computer print when given these statements?

```
      WRITE (6,8) B
    8 FORMAT (1X,F10.2)
```

15. Refer to Question 14. In what print position will the decimal point print?

16. Assuming a line has a capacity of 132 characters, what FORMAT would you give in order to have the program print "EMPLOYEE SALARY REPORT" centered at the top of a fresh page?

17. Study the two statements that follow.

```
      WRITE (6,15) R
   15 FORMAT (1X,'VALUE OF R IS',F8.2)
```

If the value of R is "34.27", in what print position will the digit "7" of the number print?

18. Change the FORMAT given below to one that uses quote marks instead of the "H" code.

```
   37 FORMAT (1H1,20X,16HEXPENSE ACCOUNTS//)
```

19. Study the WRITE and FORMAT statements given below.

```
        WRITE (6,37) P,R,T,V,D
     37 FORMAT (1X,2F10.2)
```

How many lines will the computer print?

20. Study the two statements given below.

```
        WRITE (6,40) JOE,PETE
     40 FORMAT (1X,I5,F10.1,F10.2)
```

How many lines will the computer print? What does the program do with the "extra" "F10.2" given in the FORMAT?

CHAPTER 7

Performing Calculations

CALCULATIONS

The basic data processing cycle involves three steps. The first has to do with obtaining input data; the second, with processing the data; and the third, with providing output.

We've already discussed the first and third steps. Now, let's discuss Step 2. This is the step during which data is processed. Much, but not all, of "processing data" has to do with the performing of calculations. In this chapter, we show how calculations may be performed.

Calculations to be performed are defined in assignment statements. Consider this example:

```
DIST = RATE * TIME
```

The computer is being told to multiply the last value assigned to RATE by the last value assigned to TIME. If the last value assigned to RATE was "60.5" and the last value assigned to TIME was "2.5", then the computed value is "151.25". That value is assigned to DIST. The value assigned to DIST may now be printed and/or used in further calculations.

FIVE OPERATIONS

The example shows that the asterisk (*) calls for a multiplication operation to be performed. There are five arithmetic operations which may be performed. The table on the following page shows the operations and their associated symbols:

ARITHMETIC OPERATIONS

SYMBOL	OPERATION
+	add
-	subtract
*	multiply
/	divide
**	exponentiate (raise to a power)

Note: Some FORTRAN systems permit ** *and* ↑ for exponentiations.

Here are some examples of the symbols being used in assignment statements:

```
A = B + C
D = E - 6.3
F = G * H * P * 5.8
Q = R/S + 8.76
T = U **3 + V **4.3
```

The first example shows that the last value assigned to C is to be added to the last value assigned to B. The result is to be assigned to the variable A.

The next example shows that an expression may contain the actual numeric values required. The value "6.3" is to be subtracted from E's value, and the result is to be assigned to D.

The third example shows that several operations may be given in an assignment statement. The last values assigned to G, H, and P are to be multiplied together. The result is to be multiplied by "5.8". Finally, the result is to be assigned to F.

In the next example, the value last assigned to R is to be divided by the last value assigned to S. Then, "8.76" is to be added to the result. Finally, the computed value is to be assigned to Q.

The final example shows that the computation

U^3

is to be made and that the value is to be added to the result of the computation $V^{4.3}$. The final result is to be assigned to T.

Powers may be negative. Example:

```
W = G**(-5)
```

INTEGER CALCULATIONS

All the previous examples gave real values and names. Integer values and names may also be used in programs. Hence, the statements

```
I = J + 3
K = L * M
M = N/5
KK = LL**3
```

and others involving integers are acceptable. In the example

```
M = N/5
```

the computer obtains an integer value from the calculation "N/5" by discarding the fractional part. If N holds the value "17", the value assigned to M is "3".

SEQUENCE OF OPERATIONS

An expression may contain many arithmetic operations. Consider this one:

```
AL = BET*GAM/EPS+PH-ZE**3
```

A question naturally arises as to which operation is performed first, which second, etc. The order of operations is governed by this table:

ORDER OF OPERATIONS

SEQUENCE	OPERATION
FIRST	**
SECOND	*,/
THIRD	+,-

The computer scans the expression several times moving from left to right. If, during the first scan, the computer sees exponentiations to be performed (**), it performs them as the computer sees them. This means that in the example given on the previous page, the calculation

```
ZE**3
```

is performed first. ZE is raised to the third power and the result is saved.

It is not "-ZE" which is raised to the third power. It is ZE. In FORTRAN, the hyphen (-) always means "subtract". The subtract operation in the example will have to wait until all exponentiations, multiplications, and divisions have been processed.

When all exponentiations have been processed, the computer scans the expression again from left to right. This time, it looks for multiplications (*) and divisions (/). It doesn't matter in which order the multiplications and divisions appear, the computer performs the indicated operations in the sequence that they appear. In the example, the computer multiplies the last value assigned to BET by the last value assigned to GAM. That is, it performs the calculation:

```
BET * GAM
```

The computer saves that result and immediately divides it by EPS. The computer saves that result.

In the third scan of the expression, the computer performs additions and subtractions. It adds the saved result of

```
BET * GAM / EPS
```

to the value that PH holds. It then subtracts the result of the operation

```
ZE**3
```

The final value is assigned to AL.

As you can see, the operations of additions and subtractions are performed during the third scan in whatever sequence they appear.

PARENTHESES

The normal sequence (hierarchy) of FORTRAN operations may not be acceptable to you. If so, you can *alter* the sequence by installing parentheses in expressions. Before processing the five operation symbols "+", "-", "/", "*", and "**", the computer looks for parentheses. Whenever it finds a set, it performs the operations within parentheses before going on to the remainder of the expression. Example:

```
AA = BB/(CC+DD*EE**4) + FF**3*GG
```

The computer finds a set of parentheses. In a set of parentheses, there must always be an open symbol "(" for every close symbol ")". It is possible for a set of parentheses to be nested within another set. If there are nested parentheses, the computer always zeroes in to the innermost set. While in the innermost set, the computer always performs operations according to their natural sequence; that is, exponentiations first, multiplications and/or divisions next, and additions and/or subtractions last.

In the example, the computer zeroes in on

```
(CC+DD*EE**4)
```

It performs the exponentiation first:

```
EE**4
```

Then, it multiplies DD by the result of the exponentiation and finally, adds that result to the last value assigned to CC. The result is saved.

Having taken care of calculations given within parentheses the computer finds that its next calculation must be

```
FF**3
```

This calculation is performed and the result is saved.

Then, it divides the value last assigned to BB by the result saved from the calculation within parentheses. It saves that result.

Then, the computer multiplies the result given by "FF**3" by the value last assigned to GG.

During the final scan, the computer adds the saved results of

```
BB/(CC+DD*EE**4)
      and
FF**3*GG
```

That final value is assigned to AA.

Let's see how various mathematical computations could be performed:

EXAMPLES OF CALCULATIONS

EQUATION	FORTRAN STATEMENT
$p = r+s$	P = R+S
$q = \frac{r}{s}$	Q = R/S
$h = \frac{r+s}{t}$	H = (R+S)/T
$h = r + \frac{s}{t}$	H = R+S/T or H = R+(S/T)
$x = \frac{axb}{cxd}$	X = A*B/(C*D) or X = (A*B)/(C*D)

The second to last example is correctly written as "H = R+S/T" but a user might elect to insert unneeded parentheses giving "H = R+(S/T)". It is not wrong to place unneeded parentheses in an expression. Nevertheless, a user may elect to do so because (1) he or she may not be sure of the computer's natural sequence of performing calculations or (2) he or she may believe that the insertion of parentheses provides better documentation. It actually does sometimes. For example:

$$p = \frac{\frac{r}{s}}{t}$$

may be correctly written in FORTRAN as "P = R/S/T" but it appears less confusing if it is written as "P = (R/S)/T".

A simple rule about parentheses is this: "When in doubt,

put them in." An abundance of parentheses will not hurt your program in any way (assuming that they have been correctly placed). Consider this equation:

$$f = \frac{\left[\frac{a+b}{3.5}\right]}{2.6-c} + \frac{d}{e+f}$$

The FORTRAN statement could be written

```
F = (A+B)/3.5/(2.6-C) + D/(E+F)
```

using a minimum of parentheses, or as

```
F = (((A+B)/3.5)/(2.6-C)) + ((D)/(E+F))
```

using more than the minimum.

When you have written a complicated expression involving several open and several close parentheses, you should double check the expression to make sure that it really says what you want it to say. Make sure, especially, that there are just as many open "(" parentheses as close ")" parentheses.

It's all right to rearrange an equation if you find that doing so is desirable. Thus,

$$p = \frac{q}{a} + \frac{r}{a}$$

may be written "P = Q/A+R/A" or the equation may be rearranged to

$$p = \frac{q+r}{a}$$

and written as "P = (Q+R)/A". It is well to remember that on most computers, divisions are slower than multiplications and that multiplications are slower than additions and/or subtractions. If an equation can be rearranged to remove an extraneous division or multiplication, its evaluation is expedited. Don't go overboard on rearranging equations simply to gain speed. The time you save may be only a few microseconds. (A microsecond is one-millionth of a second.) The computer time you gain is not worth your human-time investment.

SPECIAL INFORMATION CONCERNING EXPONENTIATIONS

When raising a value to an integer power, an integer name or number should be used as the power. Example:

$$p = r^5$$

should be written "P = R**5", not "P = R**5." True, the latter rendition, using a decimal point in the power, will often give the correct result. But at times, you'll have problems. The reason we advise against the latter method is because R may sometimes contain a negative value. If so, the computer will not give the desired calculation. When you write

```
P = R**5
```

the computer actually performs

```
P = R*R*R*R*R
```

Whether R is either positive *or* negative, a result is computed and assigned to P.

When you write

```
P = R**5.
```

the computer works out the problem by first obtaining the natural logarithm of R. It uses the logarithm to help compute the value for P. In mathematics, negative values *do not have* logarithms. Therefore, if the value last assigned to R was negative, the computer will not be able to give a result for "P = R**5.".

The rule to remember is this: When a whole-number power is to be used, use an integer for the power, not a real number.

Mixed powers may, of course, be used in exponentiations. All these next statements are correct:

```
 D = F**3.5
 E = G**.5
FF = H**(1./3.)
WW = R**(-8.5)
```

The important point to remember is that when a power has

a decimal point, the value being raised to that power must be a positive number. The values last assigned to F, G, H, and R in the previous examples must be positive.

Recall that the hyphen (-) in FORTRAN always means subtract. There is a difference between

```
D = -X**4
```

and

```
D = (-X)**4
```

In the former example, if the value last assigned to X was "2.0", the computer assigns "-16.0" to D; in the latter example, assuming the same value for X, the computer assigns "16.0" to D.

If an expression contains a series of exponentiations, the computer works them out from *right to left*. (This is an exception to the rule that scans are made from left to right.) If a statement is written this way:

```
T = G**I + H**2**3
```

the computer first raises G to the I power. Then, it raises "2" to the "3" power (giving "8") and then raises H to the "8" power. If H holds the value "3.0", the computed result for "H**2**3" is "6561.0". It's the same as if "H**2**3" had been written "H**(2**3)".

This calculation is certainly different from first raising H to the "2" power, then raising that result to the "3" power. One can, however, obtain the latter result by placing parentheses in the expression this way:

```
T = G**I + (H**2)**3
```

SPECIAL NOTE ABOUT MIXING MODES

You know that values in expressions should all be either in real or in integer mode. (An exception is integer powers in exponentiations.) However, many FORTRAN systems do permit mixing modes. Hence

```
F = R + K/S
```

is all right even though K represents an integer value and R and S represent real values. Be careful, however, if there is a series of pure integer values involved in division calculations. You may get an unexpected result. In the statement:

```
F = R + K/N
```

the "K/N" portion of the expression is performed in pure integer mode. If the values that R, K, and N hold are "1.2", "5", and "2", respectively, the computer will add "1.2" to "2" (not "2.5") and assign the result, "3.2", to F.

UPDATING VARIABLES

In expressions, the same variable name may be shown on both sides of the equal sign. Examples:

```
KNT = KNT + 1
SUMVAL = SUMVAL + VAL
```

In FORTRAN, the equals sign does not mean "equals". It means "is assigned the value of". Hence, "KNT = KNT + 1" should be read as "KNT is assigned the value of KNT + 1". This means that the *old* value of KNT is used to help compute its replacement value. The new value is substituted for the old one. Thus, if the old value assigned to KNT was "14", the new value assigned to KNT is "15".

In the second example, the value last assigned to VAL is added to the value last assigned to SUMVAL. The result is assigned to SUMVAL. If the value that VAL held was "3.6" and the value that SUMVAL held was "2.8", the new value assigned to SUMVAL is "6.4".

In both examples, the former values assigned to KNT and SUMVAL disappear. Obviously, one would not use these statements unless the person wanted to update KNT and SUMVAL and did not mind losing the old values that those variables held.

FUNCTIONS

There are several functions built into the FORTRAN system that enable you to easily obtain such values as sines, cosines, logarithms, square roots, and others. Later in this text, we will give a table giving all available built-in functions. In the meantime, we'll explore several of the most useful ones. These are:

TABLE OF FUNCTIONS

FUNCTION	PURPOSE
SIN	Obtains the trigonometric sine of an angle given in radian measure.
COS	Obtains the trigonometric cosine of an angle given in radian measure.
ABS	Obtains the absolute value of a numeric quantity.
SQRT	Computes the square root of a positive real value.
ALOG	Computes the natural logarithm of a positive real value.
EXP	Computes "e" (2.718281828....) raised to some desired real power.

To use one of these functions in an expression, one simply calls for it by name and supplies the value the function must have to work with. That value is called the function's "argument". Here is an example:

```
DDT = ABS (FFW)
```

The program obtains the absolute value of FFW and assigns it to DDT. If FFW holds the value "-83.6", DDT will receive the value "83.6"; if FFW holds the value "83.6", that value, in unchanged form, will be assigned to DDT.

Some additional examples:

```
WRD = P + SIN(ALPHA) + SQRT(3.6)

PL3 = ALOG(FN+SQRT(RQ+2.4))
```

```
D = EXP(SIG)
EL = SIN(A) + 2.*COS(A) + SQRT(3.1416)
```

In the first statement, the sine of ALPHA is computed. ALPHA holds an angle expressed in radians. Then, the square root of "3.6" is computed. The sine of ALPHA is added to the value last assigned to P and to the square root of "3.6". The final result is assigned to WRD.

The functions shown in the other examples compute natural logarithms, sines, cosines, and square roots. Also, in the third statement shown above, the value of "e" is raised to the SIG power. That statement could alternately have been written

```
D = 2.7182818**SIG
```

As you can see, arguments in functions may be variable names (for example, P, SIG, A), actual numeric values (for example, "3.6", "3.1416"), or expressions. In the second statement, "RQ+2.4" is the argument for the function, SQRT, and "FN+SQRT(RQ+2.4)" is the argument for the function, ALOG. Be sure to observe that arguments must always be enclosed within parentheses.

As a point of interest, you might observe that square roots can be computed in two ways. You can use the SQRT function or you can raise a value to the ".5" power. Example:

```
WDD = SQRT (F*G)
WDD = (F*G)**.5
```

Either way, the square root of "F*G" is computed and assigned to WDD. The first method is much faster.

Other roots may be computed this way:

ROOTS TABLE

ROOT	STATEMENT
cube	A = X ** (1./3.)
fourth	A = X ** .25
fifth	A = X ** .20
sixth	A = X ** (1./6.)
etc.	etc.

EXERCISES AND PROBLEMS

1. What five symbols are associated with performing calculations? Tell what each character does.

2. In the absence of parentheses, what type (or types) of calculations does FORTRAN perform first?

3. In the absence of parentheses, what type (or types) of calculations does FORTRAN perform second?

4. In the absence of parentheses, what type (or types) of calculations does FORTRAN perform third?

5. Why might you give parentheses in arithmetic expressions?

6. Is it permissible to give sets of parentheses within other sets of parentheses in arithmetic expressions?

7. Study this next expression:

   ```
   W = A + B * C + D
   ```

   What calculation will FORTRAN perform first?

8. Study this next expression:

   ```
   W = A + B * (C + D)
   ```

   What calculation will FORTRAN perform first?

9. Study these next two statements:

   ```
   R = T ** 3
   R = T ** 3.
   ```

   Which statement would you select to compute

   $$r = t^3$$

   Why?

10. Study these next two statements:

    ```
    C = (-B) ** 4
    C = -B ** 4
    ```

    Would the computer give two different results if B's value is "5."?

11. Refer to Question 10. Would the computer give two different results if B's value is "-5."?

12. Study this statement:

```
L = 21 / 4 + 3
```

What value does the program assign to L?

13. Study this statement:

```
B = V ** 4.3
```

What would you say should be true about V's arithmetic sign?

14. Study this next statement:

```
M = 2 ** 3 ** 2
```

Would you say the value assigned to M is "64" or would you say it's "512"?

15. Write a FORTRAN statement that agrees with this engineering equation:

$$d = \frac{c}{f + g} + h$$

16. Write a FORTRAN statement that agrees with this engineering equation:

$$x = \frac{w + y}{h} + \frac{d}{f}$$

17. Write a FORTRAN statement that agrees with this equation:

$$d = \sqrt[5]{f}$$

18. Define "argument" as it concerns FORTRAN functions.

19. In what measurement are trignometric angles given to function with the names SIN and COS?

20. To obtain the common logarithm of a number, you may first obtain the natural logarithm of the number, then multiply the result by ".43429448". Show the FORTRAN statement that gives you the common logarithm of "25.".

21. What is wrong with the following statement?

```
X = (A*B) + C / D + E)
```

22. Explain the meaning of the statement

```
YTD = YTD + WK
```

23. If, in FORTRAN, the equals sign does not mean "equals", as the text states, what does the equals sign mean?

24. In the statement

```
ALPHA = ABS (BETA)
```

What value is assigned to ALPHA if BETA's value is "-3.6"? What is assigned if BETA's value is "8.4"?

25. The FORTRAN expression

```
R = B / -2.8
```

is illegal because two arithmetic operators may not be given in sequence. How, then, would you code the relationship?

$$r = \frac{b}{-2.8}$$

26. Code the equation that computes A:

$$A = P\left[\left(1 + \frac{i}{q}\right)\right]^{nq}$$

This equation computes the amount, "A", of a certain principal, "P", invested at "i" percent for "n" years, compounded "q" times per year. The percent must be given as a decimal. For example, if the percent is 8½, "i" would be given as ".085".

CHAPTER 8

LOOPS

DEFINITION OF LOOP

We have seen that the basic data processing cycle involves:

(1) Obtaining data

(2) Processing data

(3) Providing output

but we didn't emphasize the fact that during the solution of a problem, the cycle is repeated many times. The cycle may be repeated hundreds, if not thousands or even millions of times.

When a program repeats a series of instructions, it is said to be "in a loop". To get a clear idea of what a loop is and what it can do for you, let us first examine a program that has no loop, then one that does.

```
      READ (5,19) GX,HY
      PZ = GX/HY
      WRITE (6,44) PZ,GX,HY
      STOP
   19 FORMAT (2F10.0)
   44 FORMAT (1X,3F15.1)
      END
```

This program reads a single punched card, computes a value for PZ, then prints a single line of results.

This program certainly has the three elements of the basic data processing cycle: input, processing, output. But, because the program has no loop, it doesn't accomplish much. The programmer who wrote this program would have been better off using a pocket calculator.

It is important to understand that a computer should not always be used for problems that involve calculations. Often, a slide rule, a desk calculator, or an electronic pocket calculator is a much better choice for a given problem. In a problem, look for the key element, repetition. If a problem does not involve the repetition of certain operations (that is, if it does not involve a loop), then a computer should probably not be used. Doing so, will surely cost more and actually take longer to obtain the solution.

Contrast the example program on the previous page with this one:

```
  8  READ (5,19,END=60) GX,HY
     PZ=GX/HY
     WRITE (6,44) PZ,GX,HY
     GO TO 8
 19  FORMAT (2F10.0)
 44  FORMAT (1X,3F15.1)
 60  WRITE (6,70)
 70  FORMAT (/1X,'END OF RUN')
     STOP
     END
```

This program introduces two new elements. First, the READ statement includes an "END=" element which we'll explain soon. Second, we meet the "GO TO" statement for the first time.

The program reads a data card (input), makes a calculation (process), then prints a line of answers (output). But the job is not yet completed. The "GO TO 8" statement tells the program to return to the statement identified with statement number "8". The entire three-step process is caused to repeat. Then repeat again. And again.

This program is designed to read and process more than one data card. It can, in fact, read and process hundreds or even thousands of data cards. The program has been written so that it operates "in a loop".

When does this loop terminate? When there are no more cards in the data deck. If the computer attempts to read a non-existent card from the data deck, the program causes the computer to jump to statement "60". The program continues from that point until it encounters a "STOP" statement.

GO TO

A "GO TO" statement is called an "unconditional transfer" statement because, upon encountering it, a program is given no choice. It *must* jump (transfer or branch) to the statement mentioned in the "GO TO". A jump may be forward or backward within a program. In the example, the jump is backward to the statement labeled "8".

"END =" IN READ

In this example, the READ statement is a bit more complex than the one given in previous chapters. Example:

```
8  READ (5,94) DL, EP, RF
```

This statement includes no "END=" element and should be used only when the program *actually expects* to find a data card to be read. If, for some reason, a data card is not available, the program *stops* and the computer gives an error message.

This type of READ statement, therefore, is not one that one should use if he or she wants to obtain several cards from a data deck. The more convenient READ form to use is

```
8  READ (5,94,END=75) DL, EP, RF
```

Now, the READ statement can be used to read data cards over and over until the cards run out. The READ statement, itself, contains a "conditional jump" to statement "75". The jump takes place only when an attempt is made to read a data card and a card is not found.

The jump is called "conditional" because the jump is made only when there is an "end of file". The term "end of file" means there are no further input data values to process.

The statement number that you place following "END=" may be any number you find convenient. There must, of course, be a portion of your program that begins with a statement having that number. In the above example, the program prints the message "END OF RUN" at end-of-file time. Statement "60" could simply have read

```
60  STOP
```

The meaning of the basic data processing flowchart, repeated in Figure 8-1, should now be quite clear to you.

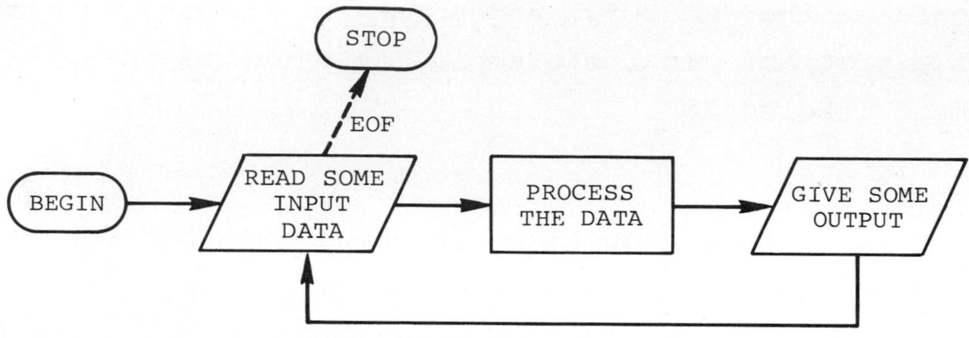

Figure 8-1

The arrow that runs from "Give some output" to "Read some input data" defines the boundaries of a loop that is to be executed many times. When the data runs out (EOF means "end of file"), the program transfers to the point labeled "STOP". As an alternate course of action, the program may continue with additional processing at end-of-file time instead of merely stopping.

"ERR=" OPTION

READ statements may be written this way:

```
2  READ (5,20,END=90,ERR=35) P,T
```

or

```
2  READ (5,18,ERR=500) T,M
```

The "ERR=" option may be used, if you wish, to define a statement to which the program is to jump if a read error occurs during reading. If, for example, a data card has been punched in such a way that the program cannot read it, the program will jump to the statement indicated at the time that the read fails.

The "ERR=" entry is an option. When used, it can precede or follow the "END=" option if the latter option is also used.

SUMMATION PROBLEM

Let's see what we can do with the ability to employ loops. Suppose we have the data deck illustrated in Figure 8-2. We may assume that there are about one hundred cards in the deck but there could be many more.

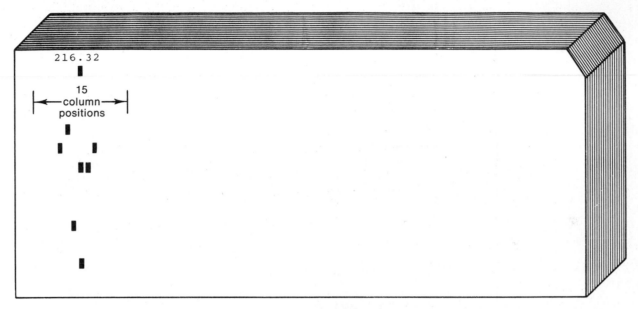

Figure 8-2

Let's assume each card contains a component cost for building a farm tractor. Assume also that each card contains only one real value punched according to "FORMAT (F15.0)". Each value has an imbedded decimal point.

Let's say we need a program to sum the values punched on the data cards. We can accomplish this task by first zeroing out a memory cell (let's call it "TOTCOS"), then adding to it the individual cost, "COST".

We haven't discussed flowcharts yet, but the one in Figure 8-3 on the following page should be easy to understand. The flowchart shows what we will ask the computer to do.

The flowchart shows that before the program goes into a loop, the value "zero" is assigned to "TOTCOS". This action is called "initializing". Actions that take place before a program's loop actually begins, come under the heading of "initialization". Additional functions that fall under the topic of "initialization" are such tasks as printing report headings, assigning initial values to program constants, and others.

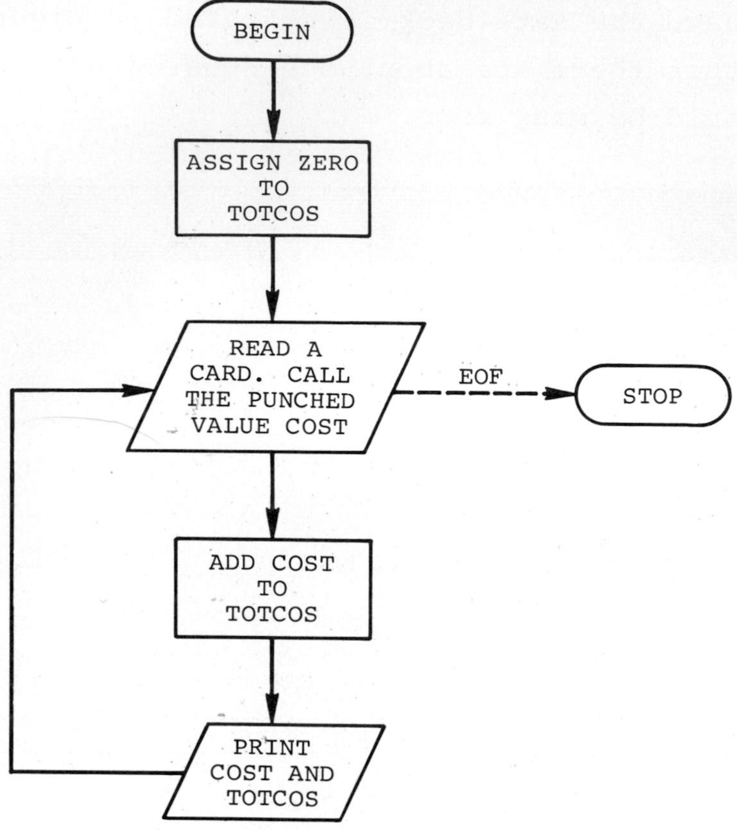

Figure 8-3

The flowchart shows that the program reads a card, assigns the value thereon to "COST". Then, it adds "COST" to "TOTCOS", prints both values, and goes back to the READ statement to repeat the cycle. At end-of-file time the program stops.

Here is the FORTRAN program that accomplishes the desired task. (Observe how the indenting of statements makes a program more understandable.)

```
      TOTCOS = 0.
   20 READ (5,30,END=80) COST
         TOTCOS = TOTCOS + COST
         WRITE (6,35) COST,TOTCOS
         GO TO 20
   30 FORMAT (F15.0)
   35 FORMAT (1X,2F20.2)
   80 STOP
      END
```

The first time the READ statement is executed, the value

"216.32" found upon the first data card is assigned to "COST". The statement

TOTCOS = TOTCOS + COST

causes that value to be added to "TOTCOS". Since the original value of TOTCOS was "zero", the new value that "TOTCOS" holds is "216.32".

When the program goes to the READ statement again, a *new* value *replaces* the old value of "COST". Suppose the next data card holds the value "113.20". That value replaces "COST" and is added to "TOTCOS". The new value of "TOTCOS" becomes "329.52".

This program prints the increasing values of "TOTCOS" as they are generated. The first few lines of output given by the program could be those shown in Figure 8-4.

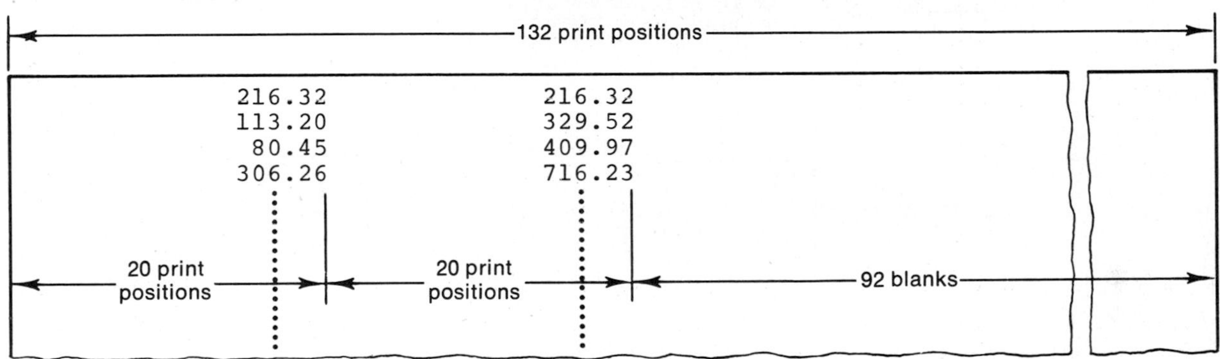

Figure 8-4

BASIC DATA PROCESSING CYCLE MODIFIED

The basic data processing cycle may always be modified to suit the requirements of the user. For example, it may be desired to have this program print only one line - the sum of all costs. If only one line of output is desired, the flowchart for the program could be written as shown in Figure 8-5 on the following page.

The program is:

```
      TOTCOS = 0.
   20 READ (5,30,END=25) COST
            TOTCOS=TOTCOS + COST
            GO TO 20
```

```
25   WRITE (6,35) TOTCOS
     STOP
30   FORMAT (F15.0)
35   FORMAT (1X,F20.2)
     END
```

The program prints only one line. That line is printed only after all the input cards have been processed and the final value for "TOTCOS" has been established.

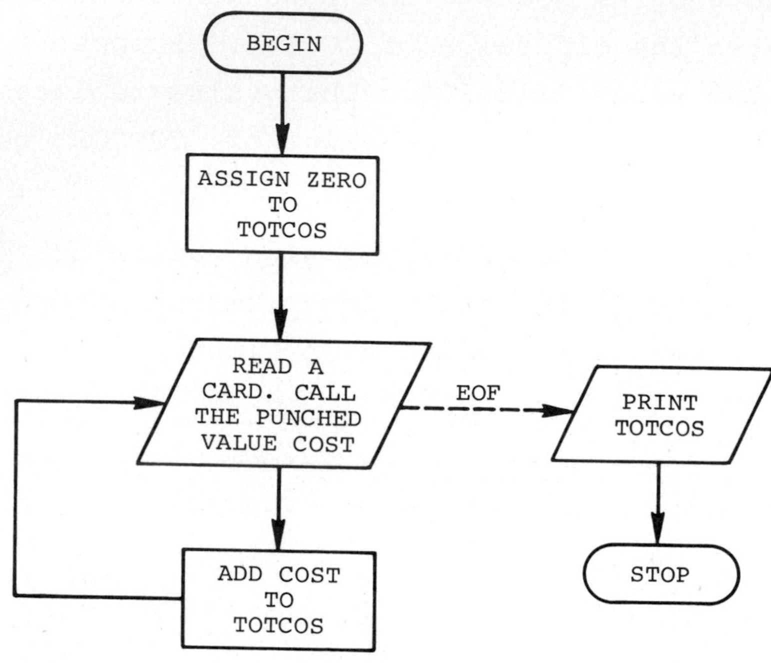

Figure 8-5

GROSS PAY PROBLEM

Let's consider another problem. Suppose we have the deck of data cards shown in Figure 8-6 on the following page.

There are about 100 cards in the deck but its actual size is immaterial in the discussion of this problem. Let's assume that each card contains pay rate per hour (the leftmost number), hours worked (the middle number) and employee pay number (the rightmost number). Two of the numbers are real; one is integer. Both real numbers have imbedded decimal points. A FORMAT that could be used to read these three values is "FORMAT (2F10.0, I10)".

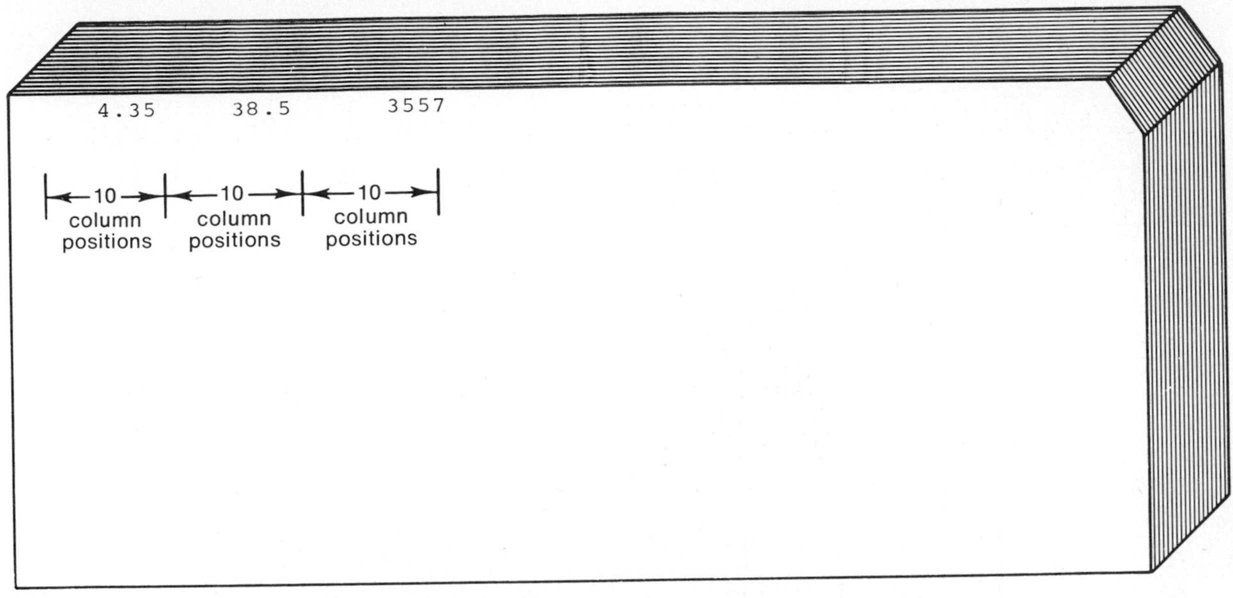

Figure 8-6

We need a program to compute gross pay by multiplying pay rate by hours worked. (We will ignore overtime payments in this simplified problem.) The report line must contain the employee number and the gross pay. The report's format should be the one given in Figure 8-7.

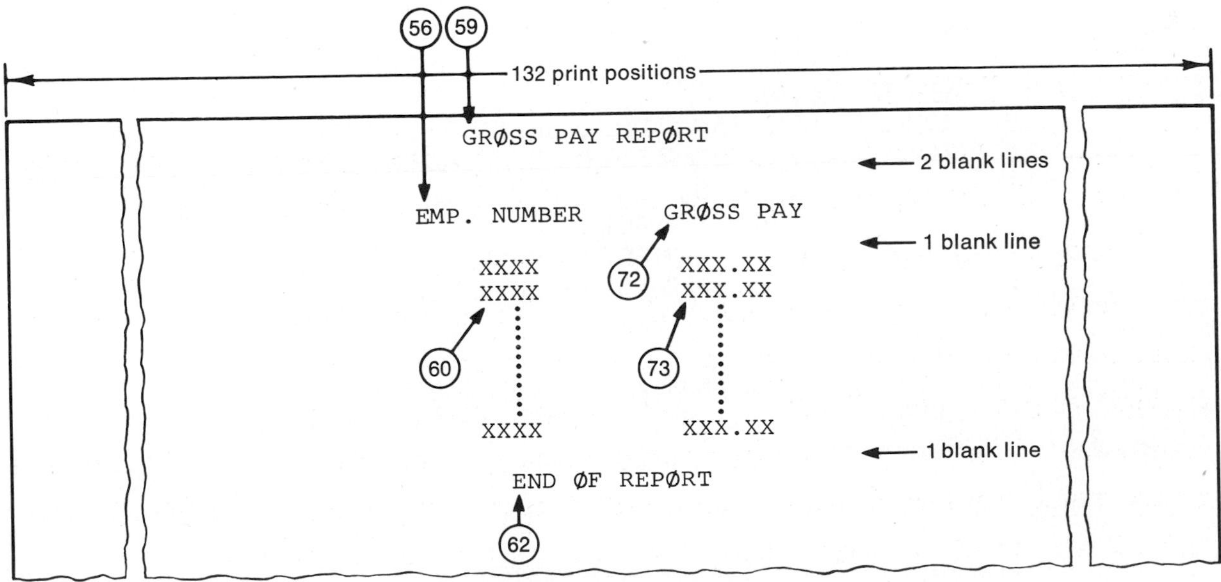

Figure 8-7

The flowchart for the program is shown in Figure 8-8.

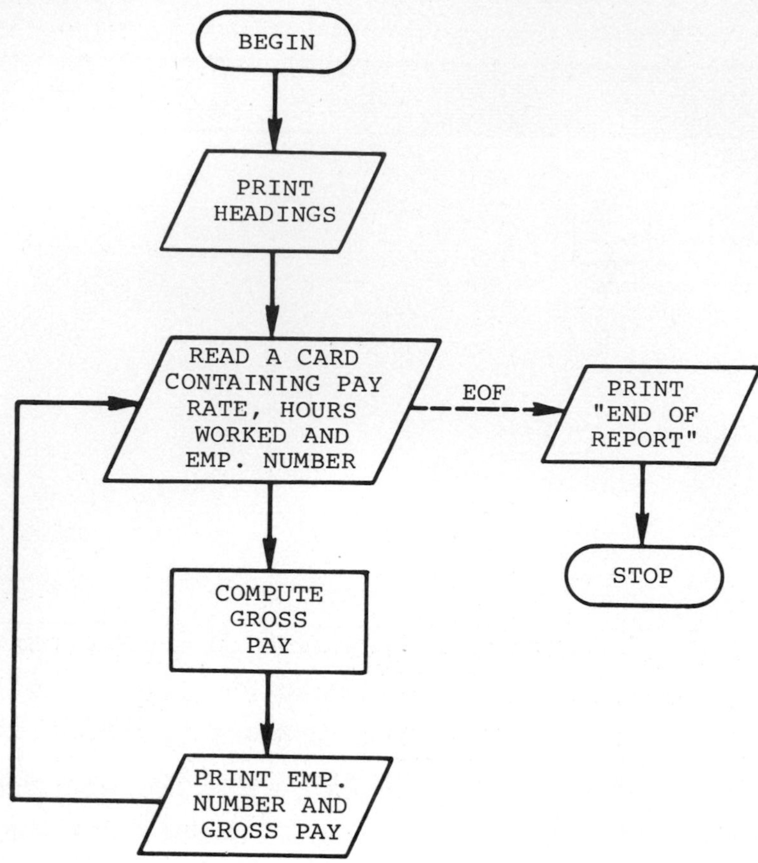

Figure 8-8

This is the program:

```
      WRITE (6,8)
  8   FORMAT ('1',58X,'GROSS PAY REPORT'///)
      WRITE (6,9)
  9   FORMAT (1X,55X,'EMP. NUMBER',5X,'GROSS PAY'//)
 10   READ (5,12,END=45) RATE, HOURS, NUMBER
 12   FORMAT (2F10.0,I10)
      GRPAY = RATE * HOURS
      WRITE (6,14) NUMBER, GRPAY
 14   FORMAT (1X,I63,F15.2)
      GO TO 10
 45   WRITE (6,46)
 46   FORMAT (/,1X,61X,'END OF REPORT')
      STOP
      END
```

<u>COMMENT STATEMENTS</u>

Interspersed with the other statements of a FORTRAN program, a programmer may give "comment" statements. A comment statement begins with the letter "C". That letter must be placed in column 1 of the coding form. See Figure 8-9.

STATEMENT NUMBER (1–5)	CONT (6)	STATEMENT (7–72)	IDENT (73–80)
C THI	S	PRØGRAM CØMPUTES GRØSS PAY	
C HEA	D	ING IS PRINTED FIRST	
		WRITE (6, 8)	
8		FØRMAT ('1', 58X, 'GRØSS PAY REPØRT'///)	
		WRITE (6, 9)	
9		FØRMAT (1X, 55X, 'EMP. NUMBER', 5X, 'GRØSS PAY'//)	
C			
C INP	U	T VALUES ARE READ NEXT	
C			
C		READ (5, 12, END = 45) RATE, HØURS, NUMBER	
12		FØRMAT (2F10.0,I10)	
C			
C NØW		GRØSS PAY IS CØMPUTED	
C			
		GRPAY = RATE * HØURS	

Figure 8-9

Anything written following the letter "C" is considered a comment and is used to explain what the program does and how it accomplishes the task. Comments may begin in column 2 and extend through column 72. As is shown in the example, comment statements may consist simply of the letter "C" followed by 71 blanks.

Comments have no effect on how a program runs. They simply give information. When the computer gives a listing of your program, as it does during the process of compilation, the comments will be included in the listing and thus serve as a documentation aid. An observer who attempts to understand your program will be greatly aided by the comments that you build into it.

Some FORTRAN systems optionally permit the asterisk (*) to be used in column 1 for the purpose of initiating comment lines. If your system allows asterisks, use them just as you would the letter "C".

STYLE

We might comment at this point regarding programming style. The beginner programmer should strive to form good programming habits. For example, a program should show regularity in spacing within statements. Most statements should begin in column

7 of the coding form. Some statements should be indented if by doing so, you will aid understanding. Example:

```
10   READ (5,14,END=90) X,Y,Z
14   FORMAT (3F10.0)
         W=(X+Y)/Z
         WRITE (6,18) W,X,Y,Z
18       FORMAT (1X,4F10.2)
         GO TO 10
90   STOP
     END
```

Statement numbers should appear in increasing sequence and, insofar as possible, increase in a regular way. This objective cannot always be easily met since programs grow and change as they are being developed. A programmer may have intended to be systematic with statement numbers but, during debugging, may have had to insert statements with statement numbers that are out of sequence.

Comments should be used extensively in programs. The larger the programs, the more complex the logic, the more is the need for comment lines. It is surprising to a new programmer how the memory dims after a few months. A program that one knows and understands very well today will often appear incomprehensible a year later. Comments help a programmer understand a program that he or she wrote in the past and in which there must now be changes made. Comments are especially appreciated by the person who must change a program that someone else wrote.

Variable names should be meaningful. In a payroll program, the name HOURS is a much better name to express hours worked than H or, worse yet, X. In an engineering program, the name RADIUS is a much better name to express radius than R or, worse yet, Z. Keep in mind that an integer name can easily be changed to a real one by adding "X" ahead of the name, and a real name can be changed to an integer one by adding "I" ahead of the name. Thus, a real name representing a maximum value can well be XMAX and an integer name for grade can well be IGRADE.

There are many other comments that we might make concerning good programming practice, but space does not permit. To develop good style, you should be alert to the improvements that you can make in your programs; improvements which will make them more efficient, easier to code, easier to understand, and easier to debug. Study well-written programs written by others. Study the programs in this text and consider how you might change them to suit your inclinations.

EXERCISES AND PROBLEMS

1. Define the term "loop".

2. Tell why most FORTRAN programs should include one or more loops.

3. Why does the READ statement, allowing the use of the "END=" option, lend itself well to FORTRAN programs?

4. Study the two READ statements shown below.

```
   15  READ (5,18) P,Q,R
   15  READ (5,18,END=65) P,Q,R
```

   Tell when you would be inclined to use the former and when the latter.

5. What does a FORTRAN program do if it runs out of data cards that are being read?

6. Tell what a "GO TO" statement does and why it is useful in programs.

7. Should a program always stop immediately when there are no more data cards to process? Explain.

8. What does the statement

```
   TOTCOS = TOTCOS + COST
```

   accomplish? Is it permissible to have the same variable name at both sides of the equals sign?

9. Explain what is meant by the term "initializing". Would you say that most programs have at least some initializing

statements?

10. Why might you sometimes indent statements in a FORTRAN program?

11. What is a "comment"? Why might you give comment lines in a program? Do comment lines affect the way that a program runs?

12. Write a program that converts 24.13 centimeters to inches. (There are 2.54 centimeters in one inch.)

13. Write a program that converts 5½ inches to centimeters.

14. Write a program that converts 3½ ounces to grams. (There are 28.35 grams in one ounce.)

15. Write a program that converts 163 grams to ounces.

16. Write a program that converts 15 miles to kilometers. (There are 1.60935 kilometers in one mile.)

17. Write a program that converts 52.3 kilometers to miles.

18. Write a program that converts 23 U.S. gallons to liters. (There are 3.785 liters in one U.S. gallon.)

19. Write a program that converts 45 liters to U.S. gallons.

CHAPTER 9

Making Decisions—
The IF Statement

MAKING DECISIONS

A program can be directed to take alternate courses of action depending upon the magnitude of certain selected values. Consider this example:

```
20  READ (5,9,END=85) P, Q
    IF (P.GT.6200.) GO TO 40
    R = Q**3 - P
    GO TO 50
40  R = Q**2 + P
50  WRITE (6,10) P, Q, R
    GO TO 20
 9  FORMAT (2F10.0)
10  FORMAT (1X,3F10.2)
85  STOP
    END
```

The IF statement is the new statement in this program. It reads:

```
    IF (P.GT.6200.) GO TO 40
```

and, in English, means:

> If the value last assigned to P is greater than "6200.", go to statement 40; if P is not greater than "6200.", go to the next statement in sequence.

This program reads a data card and finds two values punched upon it. Those two values are assigned to P and Q. The program then makes a test to determine whether the value assigned to P is algebraically greater than "6200.". *If it is,* the program jumps to statement "40" and continues processing the task from there. *If it is not* (if P is not greater than

"6200."), the program goes to the statement that follows the IF statement.

The program shows that if P is greater than "6200.", the program computes "$R=Q^2+P$", then prints the values of P, Q, and R. If P is not greater than "6200.", the program computes "$R=Q^3-P$", then prints the values of P, Q, and R. In either case, the program goes back to the READ statement to obtain two more values (P and Q), and the procedure outlined above is repeated. That procedure is repeated over and over until the data's "end of file" is reached. At that time, the program stops.

As values of P and Q are read, the program uses the IF statement to test the relationship that P has to "6200.". Sometimes, the program will jump to statement 40, sometimes the program will go to the statement immediately following "IF".

THE LOGICAL IF

The "IF" statement that you have seen illustrated in the example, is called a "logical IF". There is another type of IF which we'll explore later in this chapter. That second type is called the "arithmetic IF".

The "logical IF" statement has this general form:

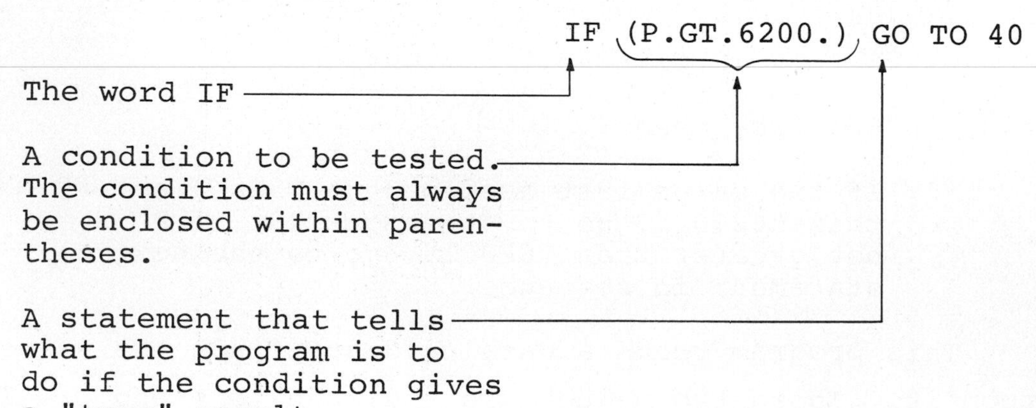
IF (P.GT.6200.) GO TO 40
The word IF
A condition to be tested. The condition must always be enclosed within parentheses.
A statement that tells what the program is to do if the condition gives a "true" result.

CONDITIONS TO TEST

Remember that a condition to be tested is *always* enclosed within parentheses.

When a condition is tested, there are only two possible conclusions which the program can make. They are "yes", the condition being tested is "true"; or "no", the condition being tested is not "true", it is "false". If the test gives a "true" result, the program takes the "true" course of action given in the IF statement. If the test gives a "false" result, the program goes to the statement which immediately follows the IF statement. That next statement might well be *another* IF statement.

In a logical IF statement, the condition that is to be tested has three parts. The parts are:

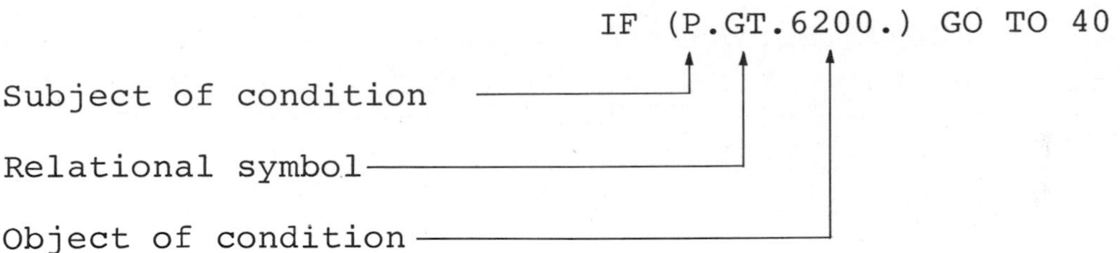

The relationship that the subject has to the object is given by the relational symbol.

The subject of a condition may be an actual numeric value, such as "3.94", "6200.", "18", etc.; a variable name, such as "P", "WDL", "NUM", etc.; or an expression, such as "B**2-4.*A*C", "(FNS+PR)/9.6", "(L+M)*N", etc.

The object of a condition may also be an actual numeric value, variable name, or expression.

RELATIONAL SYMBOLS

The relational symbol within a condition may be one of the six given in the table below:

RELATIONAL SYMBOLS

SYMBOL	MEANING
.GT.	Greater than
.LT.	Less than
.EQ.	Equal
.GE.	Greater than or equal
.LE.	Less than or equal
.NE.	Not equal

The periods on both sides of the relational symbols are integral parts of the symbols and must be included in them.

Some programmers like to place a blank on both sides of the relational symbol. Thus, an IF statement may be written

```
IF (P.GT.Q) GO TO 800
```

or

```
IF (P .GT. Q) GO TO 800
```

These next logical IF statements are all legal.

```
IF (W.EQ.A) GO TO 35
IF (FF.LE.17.6) GO TO 78
IF (K*L.NE.M+N) GO TO 40
IF (2.6.LT.PF8) GO TO 90
IF (D.EQ.(R-S)/T) GO TO 45
```

Some FORTRAN systems insist that both the subject and the object of a logical IF be in the same mode: both real or both integer. This rule is not as rigid as it once was and you should assume that mixing modes in your system is all right unless you find out differently. If it's no extra trouble on your part, do keep the modes consistent. This way, you'll avoid problems that could cause a great deal of confusion.

AN EXAMPLE

Now that we know how to form logical IF statements, let's use them in a simple problem. Suppose we have a single data card containing six different integer values that have been punched according to "FORMAT (6I10)". We can have a program read those values calling them "I", "J", "K", "L", "M", and "N". The problem is to find what is the smallest value, then have the computer print it. Suppose, for example, that the six values are the ones shown in Figure 9-1 on the following page.

The program we write should print "6". It is the object of this program to simply print the smallest value without regard to *which* of the six values it is.

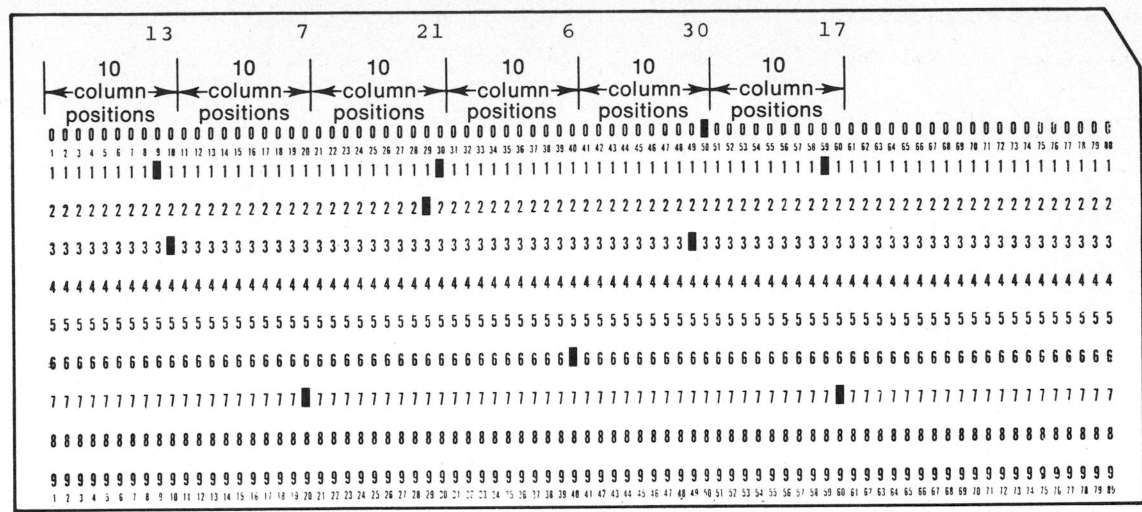

Figure 9-1

The procedure we can follow is this:

Step 1. Find out which value is smaller, "I" or "J". Assign the smaller value to "JJ".

Step 2. Find out which value is smaller, "K" or "L". Assign the smaller value to "KK".

Step 3. Find out which value is smaller, "M" or "N". Assign the smaller value to "LL".

Step 4. Find out which value is smaller, "JJ" or "KK". Assign the smaller to "MM".

Step 5. Find out which value is smaller, "MM" or "LL". Assign the result to "NN". "NN" now contains the smallest value. This is the value to be printed.

We can use the flowchart shown in Figure 9-2 on the following page.

We might comment at this point that there are better ways to determine what is the smallest value among a set of values. When we discuss arrays, you'll see that the task is much easier to accomplish using arrays than by using the method you have seen here. This problem has, nevertheless, been instructive in illustrating how logical IF statements work. Follow the flowchart and the FORTRAN program carefully. Make sure you understand both.

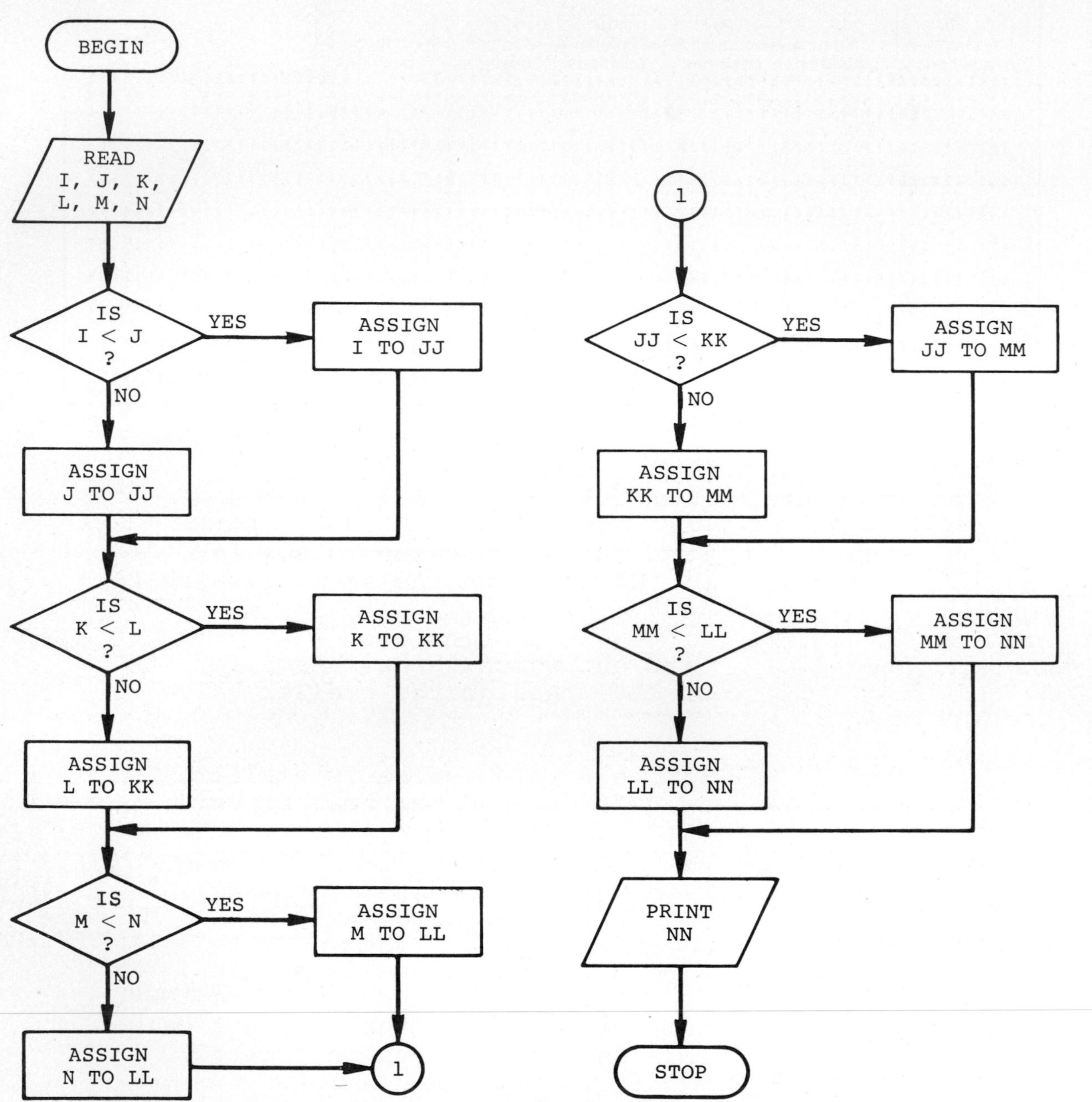

Figure 9-2

This is the program:

```
      READ (5,9) I,J,K,L,M,N
    9 FORMAT (6I10)
      IF (I.LT.J) GO TO 10
      JJ = J
      GO TO 15
   10 JJ = I
   15 IF (K.LT.L) GO TO 20
      KK = L
      GO TO 25
   20 KK = K
```

```
25   IF (M.LT.N) GO TO 30
     LL = N
     GO TO 35
30   LL = M
35   IF (JJ.LT.KK) GO TO 40
     MM = KK
     GO TO 45
40   MM = JJ
45   IF (MM.LT.LL) GO TO 50
     NN = LL
     GO TO 55
50   NN = MM
55   WRITE (6,60) NN
60   FORMAT ('1',I10)
     STOP
     END
```

DUMMY VALUE IN DATA DECK

Earlier, we explored READ statements that include "END=" options. Example:

```
80   READ (5,44,END=90) K,X
```

This type of READ statement is very useful in determining when the end of a data deck has been reached. If the FORTRAN system that your computer uses does not allow the "END=" option, then the end of a data deck has to be found in another way.

One way to find the end of the data deck is to place a "dummy" data value at the end of the deck. That value acts as a "sentinel". When found, the program knows that the end of the data deck has been reached. The sentinel, itself, is not processed.

The last card of the data deck must contain a *known* value, such as "0.0", or "999.9", or "-1000.". This value stands ready to be checked by an IF statement. When found, the program reacts accordingly. Consider a problem we discussed earlier. Suppose it is desired to sum the values in a data deck. See Figure 9-3 on the following page.

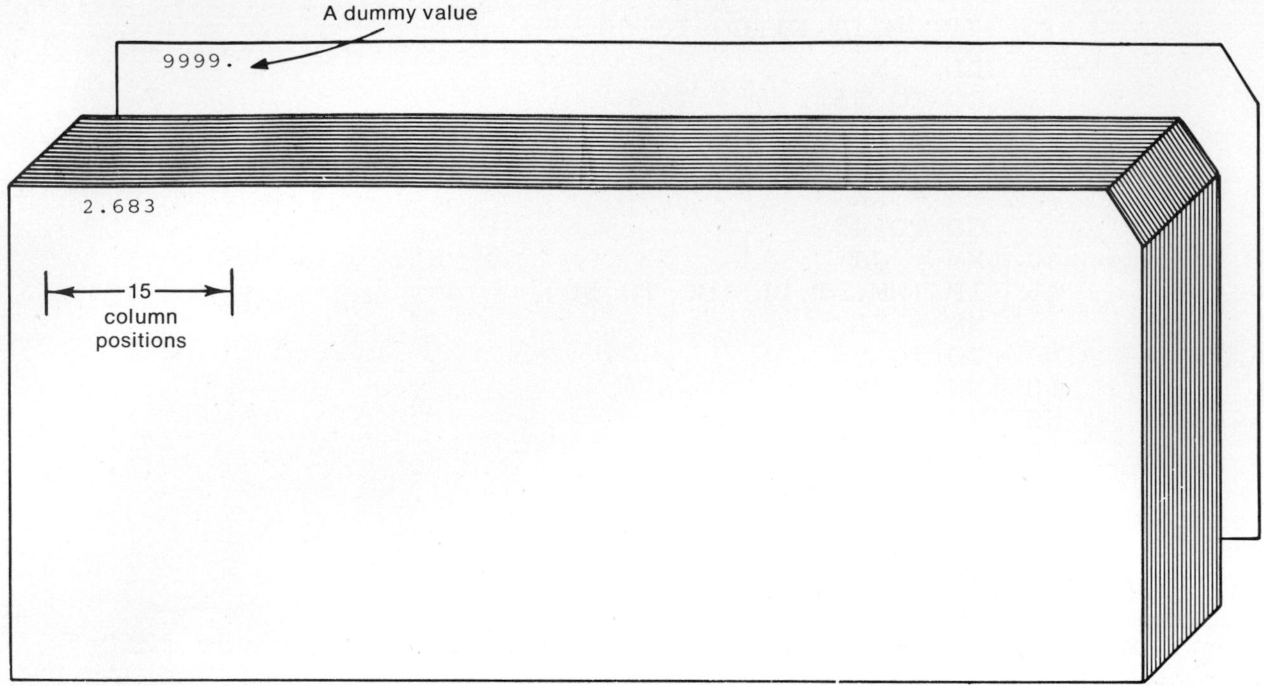

Figure 9-3

The last value (9999.) has been carefully chosen as a "dummy" value. A dummy (sentinel) value must be a value that will not accidentally be processed. For example, if the program is processing pay rates, a dummy pay rate could be "1000." or "0.". If the program is dealing with temperatures in Florida, a dummy temperature could be "-1000.". The dummy value in this problem signals the end of the data values and therefore, must not be included as one of the values in the sum to be computed. Here is the program:

```
      TOTCOS = 0.
   30 READ (5,14) COST
      IF (COST.EQ.9999.) GO TO 50
      TOTCOS = TOTCOS + COST
      GO TO 30
   50 WRITE (6,60) TOTCOS
      STOP
   14 FORMAT (F10.0)
   60 FORMAT ('1',F10.2)
      END
```

Contrast the program above with this one:

```
      TOTCOS = 0.
   30 READ (5,14,END=50) COST
      TOTCOS = TOTCOS + COST
      GO TO 30
```

```
50  WRITE (6,60) TOTCOS
    STOP
14  FORMAT (F10.0)
60  FORMAT ('1',F10.2)
    END
```

The former program must look for a dummy card (often called a sentinel card); the latter program must not look for such a card. We're sure you'll agree that the latter type of program is easier to work with and should be used if the "END=" option in READ statements is available.

Logical IF's may include other statements besides GO TO's. Examples:

```
IF (R.EQ.S) D = T+U
IF (P.LT.RR) READ (5,3)L
IF (I.NE.J) STOP
```

The statements may be assignment statements, READ or WRITE statements, STOP, and others as well as GO TO's. You *may not* use another logical IF statement within a logical IF statement.

Keep in mind that the statements shown will be executed only if the condition being tested is true. Having executed that statement, the program will automatically go to the next statement in sequence. Do not do something like this:

```
IF (R.EQ.FF) E = 2.3*H
E = 9.6*H
W = E**3
  etc.
```

If "R" is not equal to "FF", the program will assign "9.6*H" to "E" then continue. If "R" does equal "FF", the program will first assign "2.3*H" to "E", then immediately change "E" by assigning "9.6*H" to it. The value assigned to "E", therefore, is the same whether "R" equals "FF" or not. Obviously, this is wrong and not what the programmer had intended. This sequence is better:

```
    IF (R.EQ.FF) GO TO 80
    E = 9.6*H
    GO TO 90
80  E = 2.3*H
90  W = E**3
      etc.
```

Another way to accomplish the task is

```
     E = 2.3*H
     IF (R.EQ.FF) GO TO 30
     E = 9.6*H
30   W = E**3
       etc.
```

Still another way is this:

```
     E = 2.3*H
     IF (R.NE.FF) E=9.6*H
     W = E**3
       etc.
```

ARITHMETIC IF

Another type of IF statement that is available in FORTRAN is the arithmetic IF statement. It looks like this:

```
IF (F-W) 4,81,7
```

The computer first evaluates "F-W" to determine its value. If "F-W" gives a negative value, the program jumps to statement 4; if "F-W" gives "zero", the program jumps to statement 81; if "F-W" gives a positive value (but not zero), the program jumps to statement 7. The arithmetic IF statement has this general form:

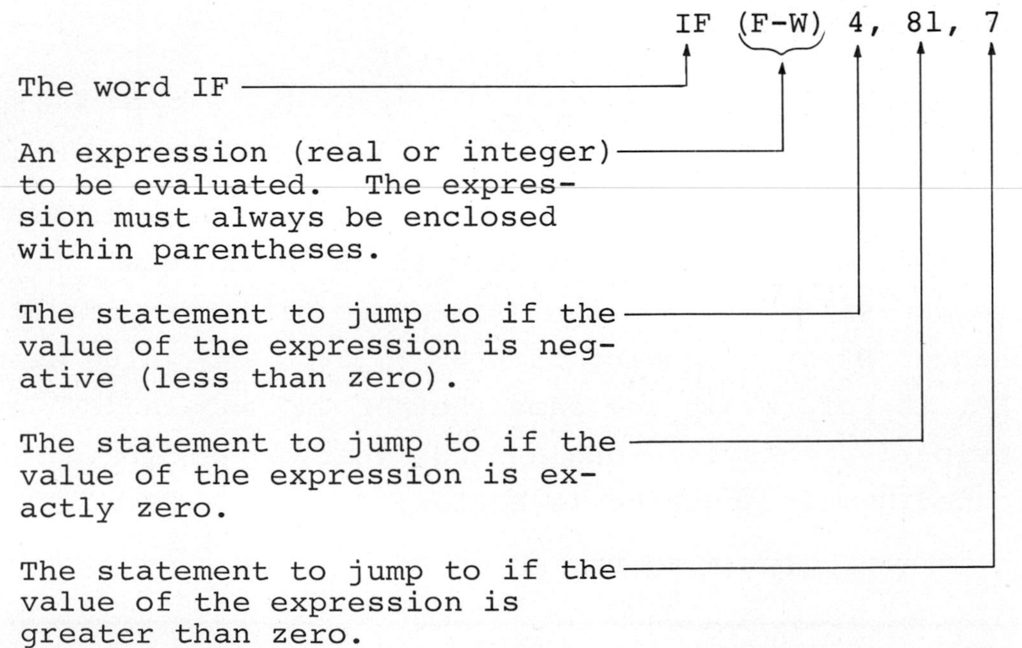

IF (F-W) 4, 81, 7
The word IF
An expression (real or integer) to be evaluated. The expression must always be enclosed within parentheses.
The statement to jump to if the value of the expression is negative (less than zero).
The statement to jump to if the value of the expression is exactly zero.
The statement to jump to if the value of the expression is greater than zero.

The three statement numbers in the IF statement must be separated by commas.

As you can see, the arithmetic IF statement provides a 3-way jump whereas the logical IF provides a 2-way jump. In a program, you may use either logical IF's or arithmetic IF's, whichever you please. You can get along very nicely using only logical IF's or only arithmetic IF's in programs. Anything you can do using arithmetic IF's, you can also do using logical IF's, and vice versa. (You may sometimes need two logical IF's to accomplish what one arithmetic IF can do for you, though).

Suppose you are using this arithmetic IF:

```
IF (D*G) 18, 14, 7
```

and you want to convert the arithmetic IF to logical IF's. You can accomplish the task this way:

```
IF (D*G.GT.0.) GO TO 7
IF (D*G.EQ.0.) GO TO 14
GO TO 18
```

(If the statement immediately following the second IF is statement 18, the "GO TO 18" statement is, of course, not needed.)

Suppose you have this logical IF:

```
IF (G.EQ.999.9) GO TO 45
```

and you want to change it to an arithmetic IF. You can accomplish the task this way:

```
IF (G-999.9) 30, 45, 30
```

If "G-999.9" equals zero, then "G" equals "999.9" and the computer will take the jump given by the middle statement number. Observe that any two of the three statement numbers in an arithmetic IF may be the same.

Consider these examples:

```
IF (R) 6,6,9
```

If "R" is less than or equal to zero, the program jumps to statement 6; otherwise, the program goes to statement 9.

```
IF ((T-V)/W) 30,13,13
```

If "(T-V)/W" is greater than or equal to zero, the program jumps to statement 13; otherwise, the program goes to statement 30.

Many FORTRAN systems always require three statement numbers in an arithmetic IF. Some FORTRAN systems have relaxed this rule. When the arithmetic IF statement appears like this:

```
IF (J-K) 9,4
```

the program uses statement 9 as the "less than zero" jump and statement 4 as the "equal to zero" jump. The program goes to the next statement in sequence if "J-K" gives a value that is greater than zero.

Similarly, in

```
IF (J-K) 9
```

the program uses statement 9 as the "less than zero" jump. When "J-K" gives any other value, the program goes to the next statement in sequence.

Further, these IF's

```
IF (J-K) ,4,20
IF (J-K) ,,20
IF (J-K) ,4,
```

are permissible. The computer takes normal jumps when applicable, but goes to the next statement in sequence when a statement number is missing. In the last example, for instance, the program goes to statement 4 when "J-K" gives a zero value; it goes to the next statement in sequence otherwise.

TESTING THE DISCRIMINANT B^2-4AC

Here is an example showing how the arithmetic IF statement might be used.

```
      READ (5,18) A,B,C
   18 FORMAT (3F10.0)
      IF (B**2-4.*A*C) 8,125,30
    8 WRITE (6,9)
    9 FORMAT ('1','ROOTS ARE COMPLEX')
```

```
      STOP
  125 WRITE (6,26)
  126 FORMAT ('1','ROOTS ARE REAL AND EQUAL')
      STOP
  30  WRITE (6,31)
  31  FORMAT ('1','ROOTS ARE REAL')
      STOP
      END
```

The program reads a single data card, then tests "B^2-4AC" to determine what form the roots of a quadratic equation must take. The three possible forms of those roots are tested and one of the descriptive messages is printed.

In passing, we might say that most programmers prefer logical IF's over arithmetic IF's since 3-way jumps are seldom needed. Further, the more exotic ways of using logical IF's are seldom employed. In your entire programming career, you may never need an IF like this one

```
IF (A.LT.B)  IF (D-E) 7,8,49
```

We have presented some of these more elaborate forms simply to inform you that they exist.

EXERCISES AND PROBLEMS

1. Name the two different types of IF statements. Give an example of each.
2. Give the six relational symbols that may be used in logical IF statements. Tell what they mean.
3. What are the three parts of a condition to be tested in a logical IF statement?
4. What are the three types of values that may be used to form the subject of a condition in a logical IF statement?
5. What are the three types of values that may be used to form the object of a condition in a logical IF statement?
6. How many FORTRAN statements can you place at the right of a condition to be tested in a logical IF statement?

7. When will the program execute the statement given at the right of a condition to be tested in a logical IF statement?

8. Refer to Question 7. When will the program *not* execute the statement given at the right?

9. What does a program do if the condition found in a logical IF statement is found to be "false"?

10. If a logical IF statement provides a "two-way jump", what type of jump does an arithmetic IF provide?

11. May you omit the parentheses surrounding a condition to be tested in a logical IF statement? May you omit the parentheses surrounding the expression in an arithmetic IF statement?

12. In an arithmetic IF statement, how many statement numbers does one normally give at the right of the expression to be tested?

13. Refer to Question 12. May any two of the statement numbers given be duplicates?

14. What is a "sentinel" value given at the end of a data deck? How should the sentinel be selected?

15. Why does the "END=" option in a READ statement make it unnecessary to provide a sentinel?

16. Study this program:

```
      READ (5,8) W
    8 FORMAT (F10.0)
      IF (W.EQ.3.5) P = 7.5
      P = 8.3
      WRITE (6,9) P
    9 FORMAT (1X,F10.2)
      STOP
      END
```

What value will the program print for P if W's value equals "3.5"?

17. Refer to Question 16. How would you change the program so that it makes more sense?

18. Study this program segment:

```
    3  READ (5,8) W
    8  FORMAT (F10.0)
       IF (W.EQ.999.) STOP
        .
        .
        .
        .
```

When does this program cease executing?

19. Study this program segment:

```
    3  READ (5,8) W
    8  FORMAT (F10.0)
       IF (W) ,,300
        .
        .
        .
        .
```

What will the program do if W's value is "-3.8"? What will the program do if W's value is "0."? What will the program do if W's value is "4.8"? (Assume that the FORTRAN system being used accepts this IF statement.)

20. Study this program segment:

```
        .
        .
        .
        .
       IF (P-Q) 3,8,4
       IF (W) 7,8,6
        .
        .
        .
        .
```

What is wrong with the segment?

21. Study this program segment:

```
       IF (W.EQ.Q) GO TO 45
   70  M = 3 + J
        .
        .
        .
        .
```

Would you agree that this next program segment gives equivalent action?

```
       IF (W-Q) 70,45,70
   70  M = 3 + J
        .
        .
        .
        .
```

22. Review the "Gross Pay Problem" given in Chapter 8 on pages 94 through 96.

Rewrite the program but this time allow payment for overtime work. If a person has worked 40 hours or less, the person gets paid only for hours worked. If the person has worked over 40 hours, the person receives "time-and-a-half" for hours worked in excess of 40 hours. That is, the pay rate for the excess is 1½ times the person's normal pay rate.

You may assume that all other conditions given in the original problem remain constant.

23. This program builds upon your solution for the problem in Question 22. Write your program so that only 30 detail lines are given on each page. The heading lines are to be repeated on each page of the report. On the top line of each page, the page count is also to be given. That is, the top line of page 1 reads "PAGE 1"; the top line of page 2 reads "PAGE 2"; etc.

You may assume that there are approximately 100 cards in the data deck.

24. A program is to be written. Assume there is a deck of cards that have been punched this way:

COLUMN POSITIONS	CONTENTS
1-4	Investment Number; an integer value between "1400" and "4999", inclusive.
10-20	A principal amount; a real value between "100.00" and "9000.00", inclusive.
21-26	An interest rate; a real value between ".065" and ".125", inclusive.

There are about 30 cards in the deck, but this fact is irrelevant.

Write a program that gives an investment report. The

report is to have a page heading line reading:

```
INVESTMENT REPORT
```

The report must also have column headings reading:

```
INVESTMENT NUM      PRINCIPAL      RATE      YIELD
```

There is to be one blank line between the page heading line and the column heading line.

The report is to give the "yield" obtained when the principal amount found on each data card is multiplied by the rate of interest found on the same card. Each line of the report gives the investment number, the principal, the rate of interest, and the calculated yield. The values are to fall as attractively as possible under the column headings provided.

Since there are about 30 data cards in the data deck, your report should contain that many detail lines under the page heading and column heading lines. There should be one blank line following the column heading line.

Give principal and yield values rounded to two decimal places; give interest rates rounded to three decimal places.

CHAPTER 10

Flowcharting

WHAT A FLOWCHART IS

In connection with the presentation of various problems in previous chapters, we introduced flowcharts. You saw that a flowchart is a pictorial (graphic) illustration of what you will ask the computer to do. Once firmed up, the flowchart is transformed to a series of FORTRAN statements. Now, if the flowchart was logically prepared, the program ought to run properly without much difficulty.

Perhaps it has become obvious by this time in your study of FORTRAN, that a problem doesn't solve itself. When given an assignment, *you* are the one who must sit back and do some thinking. Then, when you have an idea of how the computer is to help you with the problem solution, you code the FORTRAN program. Then you keep working with the program until the required results are obtained.

If a problem is not too complicated, you can go directly from the thinking stage to the coding stage. When problems become more difficult, though, all the complex considerations that accompany a problem become difficult to keep in the mind.

Consider an everyday example. In computing a person's paycheck, what are some of the factors that you must consider?

1. How many hours did the person work? Is he or she eligible for overtime?

2. What is the person's pay rate? Did it change during the week?

3. How much should be deducted for Federal tax? State tax? Local tax? Does it make a difference which tax is deducted first?

4. Does the person have to make an FICA (Social Security) contribution this week?

5. Is there to be a deduction for a savings plan? If so, on what amount is it based?

6. What about a retirement plan deduction?

7. A community contribution deduction?

These are only a few of the details that must be attended to before a paycheck is actually printed. None should be overlooked. The various actions must be performed in the proper sequence. It would not do, for instance, to compute the employee's FICA contribution on net pay. The contribution is based upon gross pay. Conversely, it would not be correct to base the Federal tax deduction entirely upon gross pay. A person's deductions for family exemptions must be taken into account.

In the business world, the preparation of a person's paycheck is such a complex undertaking, that attempting to write a program without first having thought out everything ahead of time would be foolhardy. Prior planning to assist in this undertaking is an absolute necessity. Flowcharts help with this planning.

In discussing flowcharting, we will begin with simple examples, then progress toward more difficult ones. While few programmers would ever take the trouble to prepare simple flowcharts for simple programs, we will go through the motions of actually doing so in order to gain a mastery of the subject in easy stages.

AN EXAMPLE

Suppose we want to write a program that computes the sine of "2.67", then prints the result. The flowchart is this: (Figure 10-1)

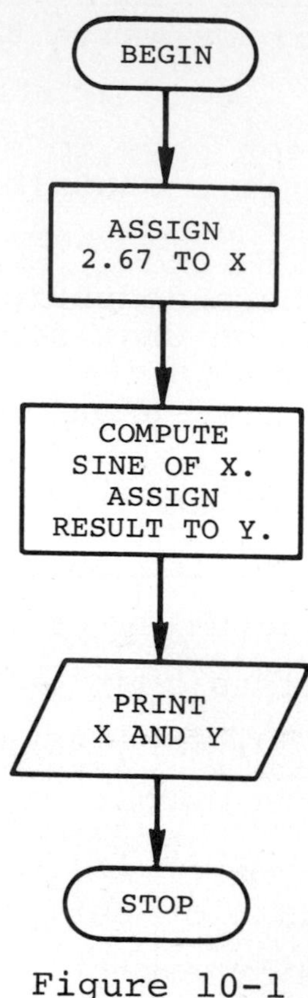

Figure 10-1

BEGIN SYMBOL

Flowcharts begin with the "BEGIN" symbol: (Figure 10-2)

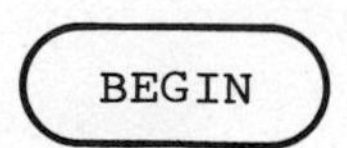

Figure 10-2

Usually, the symbol (an oval) is located in the upper lefthand corner of the flowchart. The "BEGIN" symbol shows where persons are to commence when studying your flowchart or when writing a program from it. The "BEGIN" symbol has no corresponding FORTRAN statement.

ASSIGNMENT SYMBOL

The flowchart gives an arrow leading from the "BEGIN" symbol to a rectangle with the inscription "ASSIGN 2.67 to X". The rectangular symbol is reserved for indicating assignment statements. The FORTRAN statement that ensues from the assignment symbol is the assignment statement - in this example

```
X = 2.67
```

An arrow leads to another rectangle. This one calls for another assignment statement:

```
Y = SIN (X)
```

READ/WRITE OR INPUT/OUTPUT (I/O) SYMBOL

Next an arrow leads to a parallelogram. This symbol is reserved for READ and WRITE statements. The example calls for a WRITE statement. This one:

```
      WRITE (6,8) X,Y
    8 FORMAT ('1',2F10.2)
```

The READ/WRITE symbol assumes accompanying FORMAT's. No special symbols are needed for FORMAT's.

The final symbol is the "STOP" oval. You can see that the oval is used for the "BEGIN" point of a flowchart and for any "STOP" points there might be. (There may well be more than one "STOP" symbol in a flowchart.)

The flowchart given above leads to this FORTRAN program:

```
      X = 2.67
      Y = SIN (X)
      WRITE (6,8) X,Y
    8 FORMAT ('1',2F10.2)
      STOP
      END
```

A flowchart never requires a symbol for a program's "END" statement.

FLOWCHART ORGANIZATION

In this example, the flowchart extends from top to bottom. Many flowcharts extend from left to right. The above flowchart could have been written this way: (Figure 10-3)

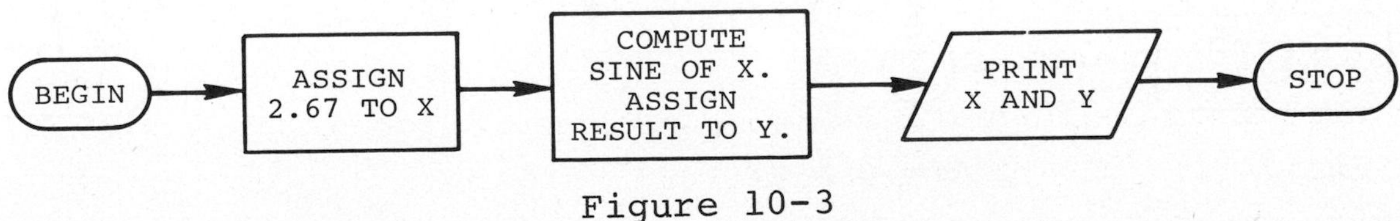

Figure 10-3

Larger flowcharts that extend from left to right, might look like this: (Figure 10-4)

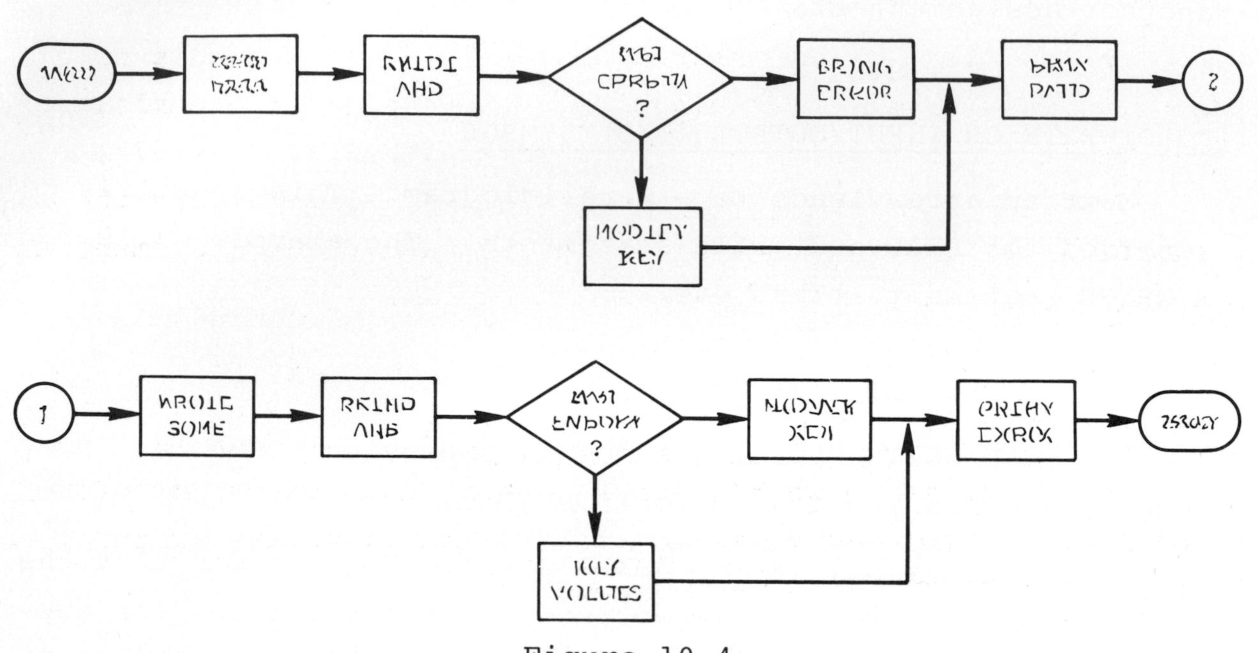

Figure 10-4

Larger flowcharts that extend from top to bottom, might look like this: (Figure 10-5)

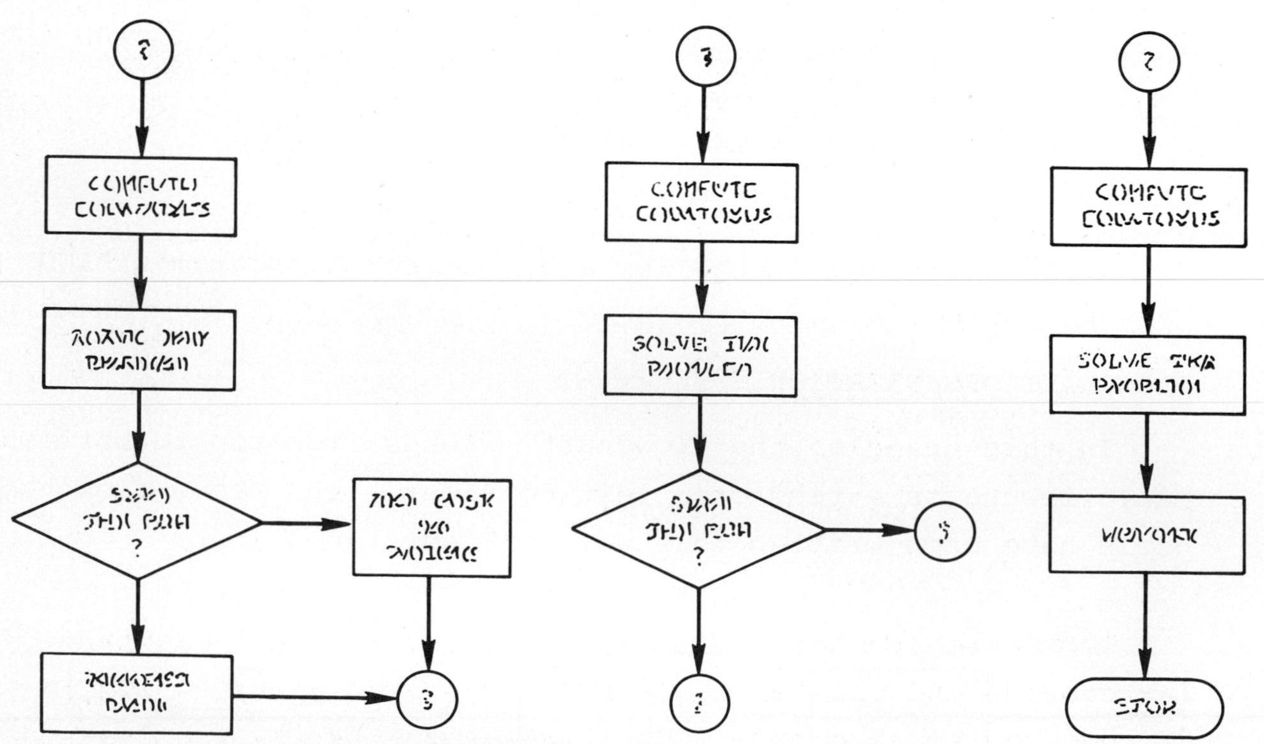

Figure 10-5

In flowcharts, arrows are very important. They show which FORTRAN statement is to be executed first, which second, etc. Arrows give logic flow information in flowcharts.

Observe that the words you place within the symbols have no rigorous format. In an assignment symbol, for example, you may write "ASSIGN 2.67 to X", "STORE 2.67 in X", "X=2.67", "2.67→X", or anything else you please. In transforming the symbol to FORTRAN, you must, of course, write the statement in accordance with FORTRAN rules.

ANOTHER EXAMPLE

Now, suppose we want to read several data cards, printing the single value found on each card. The flowchart is this: (Figure 10-6)

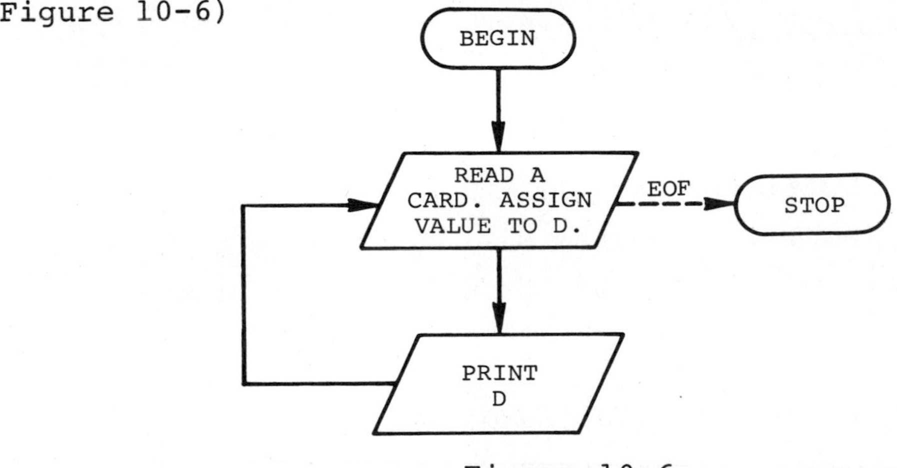

Figure 10-6

The FORTRAN program is this:

```
10   READ (5,25,END=50) D
25   FORMAT (F10.0)
     WRITE (6,30) D
30   FORMAT (1X,F20.3)
     GO TO 10
50   STOP
     END
```

The flowchart has two parallelograms, one for the READ instruction and one for the WRITE. The READ symbol shows a dotted line labeled "EOF". The end-of-file exit from the READ statement is to be executed only when an attempt is made to read a data card but no more data cards are available.

Some programmers indicate the end-of-file test with a separate decision diamond. Like this: (Figure 10-7)

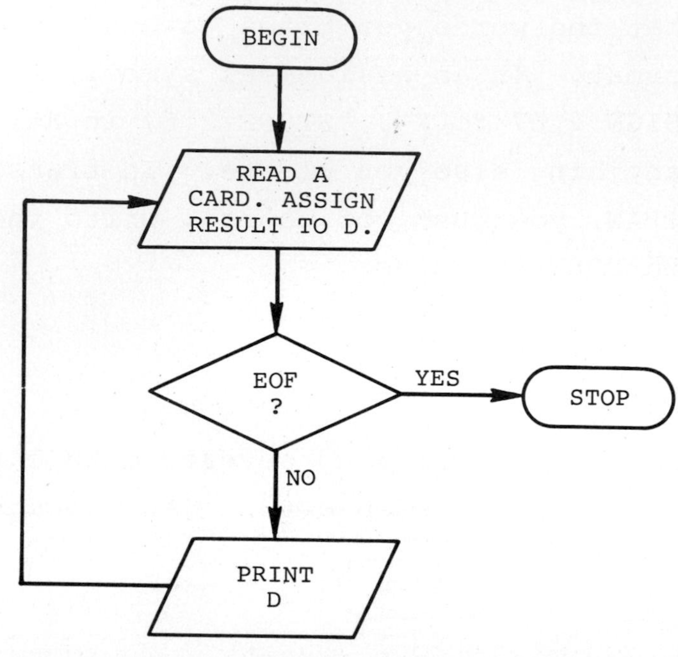

Figure 10-7

The program will process all the data cards until there are no more. Then, the program will take the end-of-file jump. Both ways of indicating the end-of-file jump are correct.

GO TO LINE

Observe that the line that leads from the WRITE symbol *back* to the READ symbol is transformed in FORTRAN to a "GO TO" statement.

Some programmers do not place arrowheads on lines leading from one symbol to another if the direction of flow is "obvious". We suggest you place arrowheads on all lines leading from one symbol to another.

STATEMENT NUMBERS ON FLOWCHARTS

After a FORTRAN program has been written, using a flowchart as a guide, the programmer should go back to the flowchart to place key statement numbers next to their associated symbols.

The flowchart in Figure 10-7 would be changed as shown in Figure 10-8.

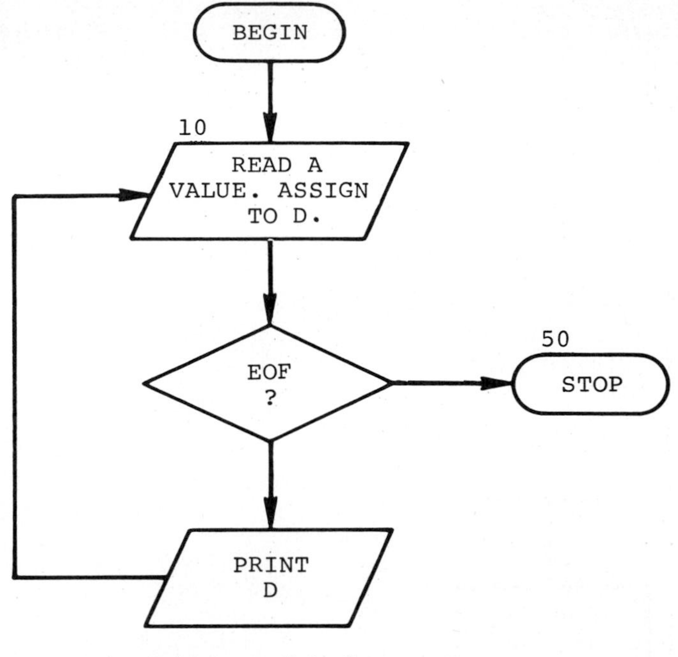

Figure 10-8

Note where the statement numbers "10" and "50" have been placed. Adopting the technique of appending statement numbers on flowcharts will enable you to debug programs easier.

DECISION SYMBOL

A diamond is the decision-making symbol. You write within the diamond a condition that has to be tested. Then you show what to do if the condition is "true", and what to do if the condition is "false". The decision diamond:

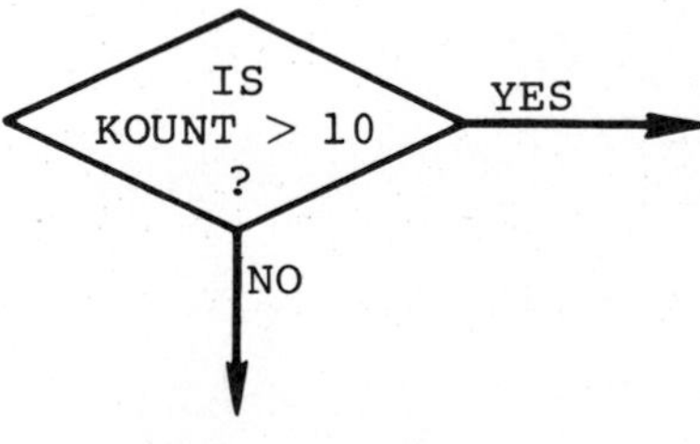

Figure 10-9

is transformed to

```
IF (KOUNT.GT.10) GO TO 70
```

If the condition is found to be "true", the program takes the course labeled "yes" on the flowchart; if the condition is found to be "false", the program takes the course labeled "no". Recall that where a logical IF statement is used, the "no" course of action *immediately follows* the IF statement.

A COUNTING EXAMPLE

Suppose we want to read exactly ten data cards, double the value found on each card, then print out each original value and each doubled value. When all ten cards have been processed, the program is to print "JOB ENDS".

Here's the flowchart:

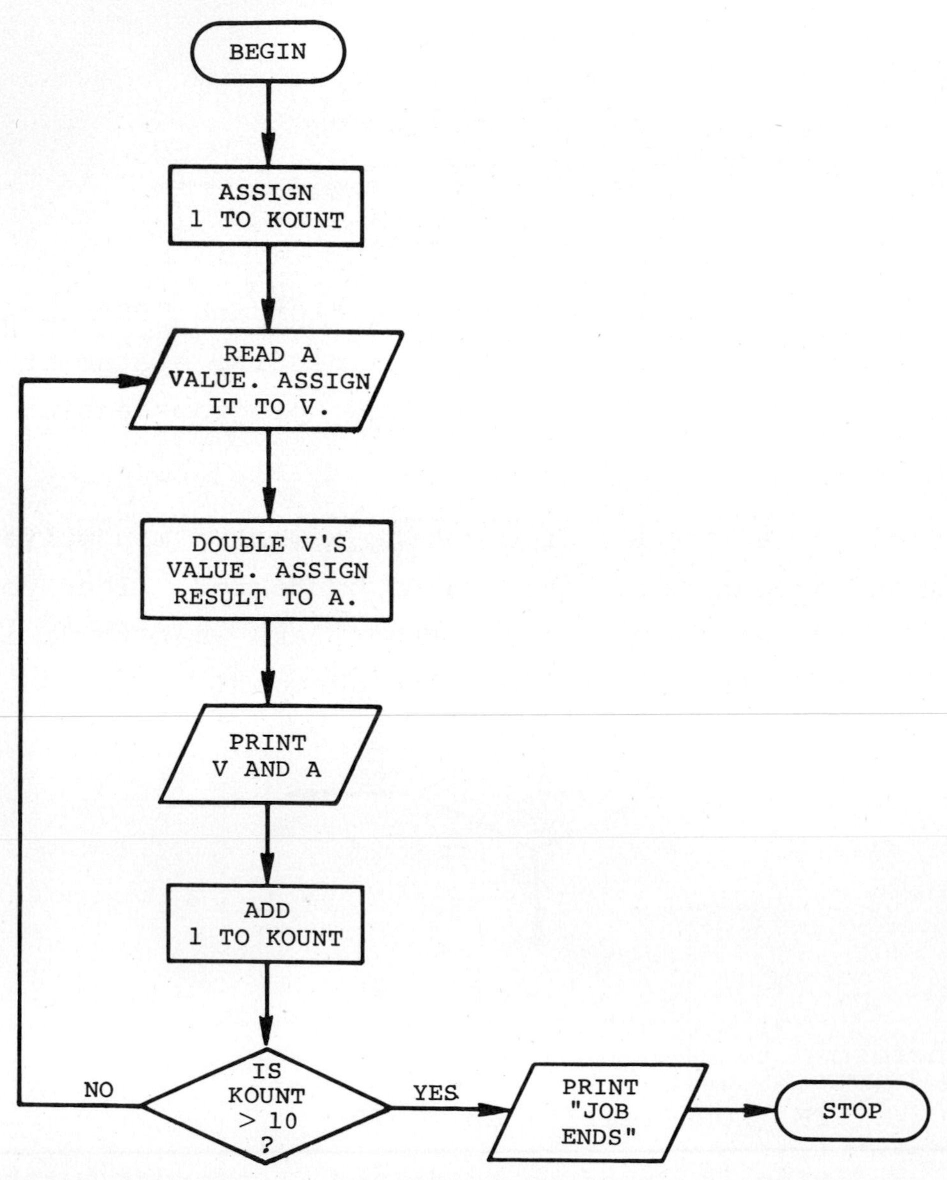

Figure 10-10

The FORTRAN program is this:

```
      KOUNT = 1
   18 READ (5,35) V
   35 FORMAT (F15.0)
      A = V + V
      WRITE (6,45) V,A
   45 FORMAT (1X,2F10.2)
      KOUNT = KOUNT + 1
      IF (KOUNT.GT.10) GO TO 70
      GO TO 18
   70 WRITE (6,75)
   75 FORMAT (1X,'JOB ENDS')
      STOP
      END
```

In following this program, observe that a counter is initialized with the value "1". The name of the counter is "KOUNT", an integer name. (Computers compute faster using integers than they do when using real numbers. That's the reason an integer counter was created, rather than a real one.)

The counter stays in step with each card read. That is, when KOUNT equals "1", the first data card is read and processed; when KOUNT equals "2", the second card is read and processed, etc. When KOUNT equals "10", the tenth card is read and processed. Immediately after the tenth card is processed, the value of KOUNT is increased to "11". Since this value is greater than "10", the IF statement detects the termination condition and the program jumps to statement "70", where the final message is printed.

CONNECTOR SYMBOL

The example flowchart on the following page shows the circular connector symbol. A connector is used to cut down on messy lines running this way and that all over a flowchart. Consider the flowchart skeleton given in Figure 10-11.

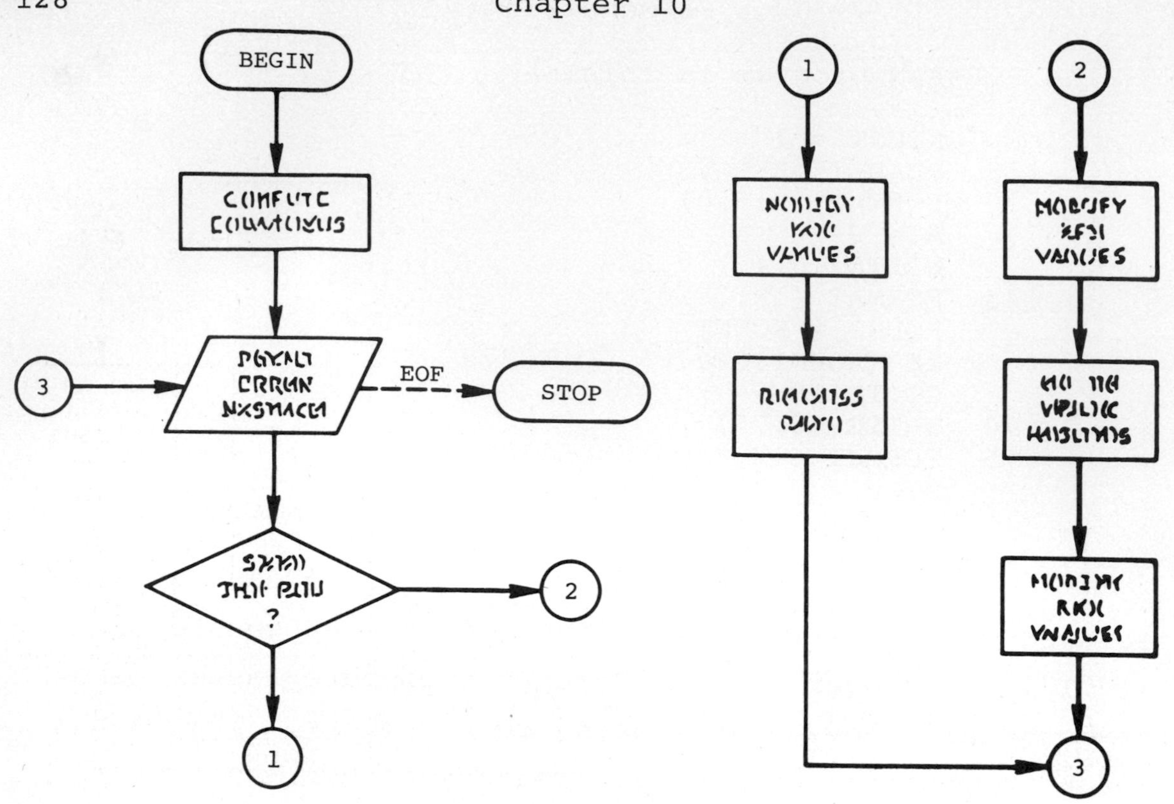

Figure 10-11

If we had elected not to use connectors, the flowchart could have looked like the one in Figure 10-12.

In this simple flowchart, extra lines don't cause much of a problem; in more complicated ones, they could cause a great deal of confusion

Contrast the flowchart given in Figure 10-11 with the one shown in Figure 10-12. Note that the flowchart in Figure 10-12 appears cleaner and easier to understand than the one in Figure 10-11.

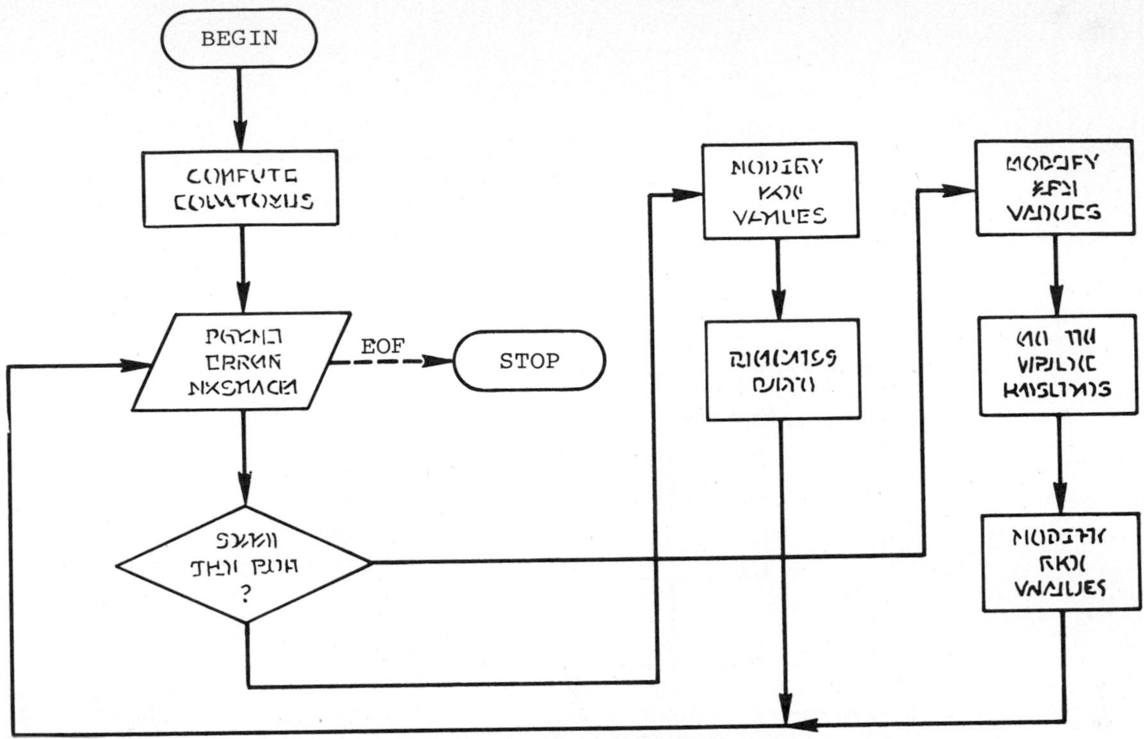

Figure 10-12

FLOWCHARTING TECHNIQUES

Flowcharts do not write themselves. There is much trial-and-error involved. One might begin a flowchart, then notice an error and do some erasing. Next, the person might see a better way of performing a particular portion of the task and scratch out the old way while squeezing in the new. At times, the programmer could decide to crumple up the work sheet and start all over.

A technique that many programmers use is to give a big picture, then refine it. For example, the person might jot down the general outline shown in Figure 10-13.

The programmer gives the major modules that constitute the major tasks that have to be accomplished. These tasks are termed "modules".

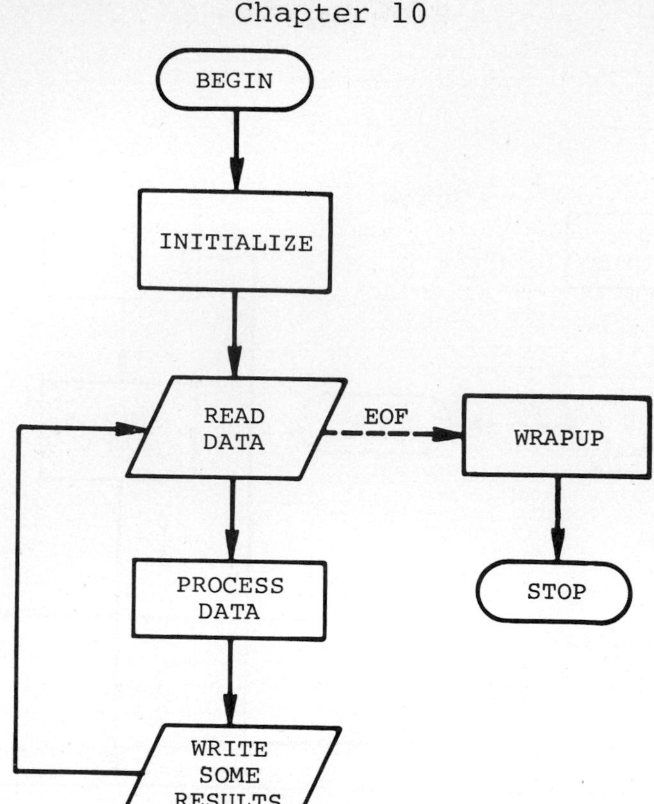

Figure 10-13

Then the programmer might select one of the modules of the program, not necessarily the first one, and amplify it. For example, the programmer might elect to work on the PROCESS DATA module. Expanding that portion of the flowchart, he or she could come up with the flowchart shown in Figure 10-14.

The flowchart shows that there are five major tasks. They are:

1. initialize
2. read data
3. process data
4. write results
5. final processing

The flowchart is given to show the relationships that these modules have with each other.

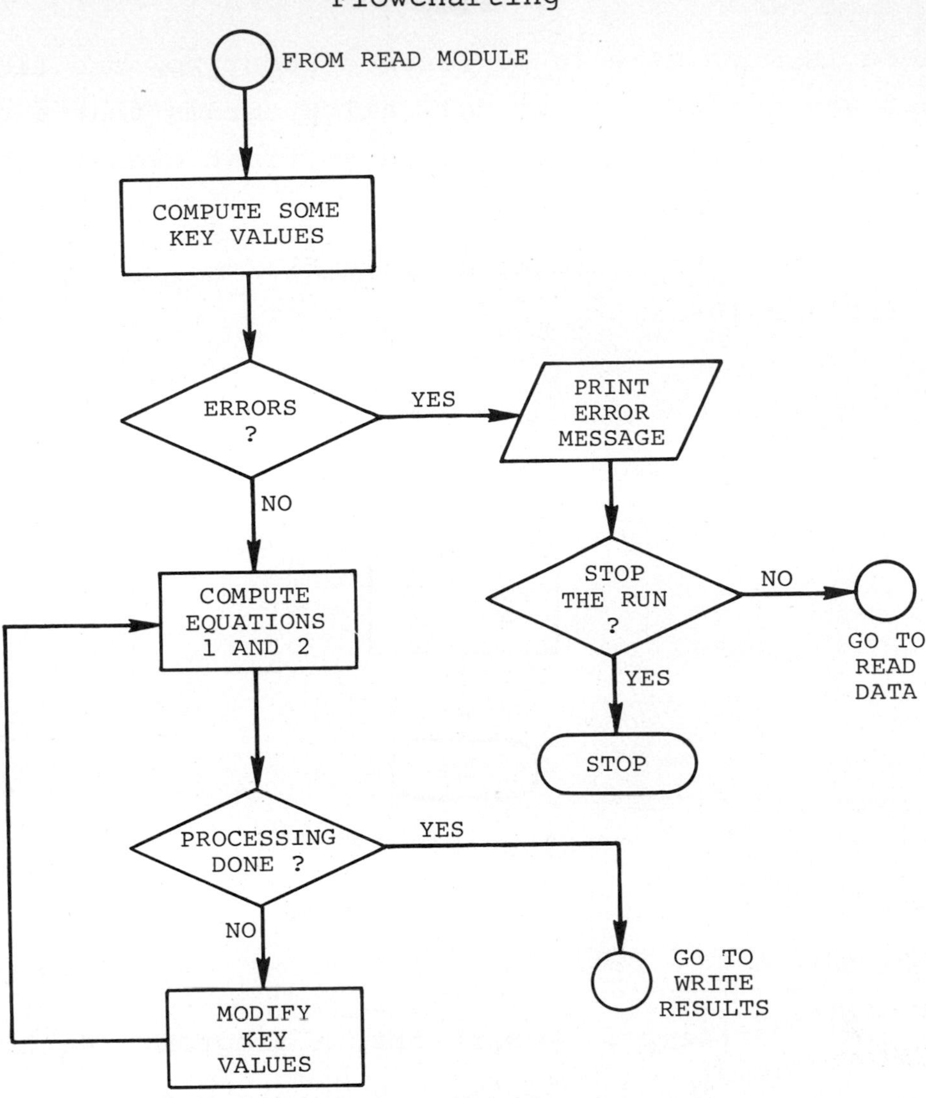

Figure 10-14

Now, any portion of the flowchart could be amplified. The programmer might, for example, amplify the portion that defines how errors are to be detected.

As the programmer works upon and completes each module, the interrelationships of all portions of the flowchart become more clear. The programmer will be able to refine, polish and finally complete the flowchart. Then, he or she can test the program by "playing computer". That is, the programmer assumes some data values and follows the flowchart as if the human were the computer. The action of the program is studied in detail. Any errors in logic should show up quickly. If the flowchart passes this test, the programmer may begin coding from it.

There is much more to be learned about how one flowcharts. The best way to learn is to do! All programs that a programmer works on should be flowcharted at first even if the assignments are simple.

If you don't know how to begin a flowchart, try doing this: (Figure 10-15)

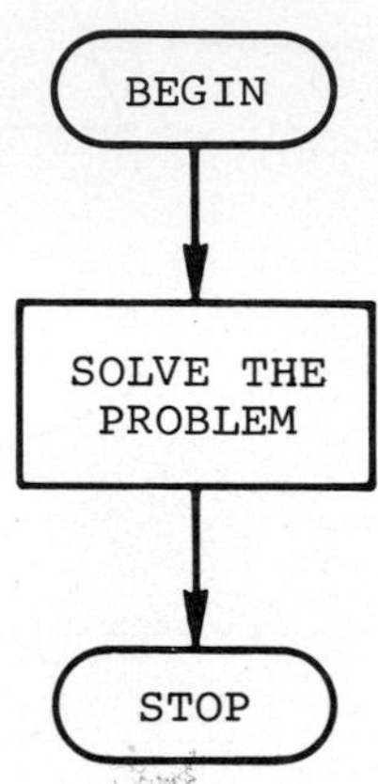

Figure 10-15

then take it from there.

WRITING A FLOWCHART FROM A PROGRAM

Now let's write a flowchart from a program. We can do this even though we may not fully understand what the program does. Consider this program:

```
       WRITE (6,9)
   9   FORMAT ('1','PROGRAM COMPUTES MEAN'//)
       SUMSCO=0.
       KOUNT=0
  10   READ (5,12,END=90) SCORE
  12   FORMAT (F15.0)
       SUMSCO=SUMSCO+SCORE
       KOUNT=KOUNT+1
       GO TO 10
  90   COUNT=KOUNT
       XMEAN=SUMSCO/COUNT
       WRITE (6,95) XMEAN
  95   FORMAT (1X,F15.1)
       STOP
       END
```

Give symbols for FORTRAN statements. Connect various symbols with logic flow lines. Your flowchart may now look like this: (Figure 10-16)

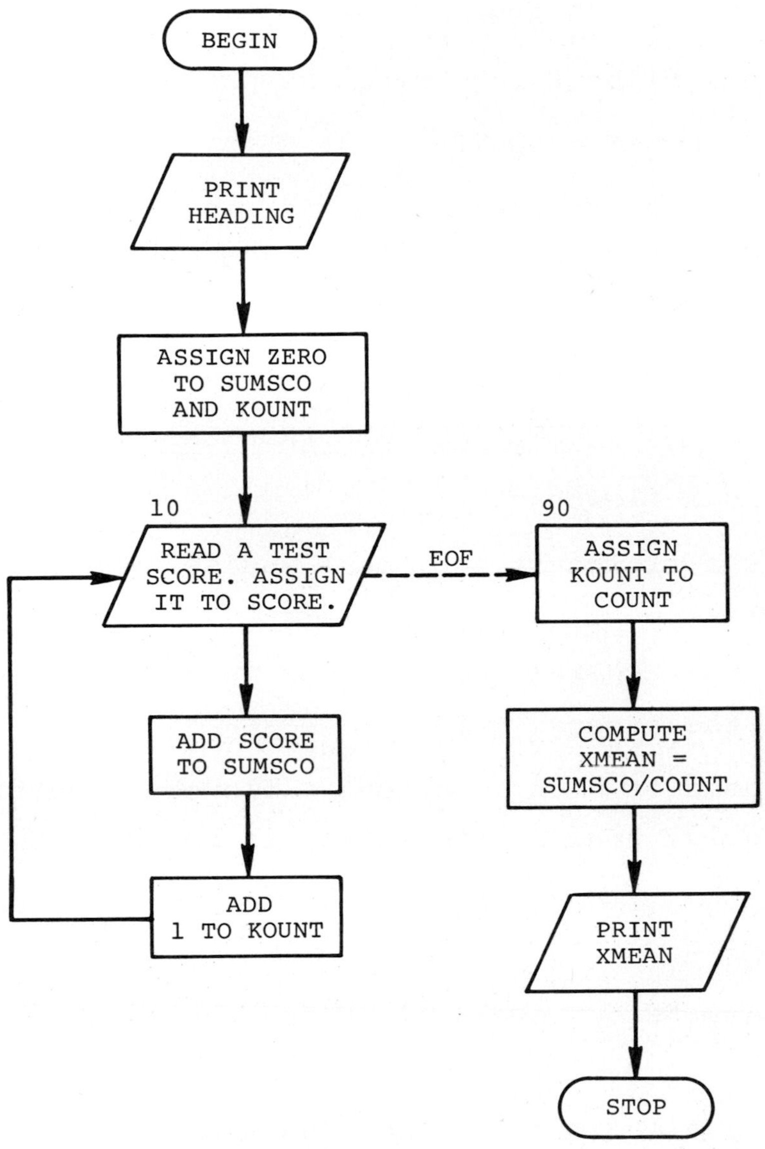

Figure 10-16

This program reads several test scores from a data deck. It adds the value of each test score to "SUMSCO" (sum of scores). Whenever a value is added to "SUMSCO", "1" is added to "KOUNT" (a counter of test scores). When the end of the data deck is found, the program computes the average (mean) of the scores. It first converts the value that "KOUNT" holds to the real value "COUNT". This is done so that the calculation

```
XMEAN = SUMSCO/COUNT
```

can be made without mixing modes. If the FORTRAN system being used permits mixing modes, the calculation

```
XMEAN = SUMSCO/KOUNT
```

could be made without requiring the preliminary

```
COUNT = KOUNT
```

The latter statement, of course, assigns the integer value that "KOUNT" holds to the variable "COUNT". The real version of "KOUNT"'s value is thus obtained.

EXERCISES AND PROBLEMS

1. What is a flowchart?
2. Why is a flowchart an almost indispensable aid in programming?
3. Give the standard symbols used in flowcharting and explain their uses.
4. What does it mean to orient a flowchart vertically? Horizontally? Which orientation is better?
5. Where on a flowchart would you expect to find the "begin" oval?
6. How many "stop" ovals might you expect to find in a flowchart?
7. What is a logic flow line? Should you put arrowheads on all flowlines?
8. How many flowlines would you expect to see exiting from a decision diamond?
9. How important is what you write within the symbols of a flowchart? Is there any standard way that you must give inscriptions within those symbols?
10. What is the reason for using connector symbols in flowcharts?

11. What is an "I/O" symbol? For what purpose is it used?

12. Why would you write statement numbers on a flowchart once the corresponding FORTRAN program has been written?

13. Do FORMAT statements have corresponding symbols in flowcharts? END statements? Why?

14. What does it mean to "play computer" in checking out a flowchart?

15. Write a flowchart from the FORTRAN program given below. Note: it is assumed that "XN" is never negative.

```
10  READ (5,15,END=35) XN
15  FORMAT (F10.0)
    G1 = XN/2.
20  G2 = (G1 + XN/G1)/2.
    IF (ABS(G1 - G2).LE..0001) GO TO 25
    G1 = G2
    GO TO 20
25  WRITE (6,30) XN,G2
30  FORMAT (1X,2F10.2)
    GO TO 10
35  STOP
    END
```

16. Write a flowchart from the FORTRAN program given below. Note: it is assumed that "A" is never zero.

```
10  READ (5,15,END=40) A,B,C
20  FORMAT (3F10.0)
    D = (B**2 - 4.*A*C)
    IF (D.LT.0.) GO TO 30
    R1 = (- B + SQRT(D)) / (2.*A)
    R2 = (- B - SQRT(D)) / (2.*A)
    WRITE (6,25) A,B,C,R1,R2
25  FORMAT (1X,5F10.2)
    GO TO 10
30  WRITE (6,35) A,B,C
35  FORMAT (1X,3F10.2,20X,'ROOTS ARE IMAG')
    GO TO 10
40  STOP
    END
```

17. Write a flowchart that shows how the first 20 numbers of the Fibonacci series would be computed. The series begins with the numbers

0, 1, 1, 2, 3, 5, 8, etc.

As can be seen, each new entry of the series is made up of the sum of the previous two numbers.

18. Write the FORTRAN program that agrees with the flowchart in Question 17.

19. If a person works for $.01 on Day 1; $.02 on Day 2; $.04 on Day 3; $.08 on Day 4; etc., doubling the amount with each subsequent day, how much will the person earn during the 30 days of June? Give the flowchart that shows how the problem would be solved.

20. Give the FORTRAN program that agrees with the flowchart in Question 19.

CHAPTER 11

More About LOOPS

READ LOOPS

In previous chapters, we began a study of "loops". You'll recall that a loop exists when there are several or many FORTRAN statements that are executed over and over.

A special form of the READ statement, for example, has a built-in option especially oriented toward loops:

```
80  READ (5,70,END=200) P,FL,K
```

Here the program executes and returns to execute the READ statement not just once but many times. Whenever the statement is executed normally, a data card is read and the three values punched upon it are assigned to P, FL, and K. Then the program processes the values read. Next a "GO TO" statement directs the computer to return to statement 80. If a data card is available to be read, the READ statement behaves in the manner just described; but when the data cards have run out, the READ command automatically causes the computer to take the "END=" jump.

A diagram showing the action of the above loop is:

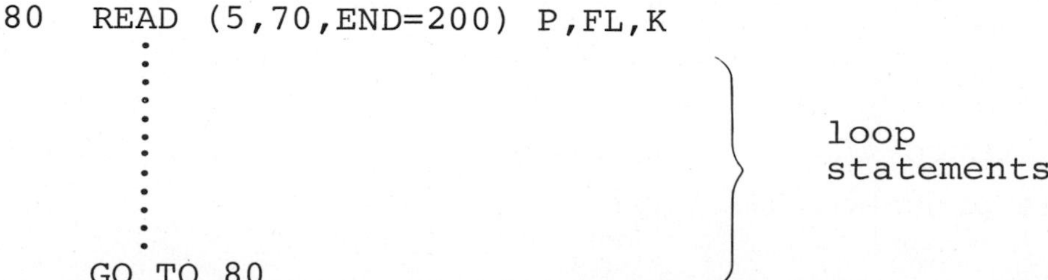

Chapter 11

LOOPS TERMINATING CONDITIONALLY

Another type of loop depends upon the fulfillment of a condition in order to terminate. Consider this example:

```
      N = 1
    5 NSQUAR = N*N
      WRITE (6.9) N,NSQUAR
    9 FORMAT (1X,2I10)
      N = N+1
      IF (NSQUAR.GT.200) GO TO 20
      GO TO 5
   20 STOP
      END
```

This program begins by assigning "1" to N. Then it squares N. Next N and its square are printed. N's value then increases to "2" and the process is repeated. The output given by this program is shown in Figure 11-1.

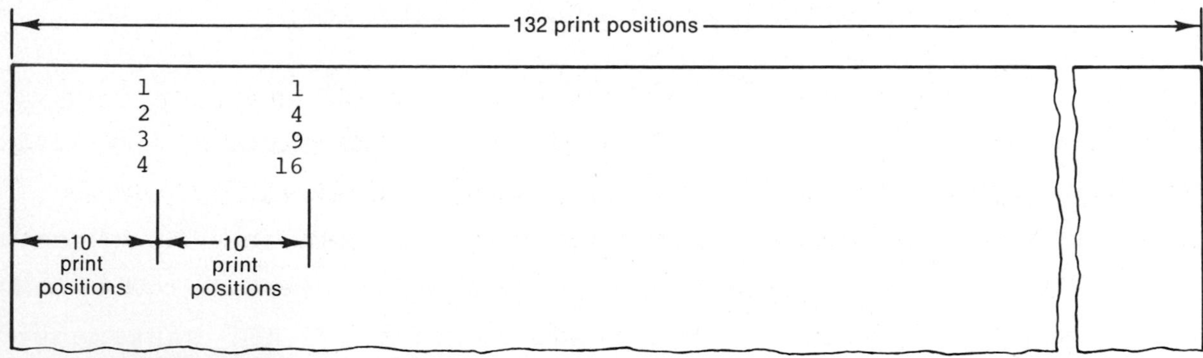

Figure 11-1

When does the report terminate? The termination of the report depends upon the value of NSQUAR. When the value of NSQUAR exceeds "200", the program jumps to the STOP statement. This means that fifteen print lines will be given by the program since "15" squared is "225", and "14" squared is only "196".

Incidentally, while studying the example program, you may have noticed that it can be shortened by one statement by writing the program this way:

```
      N=1
    5 NSQUAR=N*N
      WRITE (6,9) N,NSQUAR
    9 FORMAT (1X,2I10)
      N=N+1
      IF (NSQUAR.LE.200) GO TO 5
      STOP
      END
```

So long as the value of NSQUAR remains equal to or less than "200", the program continues. When N has the value, "14", the value of NSQUAR is "196". Since this value is not greater than "200", the program gives one more print line.

The outline for the loop of the program on the preceding page is:

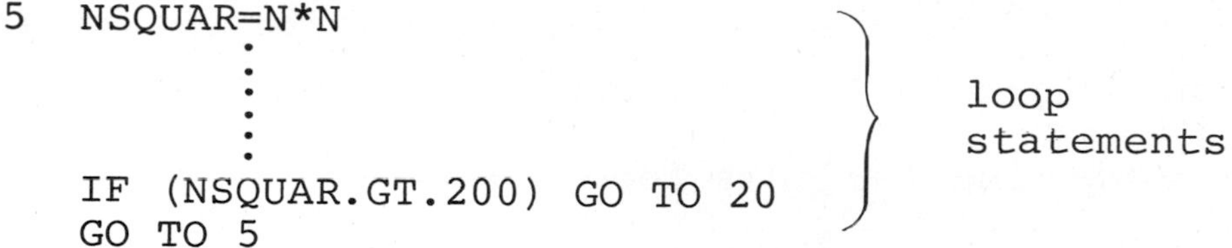
5 NSQUAR=N*N
IF (NSQUAR.GT.200) GO TO 20
GO TO 5
loop
statements

You can see that the condition upon which the loop is to terminate must be very carefully chosen. If the condition can never be met, then the loop will attempt to execute forever. Suppose the IF statement had been incorrectly written as:

```
      IF (NSQUAR.EQ.200) GO TO 20
```

NSQUAR will never attain the value "200". The program could run for hours giving thousands upon thousands of output lines. In actual practice, runaway programs are rare. The "$ LIMITS" JCL card covered earlier in this text acts as a safety valve. It stops the program when a predetermined length of computing time has been reached or when a predetermined number of output lines have been printed.

COUNTING THE ITERATIONS

A third way that a loop may be controlled is by having the computer count the number of iterations. Then, when a predetermined number has been attained, the program is directed to stop or go on to something else.

Suppose Tom Wilkins wants the computer to print his name

1000 times. (Why Tom wants the computer to do this is anyone's guess.) The program could be written this way:

```
      KNT=1
66    WRITE (6,88)
88    FORMAT (1X,'TOM WILKINS')
      KNT=KNT+1
      IF (KNT.GT.1000) GO TO 90
      GO TO 66
90    STOP
      END
```

This program employs a counter named KNT. In previous chapters, you saw that integer counting is faster than real counting. Therefore, this program counts by using integer names and numbers.

Study the program carefully to convince yourself that the program prints TOM's name 1000 times, not 999 or 1001.

The outline for this loop is:

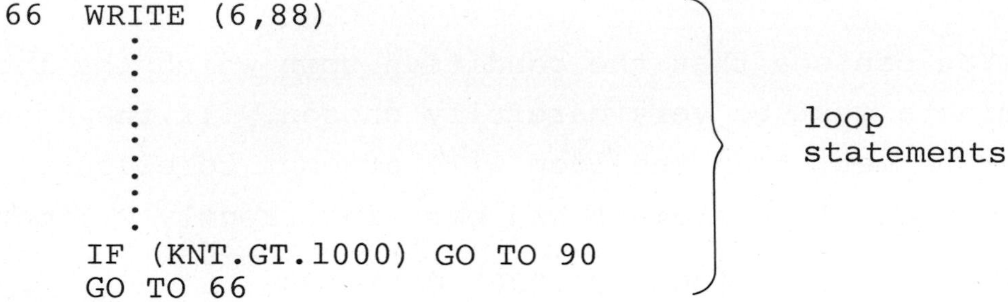
66 WRITE (6,88)
IF (KNT.GT.1000) GO TO 90
GO TO 66
loop
statements

For termination, this program depends upon the counter's value. The counter must be carefully chosen to ensure that the loop will be executed exactly as many times as required. In the example, note that the loop statements are executed once while the counter's value equals "1"; they are executed a second time while the counter's value equals "2"; etc. The loop statements are executed for the thousandth time while the counter's value equals "1000". When the counter's value is "1001", the loop terminates. The loop statements are *not* executed for the 1001'th time.

FOUR PARTS IN A LOOP

A loop that depends upon a counter for its termination has four parts. Those parts are

1. Initialization of counter.
2. Body of loop.
3. Augmenting of counter.
4. Testing of counter.

The counter to be used should be an integer name. Any name the programmer arbitrarily chooses is acceptable. The body of the loop may consist of from one to several thousand statements. An integer value is added or subtracted from the counter, then the counter is tested.

In a flowchart, those four parts can be illustrated as shown in Figure 11-2.

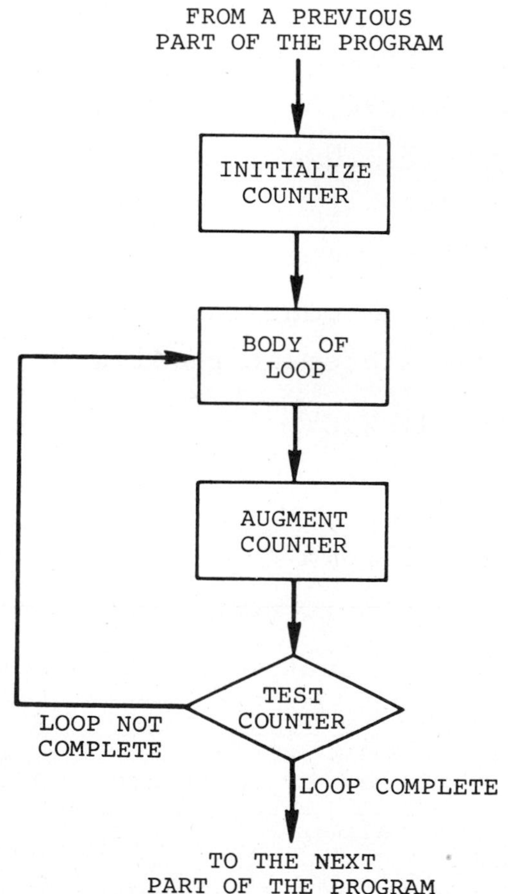

Figure 11-2

There are several ways that these four parts of a loop may be arranged. We won't explore those other ways since FORTRAN prefers this procedure. (You'll see why FORTRAN prefers this procedure when we discuss the DO and CONTINUE statements later in this chapter.)

The body of a loop is the part that must be executed

several times. It may consist of a single FORTRAN statement or it may consist of several thousand statements.

Let's consider a problem that uses the loop format given on the previous page:

```
      K = 1
  20  READ (5,24) W,S
  24  FORMAT (2F15.0)
      P = W**3
      T = S/3.5
      WRITE (6,19) W,S,P,T
  19  FORMAT (1X,4F15.2)
      K = K + 1
      IF (K.GT.200) GO TO 500
      GO TO 20
 500  STOP
      END
```

This program reads 200 data cards. From each card, it obtains values of W and S. Next, values are computed and assigned to P and T. Finally, a line of answers is printed for each card that is read.

Clearly, this program contains a loop. The body of the loop extends from the statement reading

```
  20  READ (5,24) W,S
```

to the statement reading

```
      WRITE (6,19) W,S,P,T
```

There are four statements in the body of the loop. (We normally don't count FORMAT statements when counting statements in the body of a loop.

The loop is controlled by a counter called K. Observe that K has an initial value, "1".

Just before the counter is tested, its value is augmented by "1".

The counter's value is then tested to determine whether it's greater than "200". If "yes", the loop has been completed; if "no", the loop must be executed once more. Observe that the next execution of the loop begins at the first statement of the loop's body.

AUTOMATIC LOOPS USING DO AND CONTINUE

FORTRAN gives us the ability to automate loops. The DO and CONTINUE statements are employed for this purpose. When using the statements in constructing a loop, the programmer does not need to plan all four separate parts of a loop. He or she can direct the attention mainly to the loop's body.

Consider this example:

```
      DO 95 KNT = 1,200
      WRITE (6,40)
   40 FORMAT (1X,'TOM WILKINS')
   95 CONTINUE
      STOP
      END
```

This is Tom Wilkins' program in which he directs it to print his name 200 times. Though it may not appear to do so, this program includes all four parts of a standard loop. The DO statement sets up the counter (KNT in this example) and gives it an initial value "1". (Note the "1" given in the DO statement.) The DO statement also tells what is the final value that the counter is to hold (in this example, "200").

In this example, the body of the loop extends from the statement immediately following the DO statement through the statement immediately preceding CONTINUE. There is only one statement here within the confines of the loop's body.

The body of a loop always resides within the boundries shown below:

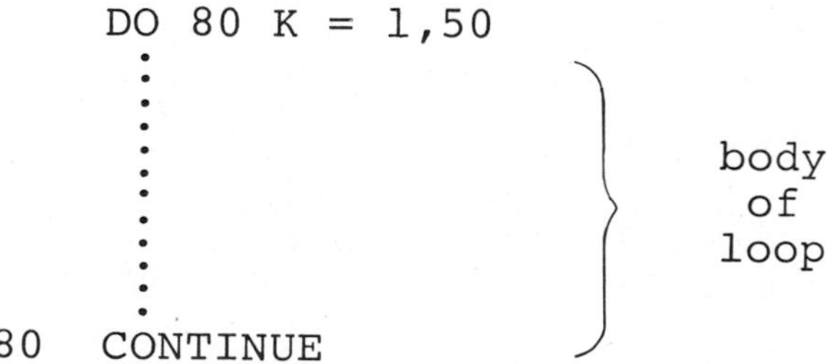
DO 80 K = 1,50
body
of
loop
80 CONTINUE

The counter's name is K. Its initial value is "1" and its final value is to be "50". Observe that there is a statement number following the word "DO" in a DO statement. The corresponding CONTINUE statement, later in the program, must contain that same statement number.

CONTINUE ACCOMPLISHES SEVERAL TASKS

The CONTINUE statement in the example loop performs these tasks:

1. Adds 1 to the counter that is named in the DO statement.
2. Checks the counter to determine if it *exceeds* the final value defined in the DO statement.
3. Stops executing the loop if the counter's value exceeds the maximum value defined in the DO statement, or causes one more execution of the loop's body.

When a program completes a loop, it is said to "escape" from the loop. "Escaping" means going to the next statement following CONTINUE. Example:

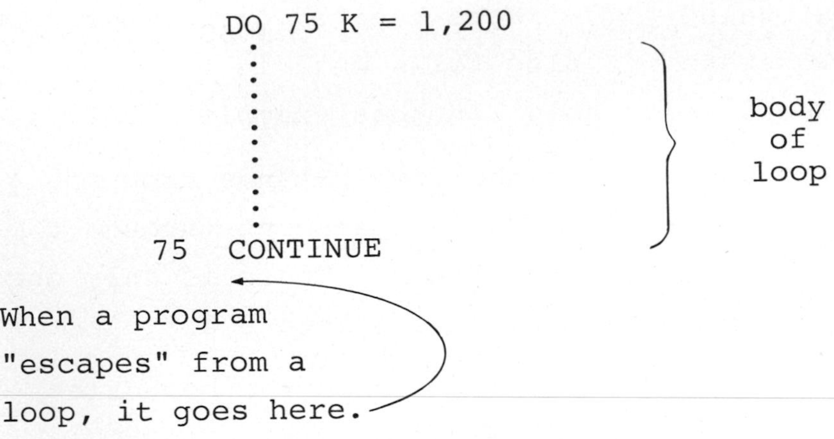
DO 75 K = 1,200
body
of
loop
75 CONTINUE
When a program
"escapes" from a
loop, it goes here.

DO LOOPS AND CONTROLLED LOOPS

A loop constructed with the aid of a DO statement is called a "DO loop". A loop explicitly containing all four parts of a programming loop is called a "controlled loop". By employing a DO loop, a programmer is relieved of much of the tedious effort required in designing a controlled loop. DO loops also provide better program documentation since loops are more clearly defined.

To review, the DO statement in a DO loop is equivalent to the initialization of a counter that is given in a controlled loop; the CONTINUE statement in a DO loop is equivalent to the augmenting and testing of a loop counter that is defined in a controlled loop. Here are the two kinds of loops side by side to illustrate that the two loops are basically very much alike:

<u>CONTROLLED LOOP</u>

```
      SUM = 0.
      N = 1
    7 READ (5,6) VIC
      SUM = SUM + VIC
      N = N+1
      IF (N.GT.100) GO TO 25
      GO TO 7
   25 WRITE (6,8) SUM
      STOP
    6 FORMAT (F20.0)
    8 FORMAT ('1',F10.2)
      END
```

<u>DO LOOP</u>

```
      SUM = 0.
      DO 80 N=1,100
      READ (5,6) VIC
      SUM = SUM + VIC


   80 CONTINUE
      WRITE (6,8) SUM
      STOP
    6 FORMAT (F20.0)
    8 FORMAT ('1',F10.2)
      END
```

<u>DO DETAILS</u>

There are a few details concerning DO statements that you should know. Here is the general format of the DO statement:

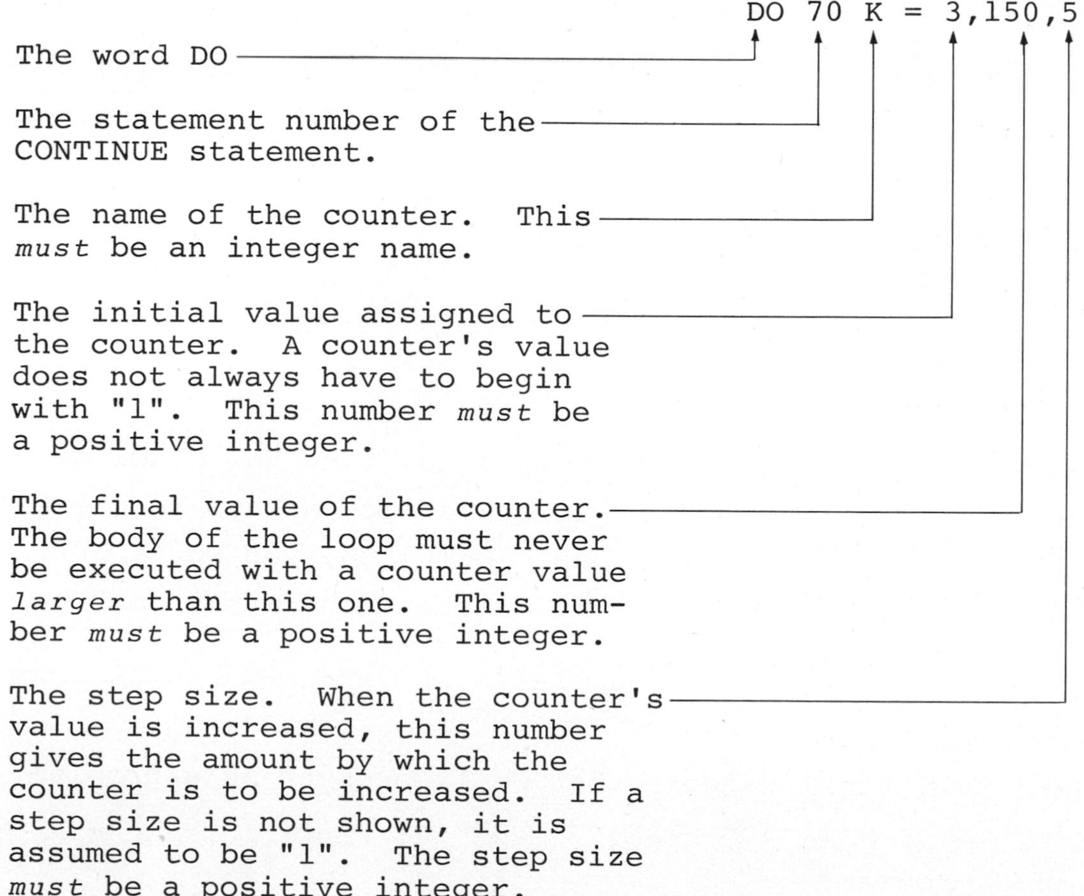

DO 70 K = 3,150,5
The word DO
The statement number of the CONTINUE statement.
The name of the counter. This *must* be an integer name.
The initial value assigned to the counter. A counter's value does not always have to begin with "1". This number *must* be a positive integer.
The final value of the counter. The body of the loop must never be executed with a counter value *larger* than this one. This number *must* be a positive integer.
The step size. When the counter's value is increased, this number gives the amount by which the counter is to be increased. If a step size is not shown, it is assumed to be "1". The step size *must* be a positive integer.

Here are some examples of valid DO statements:

```
DO 80 L = 1,350
DO 75 N = 1,300,2
DO 85 KNT = 3,L
DO 8 JJ = K,L,N
```

All numbers given in a DO statement must be integer values or integer names. All values must be positive and greater than zero. The final value given in a DO statement must be equal to or greater than the initial value. Hence in

```
DO 200 K = 10,10
```

the *body of the loop will be executed once.*

CONTINUE MAY BE OMITTED

Most statement types given at the end of a DO loop can substitute for CONTINUE. This loop, for example, is valid:

```
    DO 90 N = 1,300  ⎫
     .               ⎪
     .               ⎪   body
     .               ⎬    of
     .               ⎪   loop
     .               ⎪
90  X = Y + Z        ⎭
```

The loop could also be written this way:

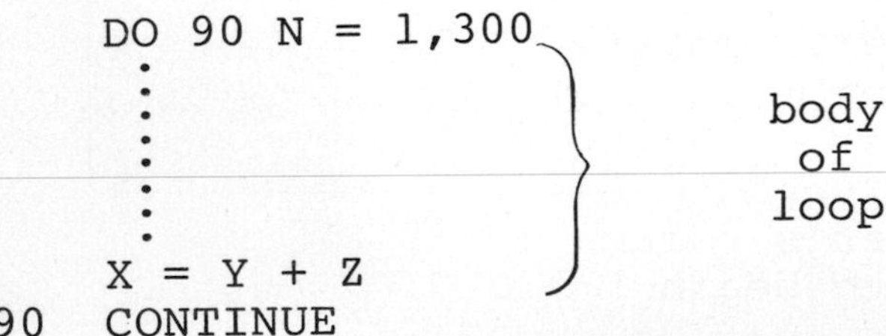
DO 90 N = 1,300
body
of
loop
X = Y + Z
90 CONTINUE

Since *not all* FORTRAN statements may take the place of CONTINUE, we suggest you make it a practice always to use CONTINUE at the end of a DO loop. Doing so, you won't ever have to worry about whether a given statement may or may not be given at the end of a DO loop.

A PROBLEM

Here is a final example that we'll present as a problem. How many times will Tom Wilkins' name be printed according to this next program?

```
      DO 800 L=5,55,3
      WRITE (6,45)
 45   FORMAT (1X,'TOM WILKINS')
800   CONTINUE
      STOP
      END
```

The answer is 17. When Tom's name is printed, the counter's values will be 5, 8, 11, 14, 17, 20, 23, 26, 29, 32, 35, 38, 41, 44, 47, 50, and 53. The value of L actually becomes "56" at one point but that value is not used since it is greater than "55".

If "L"'s value had ever actually been exactly equal to "55", it would have caused one more iteration through the loop. The body of a loop will be performed once more when the number that the counter holds *equals* the final value defined in the DO statement, but not when the counter's number *exceeds* that value.

LAST VALUE

To find the last value that the counter will actually employ in the performance of a DO LOOP, use this equation:

$$L = S \times (\text{integer} \left[\frac{F - B}{S}\right]) + B$$

HOW MANY TIMES

To find how many times the body within a DO LOOP will be executed, use this equation:

$$N = \text{integer} \left[\frac{F - B}{S}\right] + 1$$

In these equations F is the final value given in the DO statement; B is the beginning value; and S is the step size.

To give the flowchart for a program that involves a DO LOOP, give the flowchart as if the loop were a controlled loop. The flowchart for this program

```
      DO 80 N = 1,20
      WRITE (6,20)
 20   FORMAT (1X,'HELLO')
 80   CONTINUE
      STOP
      END
```

appears like this:

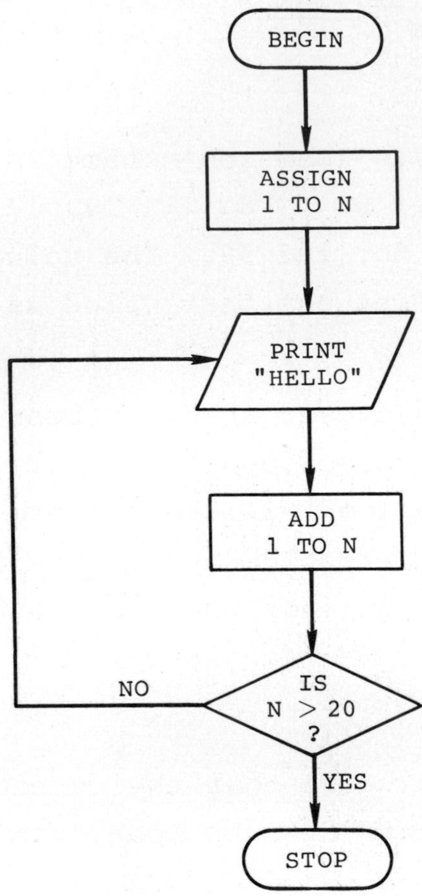

Figure 11-3

EXERCISES AND PROBLEMS

1. Why does the "END=" option in READ statements lend itself well to programs that require loops?
2. Give some ways that loops, once having begun, may terminate.
3. How many parts does a loop that counts iterations have? What are the parts?
4. How many statements might you expect to find in the body of a loop?
5. Define "controlled loop".
6. Define "DO loop".

7. What does it mean "to escape from a DO loop"?

8. In a DO loop what type variable must the counter be?

9. How many integer numbers might you expect to see to the right of the equals sign in a DO statement? Tell what each of the numbers means.

10. If a DO statement does not give a step size, what is the step size assumed to be?

11. May any of the numbers to the right of the equals sign in a DO statement be negative?

12. May the integer values to the right of the equals sign in a DO statement be represented by integer variable names?

13. Study this DO statement:

    ```
    DO 45 IK = 20,20
    ```

    How many times will the loop be executed?

14. What does the CONTINUE statement in a DO loop do? Must all DO loops include CONTINUE statements?

15. Study this DO statement:

    ```
    DO 90 NN = 23,105,5
    ```

    What value will NN hold while the loop is executed for the last time?

16. Study this DO statement:

    ```
    DO 38 M = 81,247,7
    ```

    How many times will the loop be executed?

17. Write a program that computes and prints the value of a variable named X and the square root of X when X varies from "21.6" through "23.5" in steps of ".1". Have the program print answers rounded to two decimal places. The program should use a "DO loop". Hint: begin the program this way:

    ```
    X = 21.6
    DO 40 K = 1,20     or     DO 40 K = 216,235
    ```

CHAPTER 12

Arrays

For the solution of many types of problems, it is necessary to obtain data values from punched cards and store them in consecutive memory cells. After the values have been thus located, they can be accessed again and again to solve the given problems.

If values can be processed immediately upon being read, there is no necessity to store them. Suppose, for example, you have a problem involving the punched cards shown in Figure 12-1.

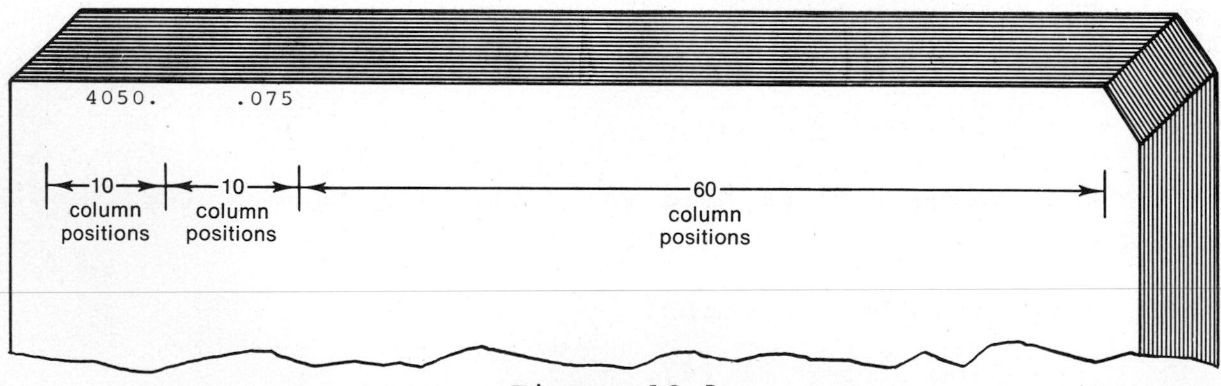

Figure 12-1

The leftmost value on each card represents a principal amount to be invested; the rightmost represents an interest rate. Assume the task is to read the cards, a card at a time, and to compute the income per investment for one year. Each investment is evaluated by multiplying the dollar amount by the interest rate.

A program that gives the desired results is this:

```
25  READ (5,30,END=95) PRINC,RATE
30  FORMAT (2F10.0)
    XINC = PRINC * RATE
    WRITE (6,35) XINC,PRINC,RATE
35  FORMAT (1X,2F10.2,F10.3)
    GO TO 25
95  STOP
    END
```

The flowchart for this program shows how the problem is solved. See Figure 12-2.

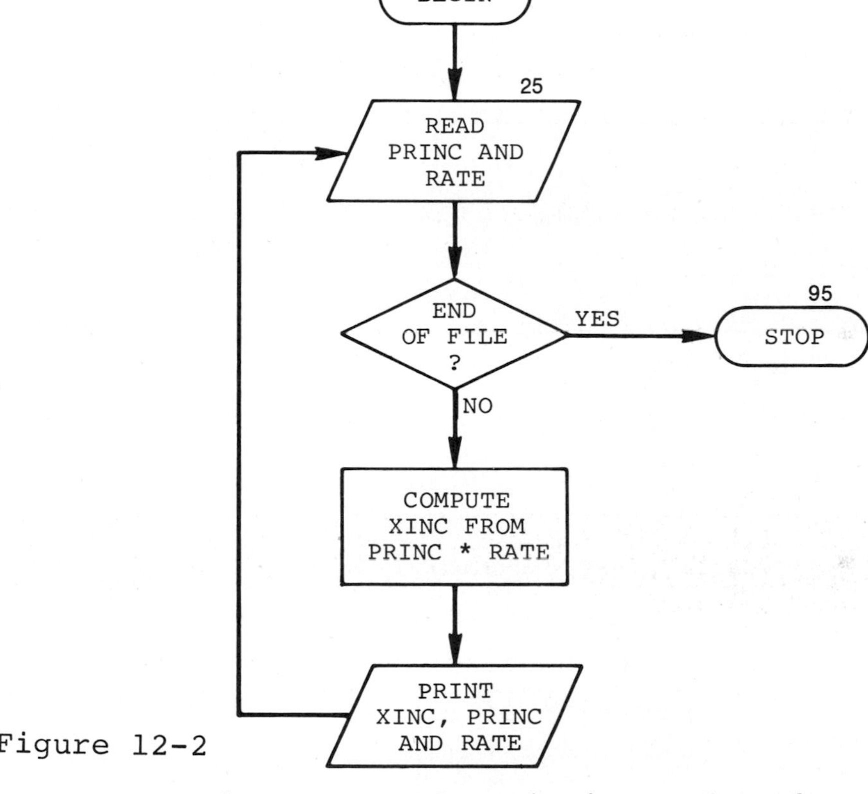

Figure 12-2

Each data card is processed as it is read. There is no attempt to read *all* data values into memory before any of them are processed. It is possible to solve the problem by storing all data values first but the solution is awkward to program and more costly to run.

Some problems *require* that all the values needed be first stored in memory. Consider an example where one hundred values obtained from one hundred data cards are to be printed in increasing sequence. When the values are first read, they are in no special sequence. The values stored in 100 memory cells might be those shown in Figure 12-3 on the following page.

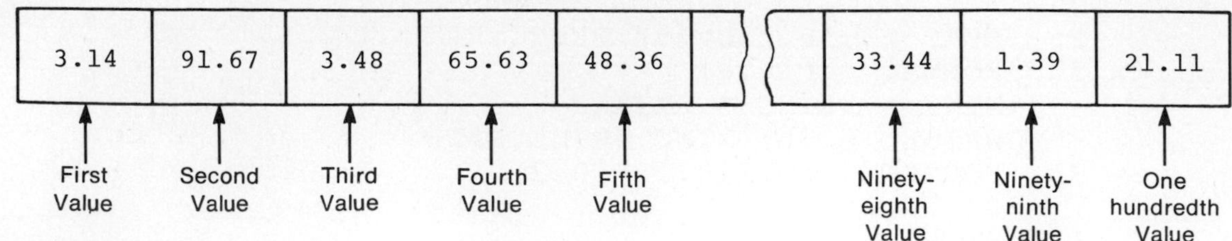

Figure 12-3

Now, by shifting the positions of these numbers from cell to cell, the numbers can be sequenced. In memory, the values will be stored in the positions shown in Figure 12-4.

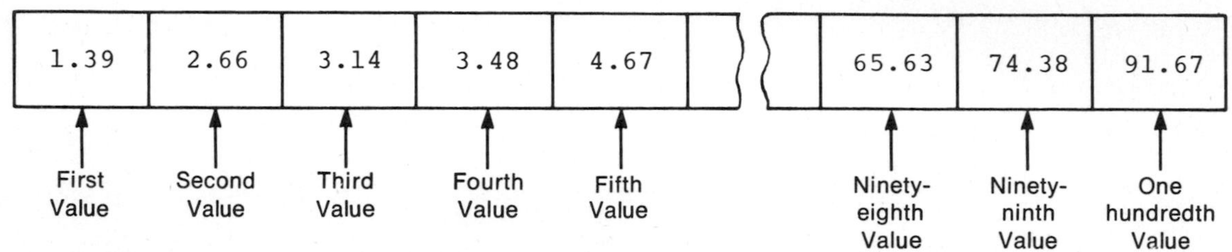

Figure 12-4

There may be hundreds, if not thousands, of positional shifts before the values are finally arranged in sequence. Once positioned, all one hundred numbers are printed and the problem has been solved.

In this chapter, we'll show how to write a program that arranges (sorts) the one hundred values in increasing sequence, then prints them. At the time that we discuss sorting, we will also discuss the creation of arrays using the DIMENSION statement. In the chapter that follows, we will continue our investigation of arrays and see where they can be used effectively.

The sorting technique we illustrate here is one that works properly regardless of whether the number of data values is as few as ten or as many as several thousand.

In order to store related data values in memory, a special area in the computer's memory has to be prepared. The special area is established by use of the DIMENSION statement. A DIMENSION statement may be written in a variety of ways. Here are some:

```
DIMENSION AP(50)
DIMENSION KF(100),PMK(20)
```

The first DIMENSION statement sets aside an area containing 50 memory cells. The area has the name "AP".

The second DIMENSION statement sets aside two areas; the first is named "KF" and contains 100 memory cells; the second is called "PMK" and contains 20 memory cells.

You may include as many DIMENSION statements in your program as you need. Each DIMENSION statement may define one or many memory areas. (DIMENSION statements may be continued in the same way as other FORTRAN statements.) A DIMENSION statement may be given anywhere in a program providing it is given before the defined area is used.

An area reserved in memory with the use of a DIMENSION statement has three attributes:

1. The area has a name. Examples:

   "AP", "KF", "PMK".

2. The area has "mode". That is, the area may be an integer area or it may be a real one. If the area's name is an integer name (for example, "KF"), the area is intended to hold integer values; if the name is real (for example, "AP"), the area is intended to hold real values.

3. The area has "size". In the DIMENSION statements, the numbers shown within parentheses tell how many memory cells are associated with each area. The size of an area may be as little as "2" or as large as several thousand.

Let's see how these attributes apply to a representative area.

```
DIMENSION ROOTS(250)
```

The name of the area is "ROOTS"; its mode is "real"; its size is "250". It has the appearance shown in Figure 12-5 on the following page.

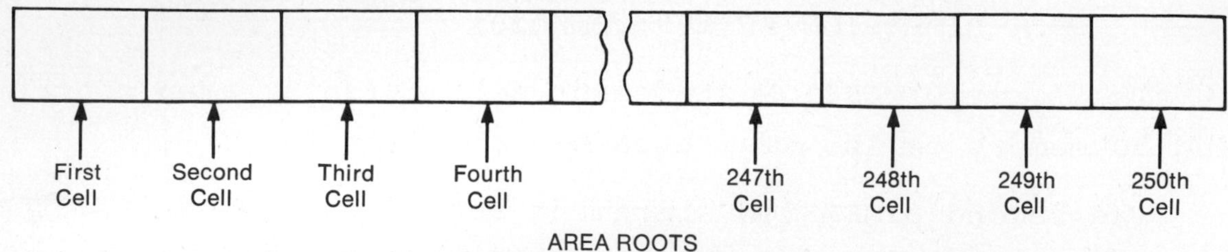

Figure 12-5

An area in memory (such as "ROOTS") is useless unless the area is loaded with some values to work with. Those values may be given to the memory cells one at a time (using assignment statements) or the values may be given several at a time (using READ statements). The latter method is much more efficient.

To show how numeric values may be stored in the memory cells of a dimensioned area, let's discuss the area called "COSTS". The area has been reserved with this DIMENSION statement:

```
DIMENSION COSTS(10)
```

The area may be given values this way:

```
DIMENSION COSTS(10)
COSTS (1)  = 48.21
COSTS (2)  = 19.35
COSTS (3)  = 46.20
COSTS (4)  = 31.80
COSTS (5)  = 23.95
COSTS (6)  = 16.32
COSTS (7)  =  6.78
COSTS (8)  = 11.45
COSTS (9)  = 51.45
COSTS (10) = 33.25
```

Each of the statements given under the DIMENSION statement is an assignment statement. In each assignment statement, the number within parentheses is called a "subscript". A subscript is always an integer value. It tells *which* member of the dimensioned area is being referenced. Thus, in the statement

```
COSTS (1)  = 48.21
```

the value "48.21" is being assigned to the first cell of the area, "COSTS". In the statement:

```
          COSTS (6) = 16.32
```

the value "16.32" is being assigned to the sixth cel
same area.

Assignments may be made in any order. The ten assignment statements could have been scrambled in any sequence but the end result would have been the same. Any cell which has never had a value assigned to it, holds the initial value "0." (for real areas) or "0" (for integer areas).

Values in dimensioned areas may be changed as required. If the statement

```
          COSTS (7) = 19.90
```

is given at a later point in the program, the value "19.90" replaces the value "6.78" that the seventh cell of "COST" held earlier.

A dimensioned area that is no longer empty - that has had numeric values stored in it - is called an "array". When "COSTS" has been given values, for example, it is referred to as the "COSTS array".

You can see that loading an area by the use of assignment statements is quite tedious. An array of only ten values needs only ten assignment statements, but an area of one hundred or one thousand memory cells would require far too many assignment statements. An easier way to create an array is to read values into the cells from data cards. Here's an example:

```
          DIMENSION RATES(100)
          READ (5,9) RATES
        9 FORMAT (F10.0)
```

The program reads, not one, but one hundred data cards. Each card has a single numeric value punched upon it. The value on the first card is stored in cell "1" of "RATES"; the value on the second card is stored in cell "2", etc.

Note carefully that a READ statement that gives the name of a dimensioned variable is processed differently from a READ statement that gives the name of an undimensioned variable.

In the statement

```
READ (5,4) QTY
```

the program reads a *single* card and stores the value punched thereon to QTY. (We assume that QTY is not dimensioned.)

In the statement

```
READ (5,9) RATES
```

the program reads enough cards to completely fill the array "RATES". The FORMAT tells how many values to obtain from each card. If the FORMAT is

```
9  FORMAT (F10.0)
```

the program obtains only one value per card. That value is stored within the leftmost ten columns of the card. See Figure 12-6.

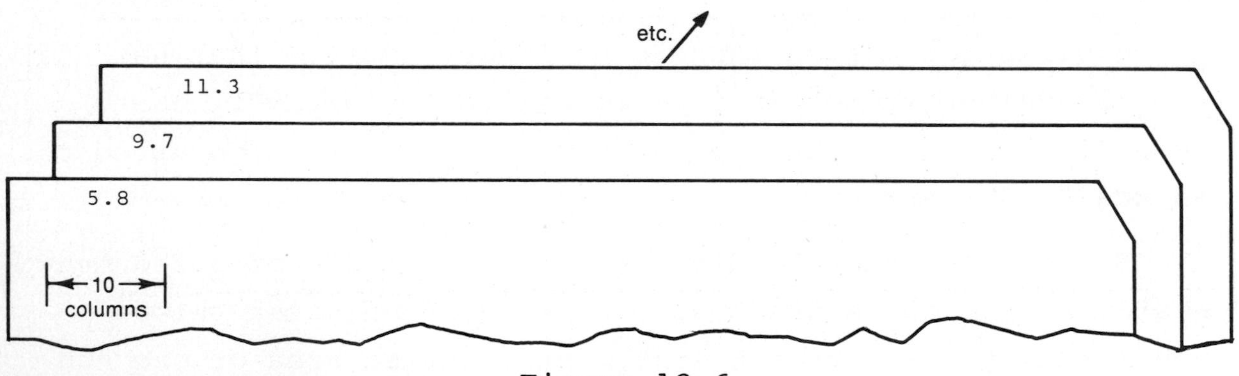

Figure 12-6

If the FORMAT is

```
9  FORMAT (2F10.0)
```

then *two* values are obtained from each card. Only 50 cards are needed to create the entire array. The cards are punched as shown in Figure 12-7 on the following page.

A FORMAT can be designed in any way that is convenient. It may call for five numbers per card, ten, or even more. The more values that are punched on a card, the fewer the number of cards that have to be read. Suppose we wish to punch eleven numbers per card. These statements will load the RATES array:

```
      DIMENSION RATES(100)
      READ (5,9) RATES
    9 FORMAT (11F7.0)
```

The cards would be punched as shown in Figure 12-8.

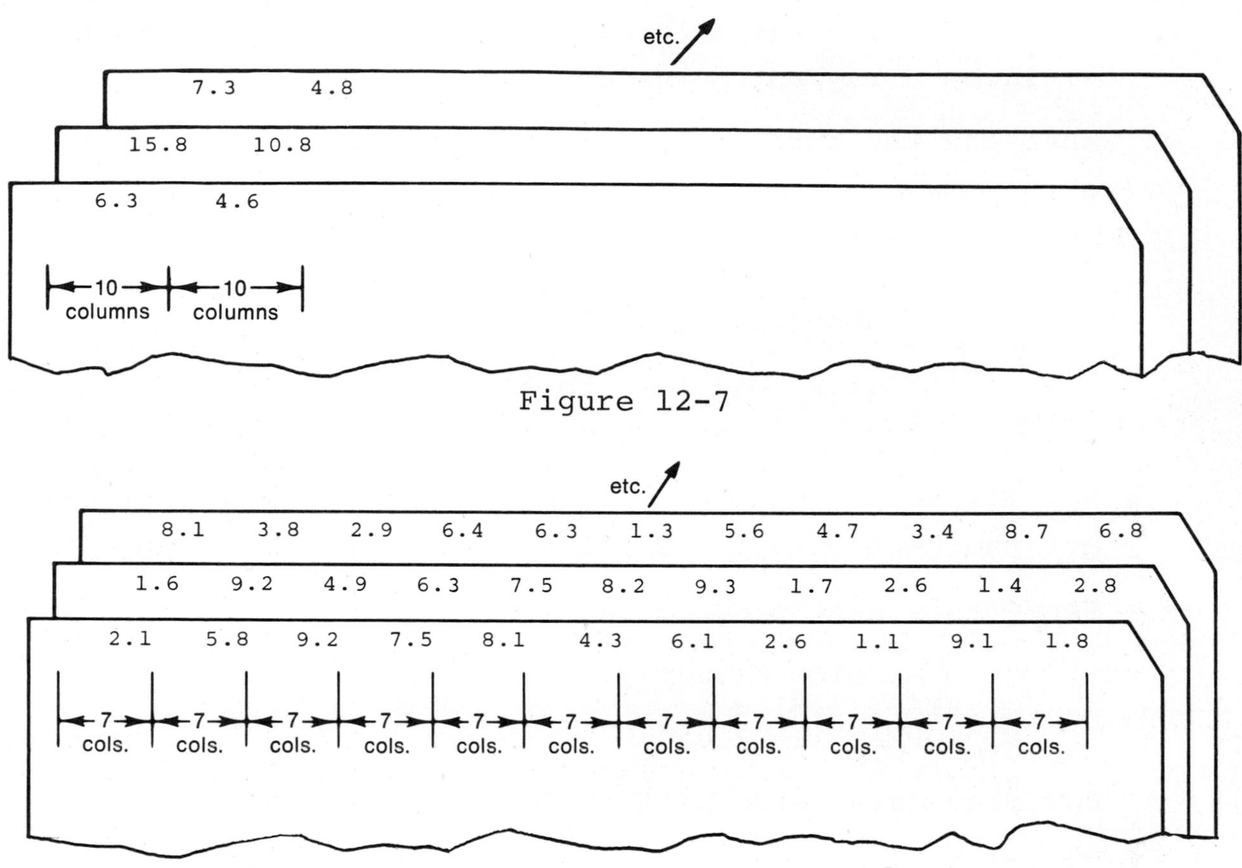

Figure 12-7

Figure 12-8

There are eleven values punched per card, each value occupying seven column positions. (Altogether, 77 column positions of each card are used. Columns 78, 79, and 80 are not used.) To load the entire array, ten cards are needed. The values for array cells 1 through 99 are found upon the first nine cards. The tenth card contributes only one value - the one for array cell 100. Any values punched to the right of column 7 in the last data card are ignored.

EXERCISES AND PROBLEMS

1. Define the term array.

2. In a FORTRAN program how is space for an array defined?

3. When would you use an array to solve a problem? When would an array not be needed?

4. What are the three attributes that space reserved for an array has?

5. What names may you give to space reserved for an array?

6. What is a subscript?

7. Why is it not a good idea to load values into an array using assignment statements?

8. How may large amounts of data be stored into arrays without the necessity for doing a great deal of coding?

9. Study this next program segment.

```
      DIMENSION W(500)
      READ (5,8) W
    8 FORMAT (10F8.0)
```

   How many data cards will the program read to load the entire W array?

10. Refer to Question 9. What will the program do if only ten data cards are available to be read?

11. Study the following program segment.

```
      DIMENSION J(100)
      READ (5,20) J(8)
   20 FORMAT (10I5)
```

   How many data cards will the program read?

12. Write a program that creates an array space named K having 200 locations. Then have the program store the integer values "1", "2", "3", ..., "200" into the array. Have the program stop at that point. (Do not use data cards.)

13. Write a program that creates an array space named L having 5 locations. Then have the program store the integer

values "21", "56", "95", "32", and "74" into the five cells of the array. Have the program stop at that point.

14. Write a program that creates an array space named X having a size of 75. Then have the program read values into the array from data cards. Each data card has eleven values punched upon it with the FORMAT "11F7.0". Have the program stop at that point.

15. Begin a program this way:

```
      DIMENSION T(100), V(100)
      READ (5,8) T
    8 FORMAT (10F8.0)
```

Continue the program by *copying* the T array into the V array. Have the program stop at that point.

16. Begin a program this way:

```
      DIMENSION T(100), V(100)
      READ (5,8) T
    8 FORMAT (10F8.0)
```

Continue the program by *copying* the T array into the V array in *reverse* order. Then have the program print the entire V array and stop.

17. Begin a program this way:

```
      DIMENSION T(100), V(100)
      READ (5,8) T
    8 FORMAT (10F8.0)
```

Continue the program by creating a V array. Every cell in the V array is to have double the value that the corresponding value has in the T array. Have the program print the entire V array and stop.

18. Write a program that begins this way:

```
      DIMENSION J(100)
      READ (5,9) J
    9 FORMAT (10I8)
```

Then continue the program by counting the number of zero values that are located in the 100 cells of the J array. Have the program print that count and stop.

CHAPTER 13

Using Arrays

Arrays are needed only if you intend to use the data punched on the data cards more than once. If you need to process the data only once, there is no need to create an array. Consider this example that sums several values punched upon several cards:

```
      SUM = 0.
    2 READ (5,4,END=80) XVAL
    4 FORMAT (F10.0)
      SUM = SUM + XVAL
      GO TO 2
   80 WRITE (6,85) SUM
   85 FORMAT (1X,F10.2)
      STOP
      END
```

This program first initializes a variable, "SUM", to an initial value of zero. Then, the program reads a data card containing only one value. That value is given the name "XVAL". Next, the value just read, "XVAL", is added to "SUM". The program then returns to the READ statement to obtain another value which is, in turn, added to "SUM".

Observe that the statement

```
      SUM = SUM + XVAL
```

adds the value XVAL to the *old* value of SUM. The *new* value of SUM replaces the old one.

The program shown above has a loop. Data values are read and added to SUM until the data values are exhausted - that is, until there are no more data cards in the data deck. The program then jumps automatically to statement 80 where the final computed value of SUM is printed.

The points to observe from this program are these:

1. The cards in the data deck are read only once.

2. The final value of SUM is printed only once.

3. When the data cards run out, the program automatically jumps to statement 80.

4. There is no definite number of data cards that might be given in the data deck. There might only be one, but on the other hand, there might be 1000 or more. The program works the same regardless of how many data cards there are in the data deck.

Though this problem is virtually the same as one that we discussed earlier in this text, it is instructive since we can now contrast it with the problem that follows.

Suppose you are required to read ten data values from ten sequential data cards and print them *in reverse order*. Obviously, this next program will not accomplish the objective:

```
      DO 75 N=1, 10
      READ (5,9) V
    9 FORMAT (F10.0)
      WRITE (6,15) V
   15 FORMAT (1X,F10.2)
   75 CONTINUE
      STOP
      END
```

The ten data values that this program reads are printed in the *same* sequence that they were read. This is not what was required. In order to solve the problem, the ten data values must be read into an array, then printed from the array, bottom value first.

Here is a program that accomplishes the objective:

```
      DIMENSION V(10)
      READ (5,9) V
    9 FORMAT (F10.0)
      DO 75 N=1,10
```

```
      WRITE (6,15) V(11-N)
   15 FORMAT (1X,F10.2)
   75 CONTINUE
      STOP
      END
```

This program first reads the ten data values into the "V" array. Let's assume this is what the "V" array looks like after the READ statement has been executed:

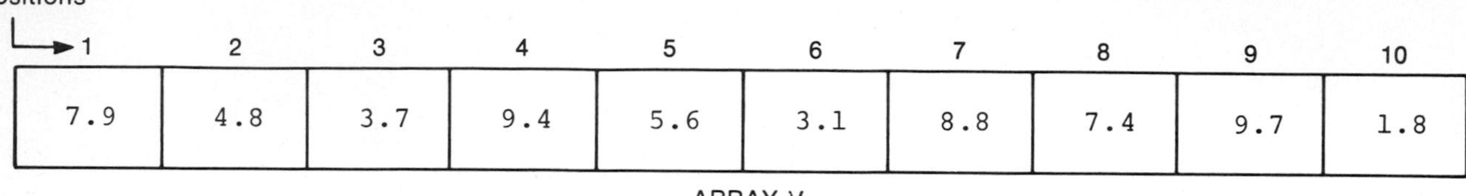

Figure 13-1

The program then executes a loop ten times. In the body of the loop, the value "V(11-N)" is printed. When the index of the loop, N, is "1", the subscript "11-N" is equivalent to "10" and the tenth value of V is printed; when the index is "2", the effective subscript is "9" and the ninth value of V is printed, etc.

Some FORTRAN's do not accept certain forms of computed subscripts. If you find that your system does not accept a subscript like "11-N", you can still give essentially the same solution. The subscript is computed separately and assigned to an integer variable name. The program above could be given this way: (Note K.)

```
      DIMENSION V(10)
      READ (5,9) V
    9 FORMAT (F10.0)
      DO 75 N=1,10
      K=11-N
      WRITE (6,15) V(K)
   15 FORMAT (1X,F10.2)
   75 CONTINUE
      STOP
      END
```

Let's consider another, more complex, problem. Suppose you are required to read ten real values from data catds, then have the computer print them in sequence from lowest to highest. Figure 13-2 shows a flowchart we may use.

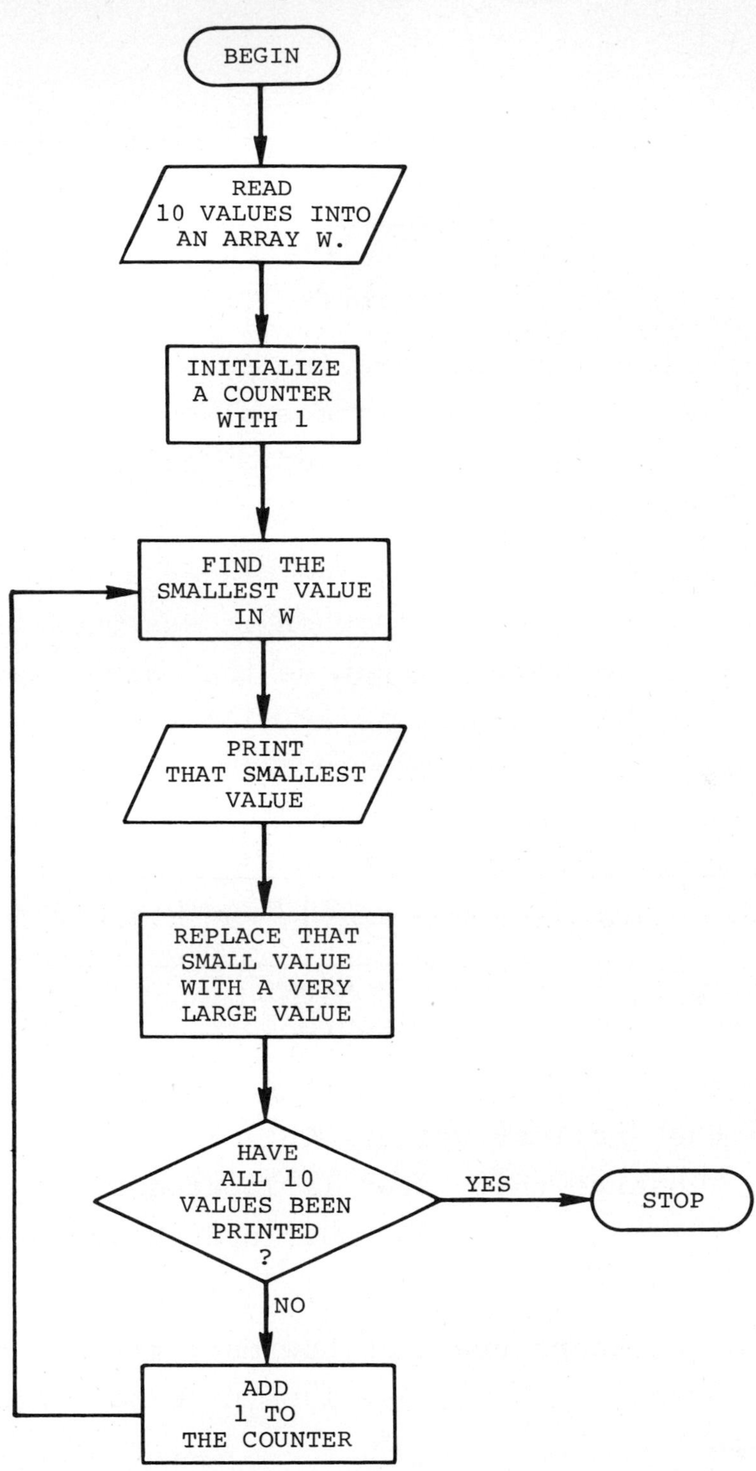

Figure 13-2

The program first reads ten values from data cards into the array called "W". Figure 13-3 shows the contents of the array after the values have been loaded.

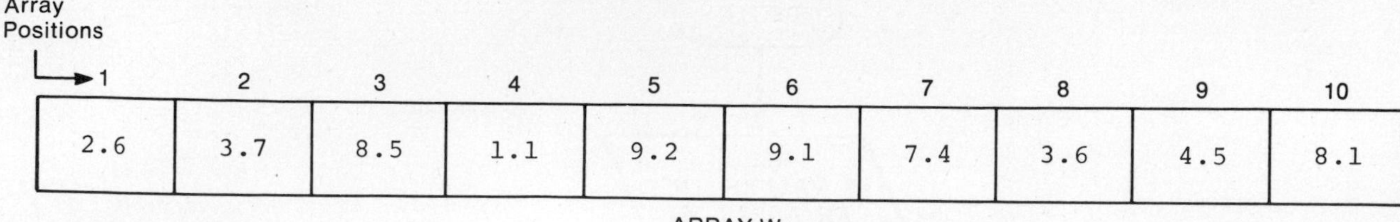

Figure 13-3

The program must now examine each value in the array looking for the smallest one. The smallest value is, of course, "1.1", and that value is printed. The value is located at "W_4" (the fourth location of "W").

Now, a large number must be placed at "W_4" so that the program will not find "1.1" when it searches the array again for the smallest value. Suppose the large number "1000000." is stored at "W_4". The W array will then appear as shown in Figure 13-4.

Array Positions

1	2	3	4	5	6	7	8	9	10
2.6	3.7	8.5	1000000.	9.2	9.1	7.4	3.6	4.5	8.1

ARRAY W

Figure 13-4

When the program again examines the W array, it finds that "2.6" is the smallest value. This is the value that will be printed. Observe that "2.6" is located at "W_1"; therefore, "W_1" is replaced with "1000000." and the program repeats the procedure.

A counter keeps track of how many times a smallest value has been printed. When 10 values have been printed, the program stops.

Here is a FORTRAN program that conforms with the flowchart given:

```
      DIMENSION W(10)
      READ (5,16) W
   16 FORMAT (F10.0)
      DO 45 N=1,10
      SMALL = W(1)
      LOC = 1
```

```
      DO 40 K=2,10
      IF (W(K).LE.SMALL) GO TO 40
      SMALL = W(K)
      LOC = K
40    CONTINUE
      WRITE (6,9) SMALL
 9    FORMAT (1X,F10.2)
      W(LOC) = 1000000.
45    CONTINUE
      STOP
      END
```

The program first reads ten values into the W array. It obtains those values from ten sequential data cards.

Next, the program executes a loop within a loop.

An illustration giving the skeletons of the two loops is this:

```
      DO 45 N=1,10                            )
      -                                       |
      -                                       |
      DO 40 K=2,10    )                       |
      -               }   inner loop          >  outer loop
      -               )                       |
40    CONTINUE                                |
      -                                       |
      -                                       |
45    CONTINUE                                )
```

The outer loop begins by assigning "1" to N, then procedes to the inner loop. There, K is set to "2"; N holds constant at "1". Then, the inner loop is executed 9 times, K cycling from "2" through "9". The program then continues by increasing N to "2". K cycles from "2" through "10" again. The program continues by increasing N to "3", recycling K, etc.

The statements in the inner loop are executed 90 times (10 times, outer loop, multiplied by 9 times, inner loop).

In this program, the index, N, counts the number of values that are printed. When N is "1", the first value is printed (the smallest); when N is "2", the second value is printed (the next smallest), etc.

The inner loop in the program finds the smallest value. To do this, the program initially assigns the first W value to SMALL. (The statement SMALL=W(1) accomplishes the task.)

Then, the location of that value is placed in LOC. Since the first value of W is assigned to SMALL, the value "1" is assigned to LOC.

The inner loop then checks the remaining nine values in the W array to determine whether one or more values therein is smaller than SMALL. If a value in the W array is found to be smaller than SMALL, that value replaces the value in SMALL. The new value's array location replaces the number in LOC.

When the inner loop has been completely executed, the value in SMALL is the smallest value in the array and LOC contains its array location. The value of SMALL is printed; then, the smallest value in the array is changed to "1000000.". The statement that causes the smallest value to take on a large value is

W(LOC) = 1000000.

The next time the inner loop is executed, the old smallest value will not be assigned to SMALL since that value is now much too large. The second smallest value is assigned to SMALL and its array location assigned to LOC. Then, that value is printed and the smallest value in the array is changed to "1000000.", etc.

The process described above repeats until the program is ready to execute the outer loop for the last time. At that time, N's value is "10". The W array appears as shown in Figure 13-5.

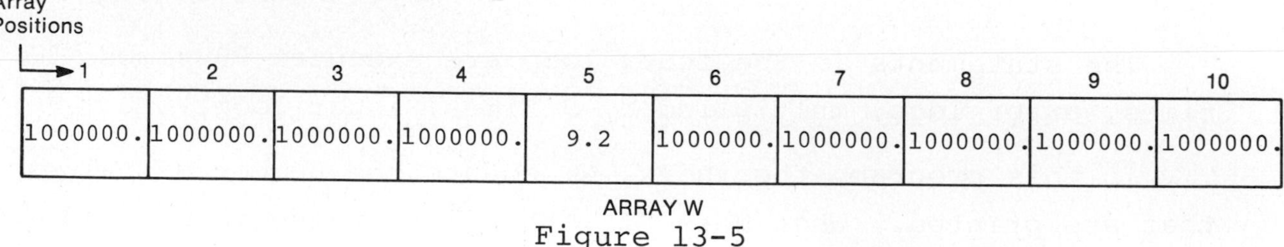

Figure 13-5

The program finds that the value "9.2" is the smallest value and prints it. Then, the fifth location of the W array is changed to "1000000." and the program stops. The output given by the program is this:

1.1
2.6
3.6
3.7
4.5
7.4
8.1
8.5
9.1
9.2

The objective of the program has been achieved.

PARTIAL LOADING OF AN ARRAY

If it is not desired to load only a portion of an array, a READ statement can be written this way:

```
READ (5,20) (T(K),K=1,25)
```

If the DIMENSION statement for the array, T, is

```
DIMENSION T(200)
```

only the first twenty-five values of the array will be loaded. The READ statement includes a "built-in DO loop" with the index, K, varying from "1" through "25". Values already in the array from cells "26" through "200" will not be affected by the execution of the READ statement shown above.

When only a portion of an array is to be read, the values must be punched on cards in the exact order that they will be read. If the FORMAT statement for the above READ statement is

```
20  FORMAT (7F10.0)
```

then the values must be punched as shown in Figure 13-6.

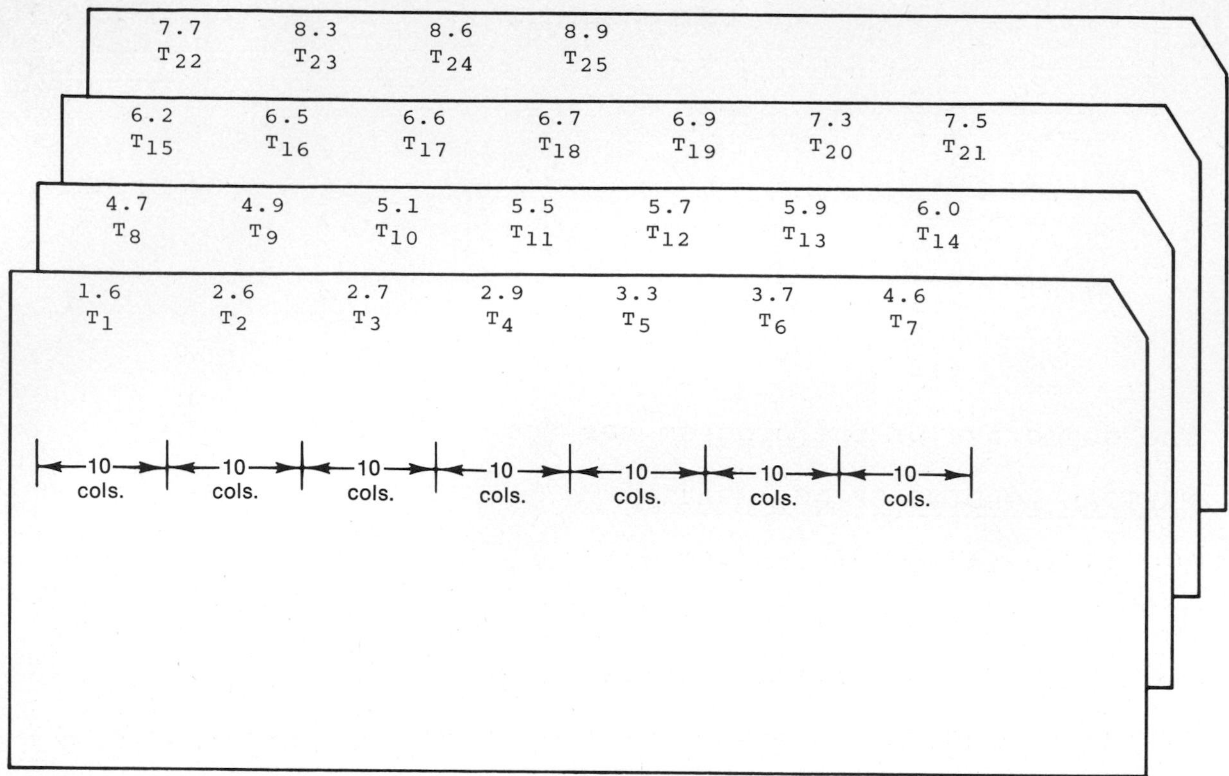

Figure 13-6

As you have seen, arrays can be partially loaded by building an implied DO loop into a READ statement. The index of the loop need not be mentioned anywhere else in the program.

Additional examples of READ statements that partially read arrays are these:

```
READ (5,77)(BETA(N),N=17,30)
READ (5,90)(SL(J),J=30,50)
```

An entire array can be read using the implied DO loop method but it is easier to accomplish the task without the DO loop. For example, if the DIMENSION of an array is:

```
DIMENSION RAD(100)
```

the entire array can be read with this READ statement:

```
READ (5,70)(RAD(K),K=1,100)
```

or this one:

```
READ (5,70) RAD
```

The latter is obviously easier to use.

ARRAYS WITH MULTIPLE DIMENSIONS

It is possible to establish arrays that have two, three, four, and even more dimensions. (Some systems permit seven dimensions, others even more.)

These DIMENSION statements are permissible:

```
DIMENSION W(5,9)
DIMENSION ALPHA (8,7,3)
DIMENSION PLD (4,7,9,2,2)
```

You can calculate the number of memory cells that are reserved for an array by multiplying the dimensions. The array W has 45 reserved memory cells; the array ALPHA has 168; the array PLD, 1008.

It is not difficult to visualize a two-dimensional array. It has length and width as shown in Figure 13-7.

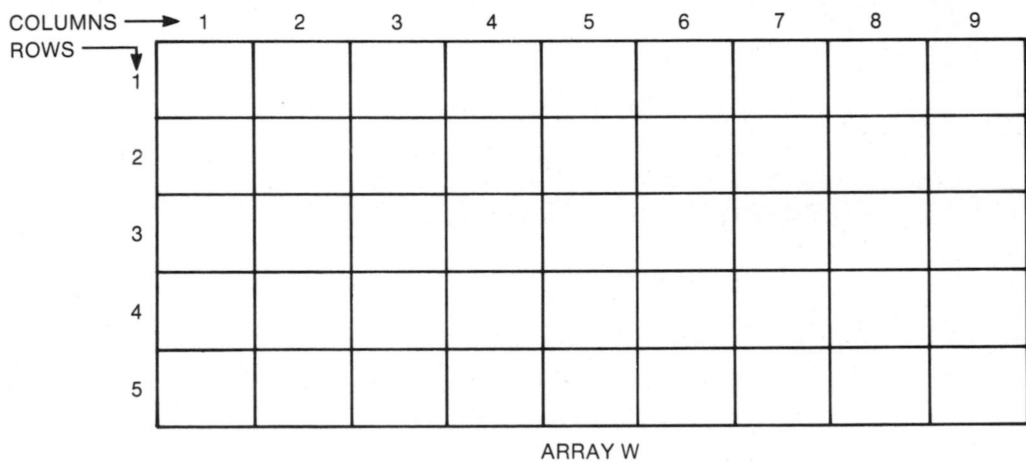

Figure 13-7

In the definition of the array,

```
DIMENSION W(5,9)
```

the leftmost number, "5", represents the number of rows in the array; and the rightmost number, "9", represents the number of columns.

In a three-dimensional array, the array has length, width, and depth. Therefore, the array ALPHA can be thought of as having the appearance shown in Figure 13-8.

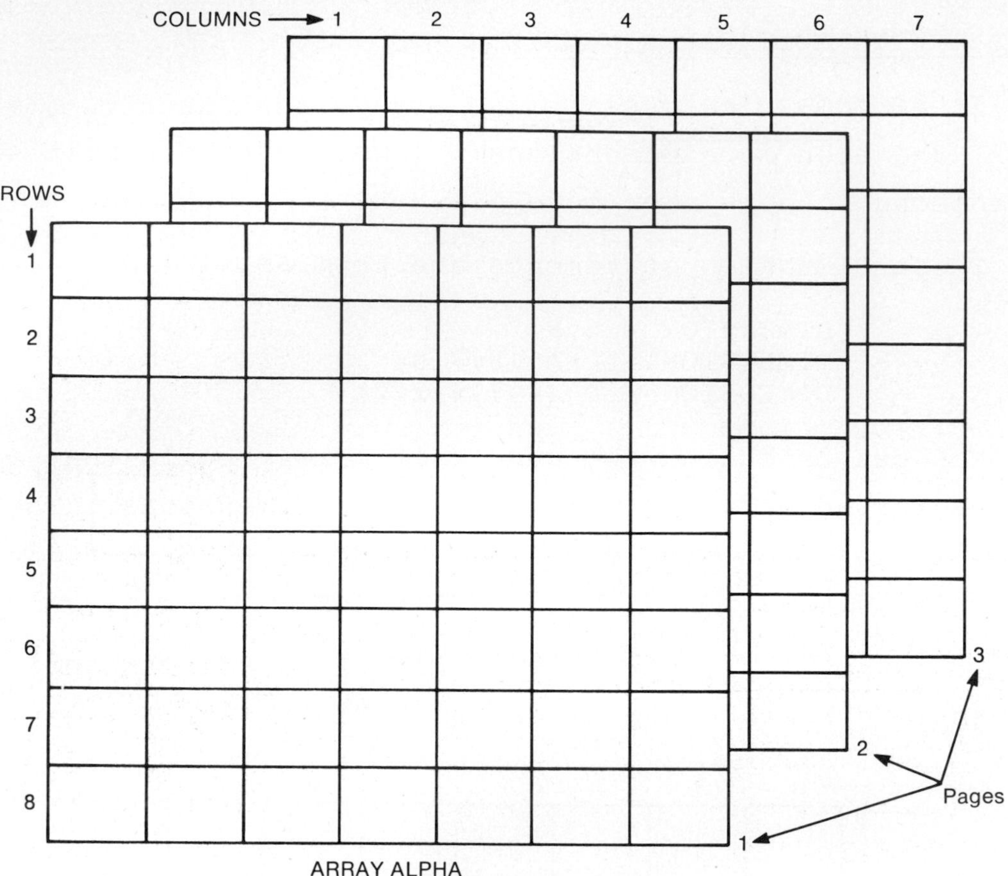

Figure 13-8

In the definition of the array,

DIMENSION ALPHA (8,7,3)

the leftmost subscript indicates the number of rows, the middle subscript indicates the number of columns, and the rightmost subscript indicates the number of pages.

Arrays having more than three subscripts cannot be illustrated very well in drawings. But they do have mathematical meanings.

In the memory of a computer, array cells are stored sequentially whether the array has two dimensions, three, four, or more. Figure 13-9 shows how the cells of a two-dimensional array are actually stored in the computer's memory.

The DIMENSION statement for the B array is this:

DIMENSION B(3,4)

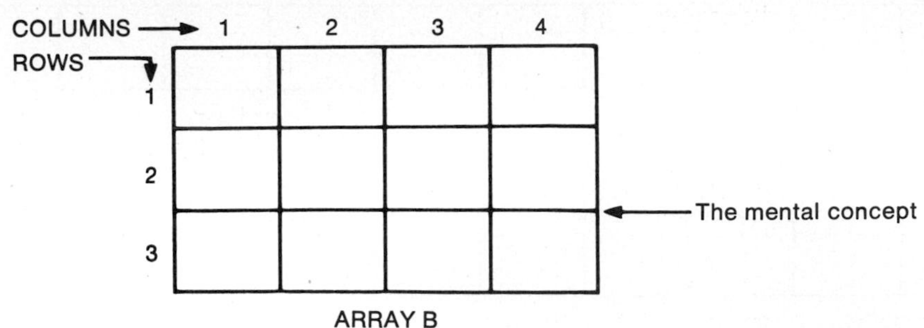

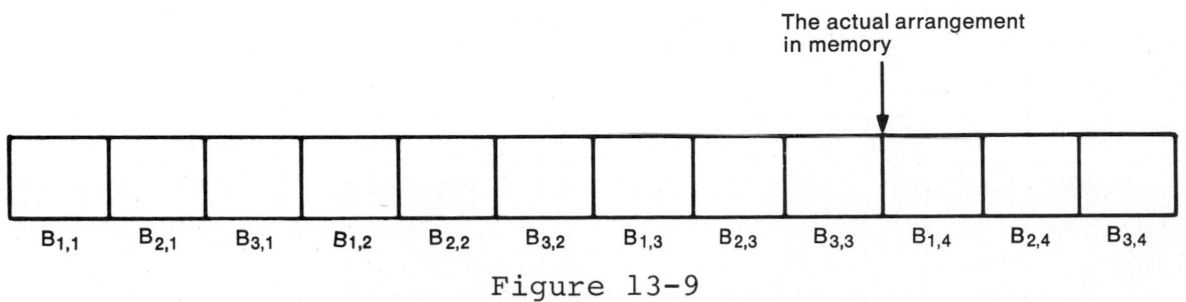

Figure 13-9

Observe that in memory, the leftmost subscript increases faster than the rightmost.

In a three-dimensional array, a similar organization exists. Consider the three-dimensional array represented by this DIMENSION statement:

```
DIMENSION R(5,2,2)
```

The mental image of the array is shown in Figure 13-10 while the actual arrangement in memory is shown in Figure 13-11.

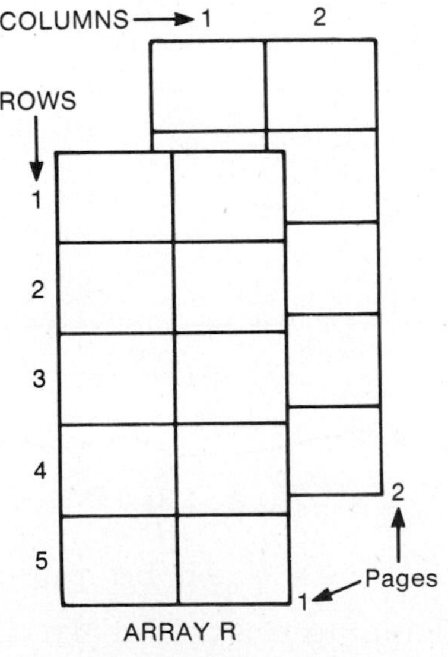

Figure 13-10

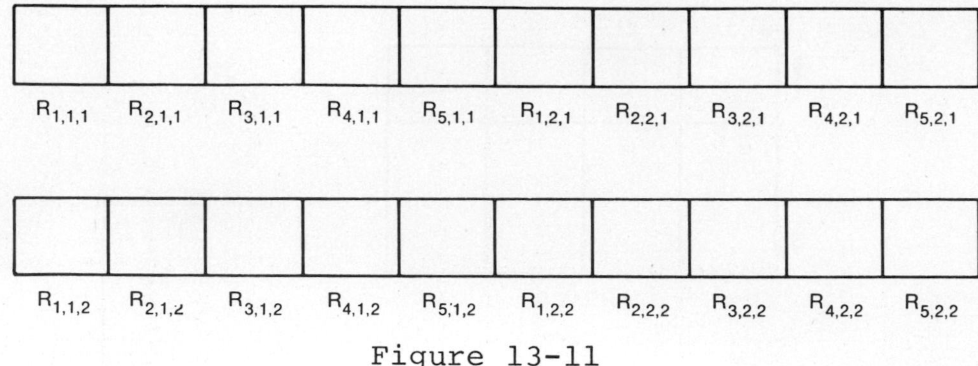

Figure 13-11

The cells of arrays having more than three dimensions are stored in memory in such a way that the leftmost subscript increases fastest while the rightmost subscript increases slowest.

Arrays having multiple subscripts can be read from cards with statements like these:

```
      DIMENSION W(5,9)
      READ (5,8) W
    8 FORMAT (8F10.0)
```

The program keeps reading cards until the *entire* array has been read. Since the W array has 45 values, the program will read six cards. The cards must be punched as shown in Figure 13-12.

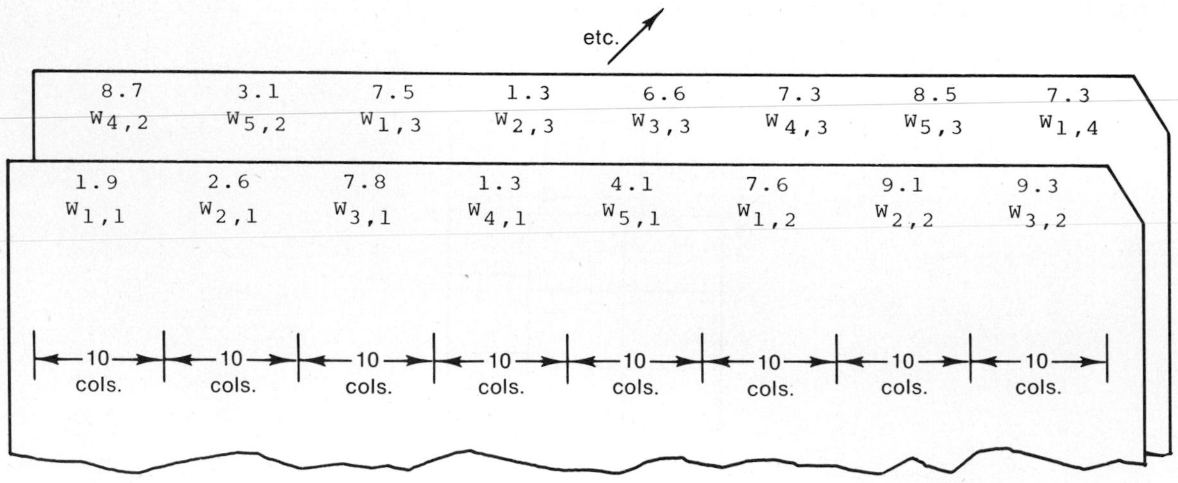

Figure 13-12

Observe that the values must be punched on cards in the same way that the values are stored in the computer's memory.

When the program reads the cards, it will store the values in the array by columns. See Figure 13-13.

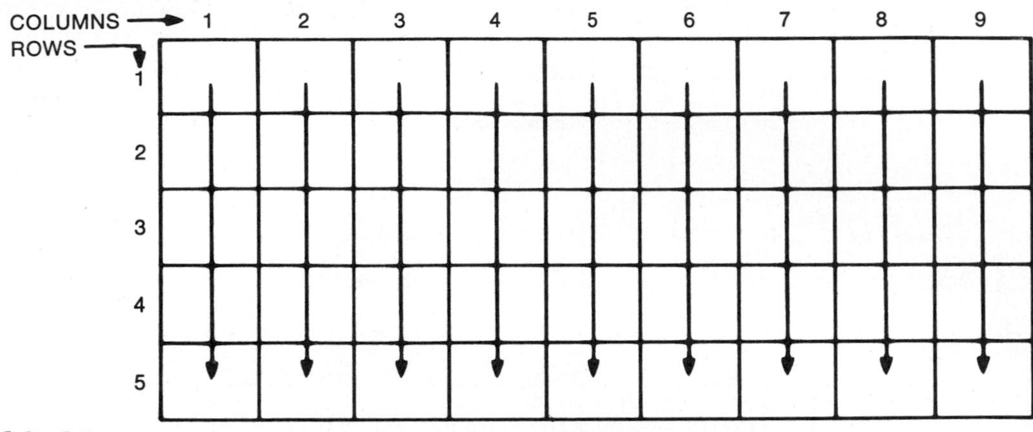

Figure 13-13

With three-dimensional arrays and with arrays having more than three dimensions, values must be punched on cards in the same order that they will be stored in the computer's memory.

Once values have been stored in arrays, work can be done with them. Suppose, for example, that it is desired to sum all the values in the W array. A program using a DO loop within another DO loop can accomplish the task this way:

```
      DIMENSION W(5,9)
      READ (5,8) W
    8 FORMAT (8F10.0)
      SUM=0.
      DO 50 J=1,5
      DO 40 K=1,8
      SUM=SUM+W(J,K)
   40 CONTINUE
   50 CONTINUE
      WRITE (6,99) SUM
   99 FORMAT (' ',F10.2)
      STOP
      END
```

As with single-dimensional arrays, two-dimensional arrays can be partially loaded. A READ statement having an implied DO loop can be written this way:

```
      READ (5,8)((W(K,J),K=1,4),J=1,3)
```

The variable J represents the index for the outer loop and the variable K represents the index for the inner loop. The values assigned to W will be in this sequence:

$W_{1,1}$ $W_{2,1}$ $W_{3,1}$ $W_{4,1}$ $W_{1,2}$ $W_{2,2}$ $W_{3,2}$ $W_{4,2}$

$W_{1,3}$ $W_{2,3}$ $W_{3,3}$ $W_{4,3}$

There will be only twelve values read and they must be punched in exactly the same sequence as shown in the above list.

Earlier in this chapter, we said that we would discuss how to sort one hundred numbers of an array. In our previous discussion of how to sort ten numbers, we actually covered also how to accomplish the task for one hundred numbers. All we have to do is retrieve the program that sorts ten numbers and change it so that it sorts one hundred.

For reference, here is the program that sorts 10 numbers:

```
       DIMENSION W(10)
       READ (5,16) W
   16  FORMAT (F10.0)
       DO 45 N=1,10
       SMALL=W(1)
       LOC=1
       DO 40 K=2,10
       IF (W(K).LE.SMALL) GO TO 40
       SMALL=W(K)
       LOC=K
   40  CONTINUE
       WRITE (6,9) SMALL
    9  FORMAT (1X,F10.2)
       W(LOC)=1000000.
   45  CONTINUE
       STOP
       END
```

Only a few statements need to be changed in order to adapt the program to the larger array. A quick glance through the program will reveal that

```
       DIMENSION W(10)
```

must change to

```
       DIMENSION W(100)
```

Also,

```
       DO 45 N=1,10
```

must change to

```
        DO 45 N=1,100
```

And,

```
        DO 40 K=2,10
```

must change to

```
        DO 40 K=2,100
```

EXERCISES AND PROBLEMS

1. Study the following program segment:

```
          DIMENSION DVAL (200)
          READ (5,50)(DVAL(K),K=51,90)
       50 FORMAT (5F10.0)
```

   How many cards will the program read?

2. Refer to Question 1. Into what locations of the DVAL array, will the program store the data values read from the cards?

3. Write a DIMENSION statement that sets up array space for a two-dimensional array. The space is to accommodate an array having eight rows and five columns. Name the array BETA.

4. Study the following DIMENSION statement.

```
          DIMENSION RAD(10,5,8,4)
```

   How many memory locations will the system reserve for the RAD array?

5. Study the following program segment:

```
          DIMENSION T(3,4,50)
          READ (5,6) T
        6 FORMAT (10F8.0)
```

   How many data cards will the program read?

6. Refer to Question 5. Tell how the data cards should be punched. That is, give the sequence that the T values should be given.

7. Begin a program this way:

```
      DIMENSION V(50,50)
      READ (5,7) V
    7 FORMAT (10F8.0)
```

Continue the program with statements that cause all values in the array to be summed. Have the program print the sum, then stop.

8. Begin a program this way:

```
      DIMENSION V(50,50)
      READ (5,7) V
    7 FORMAT (10F8.0)
```

Continue the program with statements that compute the sum of the values in the two diagonals of the array. Have the program print the two sums, then stop.

9. Begin a program with these statements:

```
      DIMENSION KARR(200)
      READ (5,20) KARR
   20 FORMAT (10I8)
```

Continue the program with statements that search for the value "87". If the program finds the value, it prints the value's location in the array (at which position within KARR was "87" found). If the program does not find the value, the program prints a message giving the fact that KARR is not in the array.

You may assume that the values stored in the KARR array are in no particular sequence.

10. Begin a program with these statements:

```
      DIMENSION KARR(200)
      READ (5,20) KARR
   20 FORMAT (10I8)
   30 READ (5,40,END=90) N
```

Continue the program with statements that find values of N and give their locations in the KARR array. You may assume there are about 40 values of N but this fact is not a significant factor in the problem's solution. You may assume that all the values in the KARR array are in *numerically increasing sequence* but that the values of N being read are in no particular sequence.

You may assume that the values of N are relatively small ranging from "150" through "585".

11. Refer to Question 17 in Chapter 11. Write the same program except have the program print the lines in reverse order - that is varying X from "23.5" through "21.6" in steps of "1".

12. Write a program to compute the sum of the digits from N = 45 through N = 125. Use a DO loop.

13. Refer to Questions 17 and 18 in Chapter 10. Rewrite the Fibonacci Series program using a DO loop.

14. Refer to Questions 19 and 20 in Chapter 10. Rewrite the earnings program using a DO loop.

CHAPTER 14

Timesharing FORTRAN
Part I

So far, everything we've said about FORTRAN has applied to the batch mode of operation. In the batch mode, a person wishing to execute a FORTRAN program must first code the program on a coding form, have cards punched, thus obtaining a source deck, provide input data, then submit the program to a local computer for a compile and execute. The results that the program gives are printed on computer paper and delivered to the programmer.

Another mode of processing a computer program is via the timesharing mode. In timesharing, a person sits at a typewriter-like terminal. The person picks up an ordinary phone and dials the computer. The computer responds by emitting a high-pitched tone through the receiver. When the user hears the tone, he or she places the receiver in a special receptical (acoustic coupler) located on the terminal, then types the program. Alternately, the program may be entered via paper tape.

After the program has been entered, the user tells the computer to run the program. The computer begins to obey at once. If the user has made any mistakes in entering the program, the computer gives this fact and allows the user to make changes. The changes are entered and another attempt is made to process. Eventually, when the program has been correctly entered, the computer executes it and the user obtains the results that were needed.

The major advantage that timesharing offers over batch is

that very fast results are obtained. A programmer may keep working on a program, in one sitting, until it is right. In the batch mode, a programmer has to wait several hours after he or she submits a program before the person can find out how he or she did. If the programmer made mistakes, he or she won't find out about them until results are received. The programmer may then make corrections and try again. At times, a programmer may spend several weeks trying to get a program to run correctly. The same objective can be accomplished in timesharing over a span of only a few minutes or hours.

The foregoing remarks are not meant to imply that timesharing is always better than batch. Each mode has its advantages and disadvantages. Timesharing is far more expensive than batch, for example. A job that costs $10 in batch could cost ten times as much in timesharing.

Where output is concerned, timesharing gives much slower printouts than batch. In timesharing, the computer can give a maximum of about 120 lines of output per minute. In batch, 1200 lines per minute is not unusual.

FORTRAN used in timesharing is very similar to FORTRAN used in batch. There are, however, a few differences that the user must be aware of. To illustrate, let's consider an actual "conversation" between a computer and a human.

The human sits at a terminal and dials the computer. The computer responds with the high-pitched tone and the user places the receiver in the receptical connected to the terminal. The computer types:

```
ID--
```

The computer has asked the user to identify himself or herself. An authorized user gives a valid ID. Like this:

ID--<u>FG374-8</u>

(In these examples, the underlined text is what the user types.)

A user may obtain a valid user number by visiting the

computer center that offers timesharing services and signing a contract. The person will be billed for computer service monthly. (The computer itself prepares the bill.)

Assuming "FG374-8" is a valid ID, the computer next asks what language the user wishes to use:

```
SYSTEM--FORTRAN
```

Observe that the user has typed FORTRAN. The programmer could have replied BASIC, ALGOL, or with any of the names of a number of other programming languages. What the user responds depends upon what languages the computer center offers.

Next, the computer types:

```
OLD OR NEW--
```

The system has asked whether the user wishes to build a new program or execute an old one previously saved. Let's assume the user wishes to build a new program. This is the response:

```
OLD OR NEW--NEW
```

The computer wants to know what name the user wants to give the program:

```
NEW FILE NAME--VERT
```

The user has typed VERT. The name that a user chooses may have up to six characters. (Some installations permit eight characters for a program name.)

The computer now types

```
READY
```

The programmer may now type a new program or enter one from punched paper tape. If, when the computer had typed OLD OR NEW, the user had wanted to run an old program, the conversation could have gone like this:

```
OLD OR NEW--OLD
OLD FILE NAME--BERKL
READY
```

The programmer gives the name of the old program which was

saved in the past. In naming a program, a user may select any name he or she pleases. Even if the selected name accidentally coincides with a name selected by another user, the computer has no difficulty keeping everything straight. (The computer separates programs by user ID's.)

When the user types the name of the old saved program, the computer obtains the program from where it was saved and makes it available to the user. The user may change the program, list it, run it, etc.

When a programmer builds a new FORTRAN program, he or she enters a series of lines. Study this example:

```
ID--FG374-8
SYSTEM--FORTRAN
OLD OR NEW--NEW
NEW FILE NAME--VERT
READY
010      A=3.1416*3.5                 \
020      B=2.71828*4.5                 |
030      IF (A.GT.B) GO TO 30          |
040      WRITE (6,7) B,A               |
050    7 FORMAT (1X,2F10.2)             > Program entered
060      GO TO 40                      |  by the user
070   30 WRITE (6,8) A,B               |
080    8 FORMAT (1X,2F10.2)            |
090   40 STOP                          |
100      END                          /
RUN
      12.23      11.00
BYE
DISCONNECT
```

Examine the program and note the differences between batch FORTRAN and timesharing FORTRAN:

1. Every line typed in timesharing must have a number. These numbers, called line numbers, must be in increasing sequence. Line numbers may begin with 1 and may increase to and including 99999. Numbers may have arbitrary gaps between them, not necessarily 10 as shown in the example above. The gaps don't have to

be regular. In other words, the line numbers shown could have been 10, 12, 18, 25, 35, 40, 100, 121, 122, 99999.

2. Some FORTRAN statements must have both line numbers *and* statement numbers. In the example program, four statements have statement numbers. They are 7, 8, 30, and 40. Observe that when a GO TO is given, the program must reference a *statement number*, not a line number.

3. In timesharing, one blank is sufficient to separate the *line number* of a statement from the *statement number* and from the statement. In other words, statements do not have to begin in column 7 as in batch.

This program solves a very simple problem. It computes 3.1416 (π) times 3.5 and assigns the result to A. Next, it computes 2.71828 (e) times 4.5 and assigns the result to B. Then, it checks whether A is greater than B. If so, the program goes to statement 30 where it prints the values of A and B, then stops. If A's value is not greater than B's, the program prints the values of B and A, then stops.

After the programmer has typed the program, he or she directs the computer to execute it by typing RUN. The command RUN is a "system command". A system command tells the computer what to do with a program. Note that the system command has no preceding line number.

Other system commands that we shall discuss in the next chapter are LIST, SAVE, NEW, OLD, and others.

In this example, the computer finds that A's value is not greater than B's value. Therefore, it prints B's value followed by A's value. The values are printed according to the FORMAT at line 50 (statement 7).

EXERCISES AND PROBLEMS

1. Explain the difference between batch and timesharing FORTRAN.
2. What is the major advantage that timesharing FORTRAN offers over batch FORTRAN?
3. What is the chief disadvantage of timesharing FORTRAN?
4. How does a potential timesharing user obtain a valid user ID?
5. What should a user respond when the system asks the OLD OR NEW question?
6. What is a line number? How does a line number differ from a FORTRAN statement number?
7. Define "system command".
8. What does the RUN system command accomplish?
9. Why might a programmer want to save a program that he or she developed for timesharing use?
10. Write a complete conversation between a user and a programmer. (The programmer's ID is FG374-8.) The programmer wishes to develop a timesharing program that computes the squares and cubes of all integer values of K from K = 10 through K = 25. The programmer wants to give the program the file name "CALC" but does not desire to save the program.

    Each line of the program is to give the value of K, its square, and its cube.

    In giving the conversation, underline all entries, except the actual program, that the programmer types. Do not show the actual answers. Simply indicate where they would be located.

CHAPTER 15

Timesharing FORTRAN Part II

When executing FORTRAN programs in the timesharing mode, there are four programmer considerations:

1. How to enter FORTRAN statements.
2. How to make changes.
3. How to employ system commands.
4. How to provide input values.

ENTERING STATEMENTS

In entering FORTRAN statements, a programmer must type them or enter them from paper tape. We will not discuss paper tape entry in this text; the technique can easily be learned once a user has gained some actual "hands on" experience.

FORTRAN statements are typed using the keyboard which is an integral part of the terminal being employed. One turns the terminal "ON"; then, using an ordinary phone, dials the computer. When the characteristic high-pitched tone is heard, the phone's receiver is placed in a special receptacle located on the terminal. After going through the "handshake" sequence where the user identifies himself or herself, the computer types READY.

When creating a new program, the programmer types a line at a time. At the conclusion of a line, the user depresses the key labeled RETURN. The computer accepts the statement and returns the carriage.

MAKING CHANGES

Then, the person types another statement and depresses the

RETURN key again. The computer accepts the statement. The user then types the next statement and again returns the carriage. If a person makes a mistake when typing a statement, he or she can correct it before RETURN is depressed. Consider this example:

```
200  50 IF (A*B.EQ.RU←AD) GO TO 750
```

The programmer erred in typing "RAD". He or she began with "RU". The "U" is incorrect. The programmer depressed the backwards arrow key (←) which permitted the correction of "U" to "A". The backwards arrow permits a character to be retyped; two arrows permit two characters to be retyped, etc. Here is an example showing three backwards arrows being used:

```
450  DIS=B--2←←←**2-4.*A*C
```

The user intended to type

```
450  DIS=B**2-4.*A*C
```

but typed three characters incorrectly following B. The three backwards arrows allowed the change of "B--2" to "B**2".

Another way that corrections can be made is to *retype* the statements. Statements are identified by their line numbers. A retyped statement, having the same line number as a previously typed statement, *replaces* the old statement. Consider this example:

```
10     X=4.8
20     Q=7.9
30     Y=9.2
40     Z=X+Y
50     PRINT 7,X,Y,Z
60   7 FORMAT (1X,3F10.1)
30     Y=8.2
70     STOP
40     Z=X-Y
80     END
```

In this program, the new statement at line 30 replaces the old one having the same line number, and the new statement at line 40 also replaces an old one. This is the program that the computer now has:

```
10     X=4.8
20     Q=7.9
30     Y=8.2
40     Z=X-Y
50     PRINT 7,X,Y,Z
60   7 FORMAT (1X,3F10.1)
70     STOP
80     END
```

To delete a statement, a programmer types the statement's line number, then depresses RETURN. To enter an additional statement, the user selects a line number between two existing line numbers and enters the additional statement.

Let's assume the programmer wants to delete the statement at line 20 in the above program and wants to add a statement between lines 60 and 70. The task is accomplished this way:

```
20
62     PRINT 7,Z,Y,X
```

The computer now has this program:

```
10     X=4.8
30     Y=8.2
40     Z=X-Y
50     PRINT 7,X,Y,Z
60   7 FORMAT (1X,3F10.1)
62     PRINT 7,Z,Y,X
70     STOP
80     END
```

If the user now types RUN, the computer will execute the program and give the two output lines requested.

To summarize, a person enters FORTRAN statements one at a time. The individual may make corrections as he or she types statements by entering the backwards arrow (←) for every character that is to be replaced.

To change a line that has already been entered, a programmer retypes the line. To add a line, the user selects a line number between two existing line numbers and types the statement. To delete a line, the user simply types the line number, then depresses RETURN.

If you have begun to type a statement but want to inform the system that you want it to disregard the statement, depress the CTRL and X keys on the terminal's keyboard. Do this before you depress the RETURN key. The system will type "DELETED", and return the carriage. The statement you began to type but never completed is ignored. It's the same as if you had never begun to type it.

CONTINUATIONS

To continue statements, use the ampersand (&) immediately following line numbers; this way:

```
40   T = E + FM
50&   + XN - WT +
60&   F - Y
```

The statement will be entered as if you had typed:

```
40   T = E + FM + XN - WT + F - Y
```

Most systems allow you to give at least nine continuations to FORTRAN statements that need them. Some systems permit many more continuations.

COMMENTS

To give comment lines, begin a statement with the letter "C" as in batch programming. The letter immediately follows the line numbers; this way:

```
 .      .
 .      .
 .      .
200    X = 27.9
200C   CALCULATIONS OF R AND T FOLLOW
220    R = X - B
230    T = C + D
240C
250C
260C   RESULTS ARE PRINTED
270    WRITE (6,9) R,T,X
 .      .
 .      .
 .      .
```

RUNAWAY LOOPS

If you suspect that your program has inadvertently entered into an endless loop, depress the BREAK key. The program will stop at once. Some systems do not have a BREAK key but require you to use the INTERUPT key instead.

In this chapter we have concentrated upon how to enter statements and how to make changes to them. In the two chapters that follow we will discuss two other timesharing considerations: using system commands and providing input data.

EXERCISES AND PROBLEMS

1. In timesharing, what key must the programmer depress in order to enter a FORTRAN statement that has been typed?
2. What must a user do to change one or more characters that have been entered incorrectly on a line, and the RETURN key has not yet been depressed?
3. What must a user do to change a FORTRAN line that was entered incorrectly? (The RETURN key was depressed.)
4. What must a user do to delete a line that was entered into a program but is now found to be unneeded? (The RETURN key was depressed.)
5. What must a user do to enter a line in a program that was inadvertently omitted when the program was originally entered?
6. What comments can you make about the spaces you give when you type FORTRAN statements?
7. In timesharing FORTRAN how does one continue a statement that is too long to be contained on one line.
8. How does a programmer stop a program that is suspected of having entered an endless loop?
9. Write a timesharing FORTRAN program that computes and prints the natural logarithms of all values of X from X = 2.6 to X = 4.7 in steps of ".1". Have the program print the value of X and its logarithm on each output line. The logarithms should be given rounded to five decimal places.

CHAPTER 16

Timesharing FORTRAN Part III

SYSTEM COMMANDS

System commands are instructions that a timesharing user employs to give the computer instructions concerning what to do with a FORTRAN program.

We have seen that the RUN system command tells the computer to execute a program that has been entered and that resides in a temporary working space. Other system commands besides RUN are LIST, SAVE, RESAVE, UNSAVE, OLD, NEW, BYE. These are not the only system commands that exist but they are some of the most important.

The RUN command tells the computer that a program has been entered and is ready to be executed. Here is an example:

```
ID--FLM5489
SYSTEM--FORTRAN
OLD OR NEW--NEW
NEW FILE NAME--GTLEM
READY
10      A=4.2                  )
20      B=2.1                  )
30      C=A+B                  )
40      WRITE (6,9) C          )  Program entered
50    9 FORMAT (1X,F10.1)      )  by the user.
60      STOP                   )
70      END                    )
RUN
          6.3
SAVE
READY
BYE
DISCONNECT
```

This program uses the RUN, SAVE, and BYE system commands. We've already discussed RUN. The SAVE command saves the program for later use. The program's name in this example is GTLEM. The BYE system command tells the computer that the user wishes to be disconnected. When a programmer types BYE, the computer types DISCONNECT and the timesharing session is over. All that remains for the programmer to do is hang up the phone and turn the "ON/OFF" switch on the terminal to the "OFF" position.

If at any time a programmer needs a listing of the program, he or she may type LIST. Example:

```
ID--FLM5489
SYSTEM--FORTRAN
OLD OR NEW--OLD
OLD FILE NAME--G45

READY
LIST

50        DO 85 K=1,20
60        WRITE (6,25)
70    25  FORMAT (1X,'HELLO')
80    85  CONTINUE
90        STOP
100       END

50        DO 85 K=1,5
70    25  FORMAT (1X,'HELLO THERE')

LIST

50        DO 85 K=1,5
60        WRITE (6,25)
70    25  FORMAT (1X,'HELLO THERE')
80    85  CONTINUE
90        STOP
100       END

RUN

HELLO THERE
HELLO THERE
HELLO THERE
HELLO THERE
HELLO THERE

RESAVE G45

READY

OLD

OLD FILE NAME--GTLEM

READY
```

```
UNSAVE
READY
NEW
NEW FILE NAME--HD436
READY
10       P=9.1
20       Q=P*2
30       WRITE (6,40) Q
40    40 FORMAT (1X,F10.1)
50       STOP
60       END
SAVE
READY
BYE
DISCONNECT
```

Program entered by the programmer.

This illustrated session shows how the system commands RUN, OLD, LIST, SAVE, RESAVE, UNSAVE, and NEW are used.

OLD

This command permits a user to call for an old program that was saved in the past. The programmer must, of course, know the name of the saved program. When the computer types READY, the computer indicates that the old program has been retrieved and is made available to the user in a working space. The user may now type RUN or LIST or UNSAVE. Observe that system commands are never preceded by line numbers. Any statement that is preceded by a line number is assumed to be a FORTRAN statement; any statement that is not preceded by a line number is assumed to be a system command.

SAVE

After a person has entered a program, he or she may have the computer save the program by typing SAVE.

RESAVE

After a person has made changes to a program, the individual may have the computer resave the program by typing RESAVE. The *changed version* of the program replaces the old version. (To use RESAVE, there must be an old version of the program.) The old version disappears completely.

UNSAVE

A person may unsave a program by first calling for it using the OLD command. Then, when the computer types READY, the user types UNSAVE. The saved version of the program disappears completely.

NEW

When the user types NEW, the system allows the user to begin working on a brand new program. Any program that the user was working on, but had not saved, disappears completely.

EXERCISES AND PROBLEMS

1. What are system commands?
2. Tell what the system commands RUN, LIST, SAVE, RESAVE, UNSAVE, OLD, NEW, and BYE accomplish.
3. Write a timesharing FORTRAN program. The program is to compute $\sqrt{25}$, $\sqrt[3]{25}$, $\sqrt[4]{25}$ ..... $\sqrt[25]{25}$. Recall that $\sqrt{25} = 25^{.5}$; $\sqrt[3]{25} = 25^{.3333}$; $\sqrt[4]{25} = 25^{.25}$; $\sqrt[5]{25} = 25^{.20}$; etc. Each output line is to give an integer designating the root and a real number giving the computed root. The root is to be given rounded to five decimal places.

CHAPTER 17

Timesharing FORTRAN Part IV

We have seen that programming in the timesharing world is essentially the same as programming in the batch world. For the programmer, there are four considerations:

1. How to enter programs.
2. How to make changes.
3. How to use system commands.
4. How to enter input data.

ENTERING INPUT DATA

In the previous chapters, we discussed how to enter programs, how to make changes, and how to use system commands. In this chapter, we discuss how to enter input data.

Input data is given to a timesharing program via the READ statement just as it is in the batch mode. There are no punched cards, of course, so a way has to be found that simulates the existence of one or more data decks. A programmer simulates a data deck by creating a file on magnetic disk. Here is how a file is created:

```
ID--GL9437
SYSTEM--FORTRAN
OLD OR NEW--NEW
NEW FILE NAME--08
READY
10      2.8      9.4      5.7   )  Data file
20      6.7      2.1      5.4   }  typed by
30      3.3      7.9      4.8   )  programmer
40      8.8      1.3      9.1
SAVE
READY
```

```
BYE
DISCONNECT
```

The programmer created a data file and gave it the name "08". The file was then promptly saved on magnetic disk.

The numbers on each line represent input data and are typed in exactly the same way that they would be punched on cards. The first number on each line is a line number and the remaining three values on each line are values to be read by a READ statement in a timesharing FORTRAN program.

Here is how those values could be accessed by a program:

```
ID--GL9437
SYSTEM--FORTRAN
OLD OR NEW--NEW
NEW FILE NAME--PLX
READY
10       PRINT 9
20     9 FORMAT (1X,"THIS IS A DEMO"//)
30     5 READ (08,12,END=70) A,B,C
40    12 FORMAT (2X,3F10.0)
50       D=A+B-C
60       WRITE (6,24) A,B,C,D
70    24 FORMAT (1X,F10.1,3F8.1)
80       GO TO 5
90    70 STOP
1000     END
```

(Lines 10 through 1000: Program typed by programmer)

```
RUN
THIS IS A DEMO

       2.8      9.4      5.7      6.5
       6.7      2.1      5.4      3.4
       3.3      7.9      4.8      6.4
       8.8      1.3      9.1      1.0

BYE
DISCONNECT
```

There are several points that should be carefully noted.

1. The READ statement in timesharing FORTRAN gives the name of a file. The name may be a two-digit number "01", "02", "03", etc., up to and including "63". However, file names for input must *not* be "05" and/or "06".

2. The FORMAT statement that is associated with

the timesharing READ statement must skip over the line numbers on each line of the data file. In the example, "2X" is needed in the FORMAT since each line number within the data file consists of two digits. If the line numbers had consisted of three digits, then "3X" would have been needed, etc.

3. To obtain output in timesharing FORTRAN, the same WRITE statement that is used in batch FORTRAN is used. That is,

```
WRITE (6,24) A,B,C,D
```

is acceptable. If the user wishes, he or she may employ the two digit file number, "06". Example:

```
WRITE (06,24) A,B,C,D
```

Either version of the WRITE statement is acceptable in timesharing FORTRAN. Instead of using WRITE, the programmer may elect to use the alternate command PRINT. Like this:

```
PRINT 24, A,B,C,D
```

Note the slight differences between the ways that WRITE and PRINT are used. In this text we prefer the more standard WRITE command.

4. GO TO statements must reference FORTRAN statement numbers, not line numbers. In the example, "GO TO 5" directs the computer to jump to statement number 5. Similarly, the "END=" clause in the READ statement references statement number 70, not line number 70.

5. In timesharing FORTRAN, quote marks may be either single quotes (') or double quotes (") as the user prefers. Since the programmer has the option of using both types, he or she can ask the system to print a message that includes

quotes. Example:

```
     WRITE (6,30)
30   FORMAT (1X,'OPERATOR, WHEN DONE TYPE "READY"')
```

The same FORMAT could be written:

```
30   FORMAT (1X,"OPERATOR, WHEN DONE TYPE 'READY'")
```

In timesharing FORTRAN, one may save as many data files as are needed. Each data file requires a unique name. Consider this example:

```
ID--HF84
SYSTEM--FORTRAN
OLD OR NEW--NEW
NEW FILE NAME--03
READY
10    2.43   1.64    \
20    9.11   3.24     }  Programmer types
30   -4.78   9.41    /   first file
SAVE
READY
NEW
NEW FILE NAME--07
READY
100    .053   .094   .126   \
200    .011   .048   .264    }  Programmer types
300    .156   .024   .143   /   second file
SAVE
READY
BYE
DISCONNECT
```

The programmer has created two files giving them the names "03" and "07". Now, the programmer may use those files in a timesharing FORTRAN program this way:

```
ID--HF84
SYSTEM--FORTRAN
OLD OR NEW--NEW
NEW FILE NAME--CALC
READY
```

```
10    3 READ (03,15,END=75) X,Y
20   15 FORMAT (2X,2F7.0)
30      READ (07,16) A,B,C
40   16 FORMAT (3X,3F7.0)
50      WRITE (6,17) A,B,C,X,Y
60   17 FORMAT (1X,F15.2,2F8.2,2F9.2)
70      GO TO 3
80   75 STOP
90      END
```

(Programmer types program)

```
RUN
             .05      .09      .13      2.43      1.64
             .01      .05      .26      9.11      3.24
             .16      .02      .14     -4.78      9.41

BYE
DISCONNECT
```

The first READ statement obtains values from the data file named "03"; the second READ statement obtains values from the data file named "07". Since it is assumed that the two data files have the same number of data lines, the program uses only one "END=" clause - the one in the first READ statement. When data values are exhausted from file "03", the program jumps to statement 75. At that time, it is assumed that values from both data files have been processed.

In timesharing FORTRAN, the WRITE statement has an additional special use. Instead of printing results on paper, it can write information upon a named data file. That file is on magnetic disk. Consider this example:

```
ID--HF84
SYSTEM--FORTRAN
OLD OR NEW--NEW
NEW FILE NAME--REK
READY

10    55 READ (03,60,END=200) P,Q
20    60 FORMAT (2X,2F7.0)
30       WRITE (09,70) P,Q
40    70 FORMAT (F11.2,F7.2)
50       GO TO 55
60   200 WRITE (6,210)
70   210 FORMAT (1X,"END OF JOB")
80       STOP
90       END
```

(Programmer types program)

```
RUN

END OF JOB
```

```
OLD

OLD FILE NAME--09

READY
LIST

        2.43   1.64
        9.11   3.24
       -4.78   9.41

READY
BYE

DISCONNECT
```

When the program executes, only one printed line is given - END OF JOB. The bulk of the output has been saved upon the data file "09". The data on that file may be examined immediately as shown in the example or it can be examined at some later time.

Observe that all this program does is read the values from the "03" file and store them upon file "09" in a slightly different format. The input file has built-in line numbers but the output file has no line numbers.

Observe that the FORMAT used for the storage of the output upon magnetic disk uses no slew control character. None is needed. Slew control characters are used only in connection with printed lines.

Output files may be named "01", "02", "03", etc. The name "05" should not, however, be used as the name for an output file. Recall that "6" and "06" cause the printing of results on paper, not the writing of results onto a disk file.

It is important to observe that an output file must already exist before a program can write upon it. One simple way to create output file space is to type this:

```
ID--HF84
SYSTEM--FORTRAN
OLD OR NEW--NEW
NEW FILE NAME--09
READY

10X
SAVE

READY
```

```
BYE
DISCONNECT
```

The programmer has created sufficient file space for several thousand characters of output. The name of the output file space is "09".

Files written on magnetic disk by FORTRAN programs can be read by other FORTRAN programs. In other words, the file created by program REK in the above example (file "09") can be read by another FORTRAN program using a READ statement like

```
2  READ (09,7) T,V
7  FORMAT (F11.0,F7.0)
```

In timesharing FORTRAN, the statements

```
200    3 READ (5,25) A,B,C
210   25 FORMAT (3F5.0)
```

have meaning. The "5" does not mean "card reader", though. It means "terminal". Upon encountering the statement the system types "=". The programmer enters numbers typed in accordance with the FORMAT. Example:

```
=  4.5  9.4 41.6
```

The system accepts "4.5" as the value of A; "9.4" as the value of "B"; "41.6" as the value of "C". Observe that there are no commas given to separate the three numbers.

If the program returns to statement 3, the system gives "=" again, the user types three more numbers and the program continues as before.

EXERCISES AND PROBLEMS

1. If numbers cannot be read from data processing cards, where can one obtain large volumes of data when operating in timesharing mode?
2. Study the following statements:

```
20    3 READ (07,15,END=40) D,G,H
30   15 FORMAT (3X,3F8.0)
```

Where does the program obtain the values for D, G, and H?

3. Refer to Question 2. What is the probable reason for "3X" entry in the FORMAT?

4. In timesharing FORTRAN, where does the program obtain data values in response to

```
100   38 READ (5,10) X,Y,Z
```

(Note the "5" in the READ statement.)

5. In timesharing, is it possible for a program to read data values from more than one magnetic disk data file? If so, give example READ statements that you might find in a program.

6. Contrast the two WRITE statements that follow:

```
400      WRITE (6,8) W,P,D
410    8 FORMAT (1X,3F8.1)
420      WRITE (20,9) W,P,D
430    9 FORMAT (3F8.1)
```

Tell where each WRITE statement gives its output.

7. Refer to Question 6. Why is there no printer control character in FORMAT 9?

8. Refer to Question 6. Must file "20" exist before the current program runs? How can one create a file space?

9. Refer to Question 6. Does the output given on file 20 have any line numbers?

10. Write a timesharing FORTRAN program that merges two files. The first file looks like this:

```
100   138   14.57
110   145   12.80
120   151   11.35
       .     .
       .     .
       .     .
```

The name of the file is "20". The first number of each line is a 3-digit line number; the second number is a 3-digit part number (right adjusted in a 6-character field), the third number is a 5-character price (right adjusted in an 8-character field).

The second file looks like this:

```
100   125   12.15
110   143   23.55
120   144   48.90
  .     .
  .     .
  .     .
```

The name of this file is "30". The three numbers on each line have the same meanings as they do for file "20".

It is unknown exactly how many lines there are in each file but you can assume they are less than one hundred. You may also assume that the part numbers in both files are in *increasing sequence*. You may also assume that there are *no duplicate* part numbers within each file or from one file to the other.

The program is to read lines from both files then create a third file, file "40". The new file is to begin like this:

```
100   125   12.15
110   138   14.57
120   143   23.55
130   144   48.90
140   145   12.80
  .     .
  .     .
  .     .
```

Observe that the structure of the output file is exactly the same as that of the input file. The line numbers in the output file are not automatically given. Your program must generate and write them in steps of "10".

CHAPTER 18

Subroutine Subprograms

A subroutine subprogram is a program that is called into use by another program. As an example, a program may call another program to perform some type of special processing. When the processing has been completed, the calling program resumes from where it left off.

A subprogram is a complete program which, by itself, is rarely used to solve a major problem. It usually helps a master (main) program in the solution of a problem. When the main program needs the subprogram it calls for it to perform the special subsidiary task that it has been designed to accomplish.

There are a number of different types of subprograms. In this chapter we discuss subroutine subprograms.

Suppose that at some given time, the memory of a computer has these three programs loaded into it. See Figure 18-1.

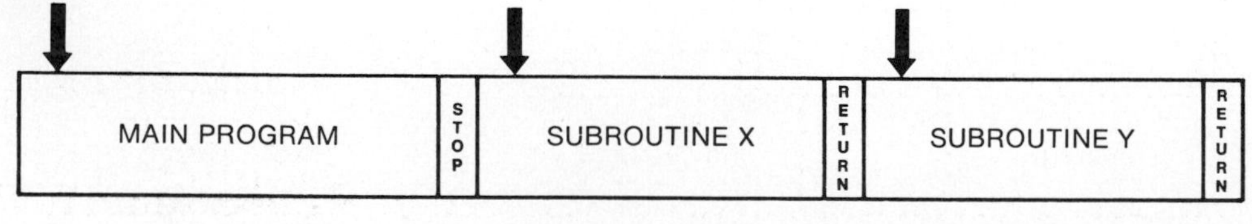

Figure 18-1

The three arrows indicate the beginning point of each program. The leftmost program is a main program. Programs X and Y are subroutine subprograms.

When there is a main program in the memory and one or more subroutines, execution of the task always begins at the beginning of the main program and proceeds toward its end. If, at any time during the execution of the main program, the main program needs the assistance of a subroutine, the main program directs the computer to go to the beginning of the subroutine. The computer then obeys the instructions in the subprogram and returns to the main program. See Figure 18-2.

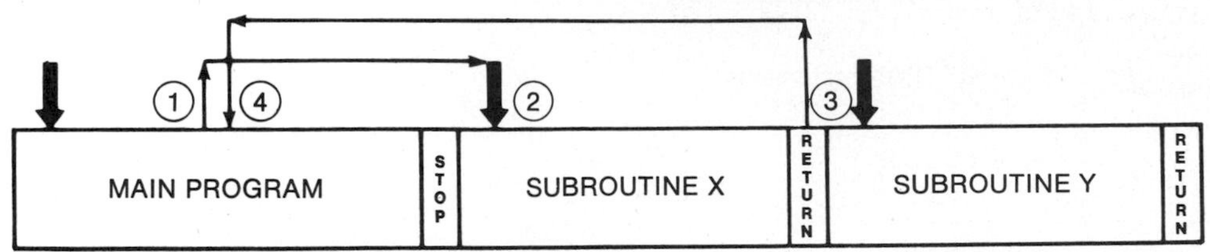

Figure 18-2

The main program has executed several instructions, then finds that it must call for the use of Subroutine X. The program directs the computer to exit from the main program. (See ①) The computer enters the subroutine. (See ②) The subroutine is executed and the computer then exits from the subroutine. (See ③) The computer returns to the main program at the point immediately following the original exit. (See ④)

The main program resumes executing. Now, another jump is taken by the computer to Subroutine X or to Subroutine Y as needed. Figure 18-3 is an illustration that shows what might happen during the processing of the job.

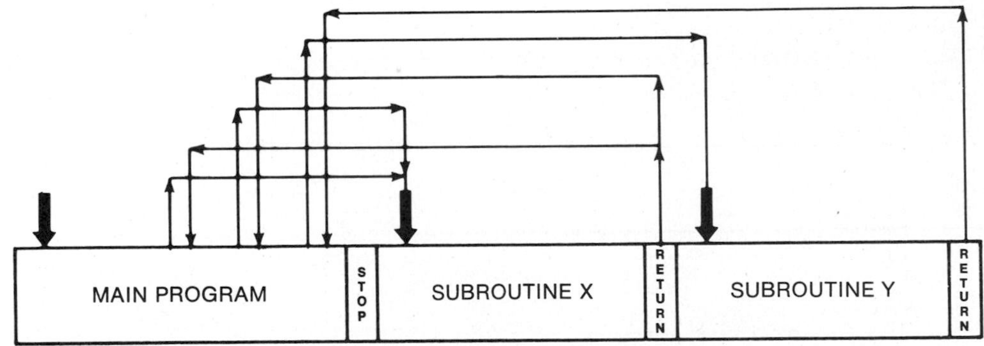

Figure 18-3

Observe that the computer exits the main program to go to Subroutine X. Later, it exits the main program to go again to Subroutine X. Finally, the computer exits the main program to go to Subroutine Y. Then, the computer concludes the main program by executing all the remaining instructions in the program.

Study the next program skeleton in Figure 18-4 which shows how subroutine subprograms might be called into use.

STATEMENT NUMBER (1–5)	CONT (6)	STATEMENT (7–72)	IDENT (73–80)
		other FORTRAN statements	
		CALL X (parameters)	
		other FORTRAN statements	
		CALL X (parameters)	
		other FORTRAN statements	
		CALL Y (parameters)	
		other FORTRAN statements	
		STØP	
		END	

Figure 18-4

The first "CALL" directs the computer to jump to Subroutine X. (Whenever a subroutine call is made, parameters must usually be provided within a set of parentheses. We'll discuss these parameters presently.) Figure 18-5 shows what Subroutine X looks like:

STATEMENT NUMBER (1–5)	CONT (6)	STATEMENT (7–72)	IDENT (73–80)
		SUBRØUTINE X (parameters)	
		other FORTRAN statements	
		RETURN	
		END	

Figure 18-5

When coded, a subroutine begins on a separate coding form and is headed with the subroutine's name. Any parameters that the subroutine needs are placed within parentheses.

A subroutine must always be headed with a statement reading SUBROUTINE. Within the subroutine there must be a statement reading RETURN and one reading END. If needed, you can supply more than one RETURN in a subroutine. The END statement must always be the last statement of the program.

We've mentioned the term "parameters". Parameters represent the values that a subroutine needs in order to operate correctly. Parameters appear within parentheses following a subroutine's call. In a main program, the call for a subroutine's execution might look like this:

```
CALL CALC (A,B,C)
```

The name of the subroutine is CALC. The parameters that are being passed on to the subroutine are A, B, and C. That is, the subroutine is to work with the values of A, B, and C. Exactly what happens to A, B, and C can be seen as we study subroutine CALC. Let's assume the subroutine is the one shown in Figure 18-6.

STATEMENT NUMBER (1–5)	CONT (6)	STATEMENT (7–72)	IDENT (73–80)
		SUBRØUTINE CALC (D,G,H)	
		IF (D.GT.G) GØ TØ 20	
		H = D * G	
		RETURN	
20		H = D/G	
		RETURN	
		END	

Figure 18-6

The subroutine accepts the parameters supplied by the main program but operates upon them under *different names*. The main program knows the parameters as A, B, and C, but the subroutine knows the same parameters as D, G, and H. The subroutine makes a one-for-one association. That is, the main program's "A" becomes the subroutine's "D"; the main program's "B" becomes the subroutine's "G"; and the main program "C" becomes the subroutine's "H".

The parameter names given in main and subroutine subprograms *may be the same*, but the fact that parameter names given in main programs *do not have to be the same* as parameter names given in the subroutines, lends flexibility to the usage of subroutines. This means that the same subroutine can be used with a variety of CALL's in the main program. For example, at several points in the main program, we might see calls like:

```
-
CALL CALC (A,B,C)
-
-
-
-
CALL CALC (R,T,E)
-
-
-
-
-
-
CALL CALC (Q,V,Z)
-
-
-
-
```

Regardless of how the call is made, the subroutine always works the same way. That is, the *same* subroutine procedure is executed but with *different* values having *different* names.

The variable names in a subroutine do not actually represent variables. They are simple "place holders" and define *how* the actual variables of the main program are to be operated upon. When the call is,

```
CALL CALC (A,B,C)
```

for example, whatever appears to happen to D within the subroutine, actually happens to A; whatever appears to happen to G, actually happens to B; and whatever appears to happen to H, actually happens to C.

You can see that the example subroutine tests the relationship of D to G. If D is greater than G, the program computes D divided by G and assigns the result to H, then directs the computer to return to the main program. If D is not greater than G, the program computes D multiplied by G and assigns the result to H. Then the subroutine directs the computer to return to the main program. The program does not actually work with D, G, and H; it works with A, B, and C. That is, if A's value is greater than B's value, the program computes A divided by B and assigns the result to C. Then the computer is directed to return to the main program. If A's value is not greater than B's value, the program computes A multiplied by B and assigns the result to C. Then the computer is directed to return to the main program.

Suppose, for example, that when subroutine CALC is called, A's value is "6.1" and B's value is "8.2". The subroutine will compute A times B (50.02) and assign the result to C. Then, the computer will return to the main program - to the statement immediately following the CALL statement. At that time, A's value will still be "6.1", B's value will still be "8.2", but C's value will have changed to "50.02".

It follows that when a call to a subroutine is made, one or more of the parameters named in the call represent *inputs* to the subroutine and one or more of the parameters represent *outputs* from the subroutine. The input and output variable names do not have to be given in any particular sequence. It is the subroutine itself, the way it works, that actually defines which variables are inputs and which are outputs. (In this example, CALL CALC (A,B,C), A and B represent inputs to CALC and C represents an output from CALC.)

The variable names used in a main program and those used in a subroutine do not conflict with each other. They are completely independent. This means that if a subroutine's call is

```
CALL VALS (R,V,W,I,N)
```

and the first statement of subroutine VALS is:

```
SUBROUTINE VALS (F,B,X,J,M)
```

there is a direct association only between the main program's R, V, W, I, and N and the subroutine's F, B, X, J, and M. If the subroutine uses variables named R, V, W, I, and N, those variables are *different* from the main program's variables having the same name.

Observe that the list of variable names in the call's parameters and the list of variable names in the subroutine's definition, must match in mode. That is, R and F are real; V and B are real; W and X are real; I and J are integer; and N and M are integer.

Suppose subroutine VALS accomplishes the tasks shown below:

```
      SUBROUTINE VALS (F,B,X,J,M)
      P=9.7
      IF (F.EQ.B) GO TO 30
      X=P*F
      J=M**3
      RETURN
   30 X=(P*F)/5.
      J=M**2
      RETURN
      END
```

It can be seen that the subroutine's place holders F, B, and M represent inputs to the subroutine. The place holders X and J represent outputs from the subroutine. The value that P needs is assigned within the subroutine itself. This assignment causes no conflict with any variable named P, should one exist in the main program. If there is a variable named P in the main program, the two P's lead independent lives.

In this example the actual values used by the subroutine for its input are R, V, and N. The results computed by the subroutine are actually assigned to W and I. If, at the time the subroutine is called, the values held by R, V, W, I, and N, are "1.5", "2.7", "4.5", "7", and "5", the values held by those variables, *after* the subroutine has been executed, are "1.5", "2.7", "14.55", "125", and "5", (R's value is an input value and does not change. V's value is also an input value and does not change. W's value is an output value and is computed from 9.7 times 1.5. I's value is an output value and is computed from 5^3. N's value is an input value and does not change.)

The actual parameters used in a CALL statement may be variable names, actual numeric values, and/or expressions. Thus, a call to VALS could be made this way:

```
CALL VALS (1.5,T*C,H,K,4)
```

The actual parameters shown above are matched with the place holders in the subroutine. The value "1.5" is associated with F; the result of "T*C" is associated with B; the value H is associated with X; the value K is associated with J; and the value "4" is associated with M. If we assume that T's value is ".75" and C's value is "2.0", then the subroutine computes new values for H and K; they are "2.91" and "16". (Since "T*C" equals "1.5", the subroutine computes "(9.7 x 1.5)/5" and assigns the result to X; and it computes "4^2" and assigns the result to K.)

Because the actual parameters given within the parentheses of a subroutine call may be variable names, numeric constants, and/or expressions these calls are all valid:

```
CALL VALS (A,B,C,J,K)
CALL VALS (2.7,9.4,W,KK,8)
CALL VALS (SQR(X),SIN(W),F,N,3*L)
CALL VALS (G(3),H(L),R,M4,NL(5))
```

It should be apparent that output parameters must always be variable names so that the results of calculations can be assigned.

The parameters in a subroutine's definition must always consist of unsubscripted variable names. Therefore, subroutine VALS may be defined as

```
SUBROUTINE VALS (F,B,X,J,M)
SUBROUTINE VALS (E,H,Y,I,J)
SUBROUTINE VALS (G,P,Q,KK,LL)
```

These names are place holders, sometimes called "dummies", and can represent values regardless of whether those values are supplied in the form of actual numeric values, variable names (subscripted or unsubscripted), or expressions. Statement numbers given within main programs and subroutines are independent of each other. This means that certain statement numbers found in a main program may duplicate certain statement numbers found in a subroutine. There is no conflict.

ALTERNATE ENTRIES INTO SUBROUTINES

A main program may direct the computer to jump to various points within a subroutine. The points at which a subroutine may be entered is identified by the word ENTRY. Consider this example:

MAIN PROGRAM

```
      X=0.0
      Y=5.6
      Z=5.6
      D=2.8
      E=9.3
      F=5.5
      CALL SUBN (X,Y,Z,D,E,F)
      PRINT, 'CAME BACK FROM FIRST CALL'
      WRITE (6,76) X
   76 FORMAT (' ',F10.1)
      CALL SUBNN (X,Y,Z)
      PRINT, 'CAME BACK FROM SECOND CALL'
      WRITE (6,76) X
      CALL SUBNNN (X,Y,Z,D)
      PRINT, 'CAME BACK FROM THIRD CALL'
      WRITE (6,76) X
      STOP
      END
```

SUBROUTINE

```
      SUBROUTINE SUBN (X,Y,Z,D,E,F)
      X=Y+Z+D-E-F
      RETURN
      ENTRY SUBNN (X,Y,Z)
      X=Y+Z
      RETURN
      ENTRY SUBNNN (X,Y,Z,D)
      X=Y+Z-D
      RETURN
      END
```

The program calls SUBN, SUBNN, and SUBNNN. Observe that there is basically only one subroutine. It is SUBN. However, two points within the subroutine have been labeled ENTRY SUBNN and ENTRY SUBNNN. The three parts of the subroutine can be accessed independently. The subroutine is, however, considered a single subprogram. GO TO's may access all three parts. Whenever any RETURN is encountered, the computer returns to the main program.

The main program and subroutine give the output shown in Figure 18-7.

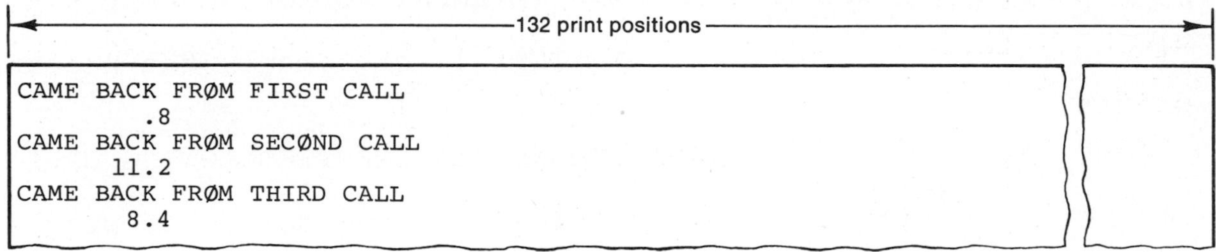

Figure 18-7

Note the use of unformatted output called for by the three PRINT statements in the main program. Unformatted output is discussed in Chapter 32.

ALTERNATE RETURNS FROM SUBROUTINES

Usually a subroutine returns the computer to the statement that immediately follows the associated CALL in the main program. Optionally, returns may be made to the second statement following CALL, the third statement, etc. Returns can also be made to statements that precede the CALL statement. Consider this example:

MAIN PROGRAM

```
      X=20.3
      Y=3.5
      Z=9.8
      CALL SUBRET (X,Y,Z,$50,$60)
      PRINT, 'PROGRAM RETURNED TO THE STATEMENT FOLLOWING CALL'
      STOP
50    PRINT, 'PROGRAM RETURNED TO A SECOND STATEMENT FOLLOWING CALL'
      STOP
60    PRINT, 'PROGRAM RETURNED TO A THIRD STATEMENT FOLLOWING CALL'
      STOP
      END
```

SUBROUTINE

```
      SUBROUTINE SUBRET (X,Y,Z,*,*)
      A=X+Y-Z
      IF (A) 44,55,66
44    RETURN
55    RETURN 1
66    RETURN 2
      END
```

If the program returns to the main program by encountering "RETURN", the program prints

PROGRAM RETURNED TO THE STATEMENT FOLLOWING CALL

If the return is made by the "RETURN 1" statement, the program prints

PROGRAM RETURNS TO A SECOND STATEMENT FOLLOWING CALL

If the return is made by the "RETURN 2" statement, the program prints

PROGRAM RETURNS TO A THIRD STATEMENT FOLLOWING CALL

By examining the program, you can see that RETURN gives the "normal" return; "RETURN 1" causes the program to return to statement 50 and "RETURN 2" causes the program to return to statement 60. Note the entries "$50" and "$60" in the CALL statement. The symbols "$50" and "$60" refer to statements 50 and 60. Observe, also, the two asterisks in the subroutine's definition. These asterisks correspond, respectively to "$50" and "$60" in the subroutine CALL.

When X's value is "20.3", Y's value is "3.5" and Z's value is "9.8", the program will give the output shown in Figure 18-8.

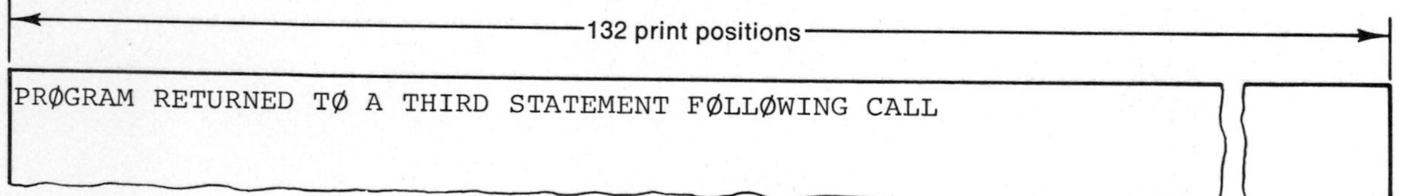

Figure 18-8

TIMESHARING SUBROUTINES

In timesharing FORTRAN, subroutines immediately follow main programs. The line numbers continue to increase without interruption. Example:

```
10      DIMENSION A(100), B(200), C(300)
20      READ (10,8) A
30      READ (12,8) B
40      READ (14,8) C
50   8  FORMAT (4X,10F5.0)
60      T=0.
70      CALL TOTE (A,80,T)
80      WRITE (6,9) T
```

```
      CALL TOTE (B,150,T)
      WRITE (6,9) T
      CALL TOTE (C,240,T)
      WRITE (6,9) T
    9 FORMAT (1X,F10.2)
      STOP
      END
      SUBROUTINE TOTE (X,J,S)
      DIMENSION X(300)
      S=0.
      DO 40 K=1,J
      S=S+X(K)
   40 CONTINUE
      RETURN
      END
```

Subroutine TOTE sums values in an array from the first value in the array through the J'th value in the array. (The actual value for J is supplied by the main program as one of the CALL parameters.)

Observe that the main program reads values into arrays A, B, and C. It obtains these values from three files: "10", "12", and "14". Array A is created from 10 lines in file "10"; Array B is created from 20 lines in file "12"; and Array C is created from 30 lines in file "14".

The main program then calls subroutine TOTE to sum the first 80 values within Array A. The call is

```
CALL TOTE (A, 80, T)
```

The list of parameters includes "A", the name of the array; "80", the number of values within Array A to sum; and "T", the variable name that receives the sum. These actual values are associated with the parameter names in the subroutine

```
SUBROUTINE TOTE (X,J,S)
```

The names X, J, and S are place holders. They are matched with the parameters A, 80, and S.

Observe that the Array X is defined and dimensioned in the subroutine. The name X is a dummy name. The DIMENSION statement *does not* actually reserve any memory space. The memory space is actually reserved by the DIMENSION statement for arrays A, B, and C defined in the main program (600 memory cells).

The subroutine has been set up to sum the values in arrays having various names. Note that the second call of TOTE requests a summation of values in Array B and a third call of TOTE requests a summation of values in Array C. The DIMENSION statement in subroutine TOTE must define an array that is large enough to permit summing all of the values in the largest array defined in the main program.

The variable J in the subroutine is used within the DO statement to indicate how many values to sum. The sum is assigned to S, the name that corresponds with the name T in the main program. The name S is a place holder. The final sum is actually assigned to T.

In the main program, the variable T is given an initial value of zero before T is used as a name within a call's parameter list. FORTRAN requires a variable to have been given some value before it appears in a parameter list even if its function is to receive output from the subroutine.

Subroutines may call other subroutines without restrictions. The RETURN statement in a subroutine always causes the computer to return to the program that called it.

EXERCISES AND PROBLEMS

1. Define the term "subprogram".
2. Define the term "subroutine". Why are subroutines used in FORTRAN programming?
3. Is it possible to design and code a main program and a subroutine at the same time? Why?
4. How does a subroutine know what values it is to work with?
5. Do the variable names in the list of parameters in a subroutine call and in the associated subroutine definition have to be the same? Explain.
6. How many times may a main program call a subroutine during

any one run?

7. May a main program call into use more than one subroutine?

8. May a subroutine call another subroutine? How are the RETURN's handled?

9. How can a subroutine be entered at optional points?

10. How can returns from a subroutine be made to various points in the main program?

11. In timesharing FORTRAN, how are subroutines built into a job?

12. Does a DIMENSION statement in a subroutine actually reserve any computer memory space? Explain.

13. What is meant by the statement that variable names given in subroutine calls and associated subroutine definitions must match by mode?

14. Is it possible for a subroutine to define its own values with statements such as

    ```
    R = 8.7
    ```

15. Do identical variable names used in main programs and in subroutines conflict with each other assuming that those names do not appear in parameter lists of subroutine calls and subroutine definitions?

16. Do identical statement numbers used in main programs and in subroutines conflict with each other?

17. Do the input and output variable names given in a parameter list have to be in any particular sequence?

18. What three forms may the values that appear in a subroutine call parameter list take on?

19. Write a subroutine that breaks up a 5-digit integer number into its component digits. Then use the subroutine in a main program to test it. The name of the subroutine is to be "COMP" and it is to be called into use this way:

    ```
    CALL COMP (N,IARRAY)
    ```

N is the 5-digit number that is being passed on to COMP. The subroutine determines what are the five digits of N and assigns those digits to $IARRAY_1$, $IARRAY_2$, etc.

IARRAY is a dimensioned variable having this DIMENSION statement in both the main program and in the subroutine:

```
DIMENSION IARRAY (5)
```

As an example of what the subroutine does, you might assign the integer number "67483" to N. This assignment is made in the main program. The main program then calls COMP. COMP breaks up "67483" into its component digits and assigns "6" to $IARRAY_1$, "7" to $IARRAY_2$, "4" to $IARRAY_3$, etc. The subroutine then returns control of the job to the main program.

The main program prints N and the five values of IARRAY.

Hint: to begin breaking up N into its component digits, N must be divided by 10.

20. Write a timesharing program that computes N factorial(N!) for all integer values ranging from zero through 10. A value of N factorial may be computed this way:

    6! = 6 x 5 x 4 x 3 x 2 x 1
    3! = 3 x 2 x 1

    Your program should show that "1!" is equal to "1" and that zero factorial "0!" is also equal to "1".

CHAPTER 19

Functions

You already know that FORTRAN offers several built-in functions. Some of them are SIN, COS, SQRT, EXP, ALOG, ABS. There are times when a programmer will need a function that FORTRAN does not offer. A programmer may *build* his own.

There are two kinds of functions that may be defined by the programmer. They are:

1. Arithmetic Statement Function (ASF)
2. Function Subprogram

The arithmetic statement function is a function that may comprise only one statement in a main FORTRAN program; the function subprogram is a function made up of two or more statements. The latter is a complete program as is the subroutine subprogram. Let us consider the arithmetic statement function first.

ARITHMETIC STATEMENT FUNCTION (ASF)

The arithmetic statement function (also called the ASF) is a function defined by a single FORTRAN statement in a main program. The definition must be given before the function is used. Once defined, the function may be used just like a built-in function.

Let's consider the tangent function first. Some FORTRAN systems do not offer a tangent function. If one is needed, a user may define one by recognizing the fact that the tangent of an angle can be obtained by dividing the sine of an angle by the cosine of the same angle. See Figure 19-1.

STATEMENT NUMBER (1–5)	CONT (6)	STATEMENT (7–72)	IDENT (73–80)
		TAN (X) = SIN (X)/CØS (X)	
		other FORTRAN statements	
		D = TAN (D) * TAN (2.3)	
		other FORTRAN statements	
		F = SQRT (G) + TAN (H-R)	
		other FORTRAN statements	
		RAD = TAN (Q) - SIN (TAN (S))	
		other FORTRAN statements	

Figure 19-1

The first statement

```
TAN(X)=SIN(X)/COS(X)
```

gives the *definition* of a function. The name of the function may be any name that a programmer selects. In this example, the name that was chosen is TAN. Since TAN is a real name, the function gives a real result.

In a function's definition, the argument or arguments are place holders. That is, they indicate the number and mode of the arguments used but they do not conflict with any actual values used in the program that may have the same names. Here, X is the dummy (place holder) argument. X shows that, when used, the TAN function must be given a real value as an argument. You'll observe from the examples of TAN, as it is being used, that the actual arguments given may be variable names (D, S, Q), literal numbers (2.3), and/or expressions (H-R).

Consider the example:

```
D=TAN(D) * TAN(2.3)
```

First, the program obtains the tangent of D. To do this, the program refers back to the definition of TAN. The definition shows that the value D is to be used as the argument in the SIN and COS functions. That is, the sine of D, divided by the cosine of D, gives the tangent of D. D must, of course, be an angle given in radian measure. It must not be an argument representing a value for which no tangent exists. For example, if D is $\pi/2$, then the cosine of $\pi/2$ is "0" and the TAN function will attempt to divide by zero, an impossible operation.

In the same statement, the program obtains the tangent of the angle (in radian measure), "2.3". To do this, it divides SIN(2.3) by COS(2.3).

The other examples given above show that tangents may be obtained with a variety of arguments.

Suppose, the programmer wishes to define a function for hyperbolic sine and one for hyperbolic cosine. The equation for hyperbolic sine is

$$\sinh = \frac{e^x - e^{-x}}{2}$$

and the ASF definition could be

```
SINH(X)=(EXP(X)-EXP(-X))/2.
```

The equation for hyperbolic cosine is

$$\cosh = \frac{e^x + e^{-x}}{2}$$

and the ASF definition could be

```
COSH(X)=(EXP(X)+EXP(-X))/2.
```

In defining an ASF, one may use any built-in FORTRAN functions but not other defined ASF's. Thus, to define a function such as

$$p = \frac{\tan(X)}{\sqrt{X}}$$

one could not do it this way:

```
TAN(X)=SIN(X)/COS(X)
P(X)=TAN(X)/SQRT(X)
```

but could, of course, do it this way:

```
P=(SIN(X)/COS(X))/SQRT(X)
```

Next is an example of two ASF's using three arguments, A, B, and C. The functions give the roots of quadratic equations having the form:

$$y = ax^2 + bx + c$$

```
QUAD1(A,B,C)=(-B+SQRT(B**2-4.*A*C))/(2.*A)
QUAD2(A,B,C)=(-B-SQRT(B**2-4.*A*C))/(2.*A)
```

Having given these definitions, a program may use them in these, and other ways:

```
D=QUAD1(B,Q,E)
E=QUAD2(B,Q,E)

ROOT1=QUAD1(2.1,9.5,1.1)
ROOT2=QUAD2(2.1,9.5,1.1)

DM=F+QUAD1(H/T,-3.5,C)
DN=F+QUAD2(H/T,-3.5,C)
```

It is the programmer's responsibility to make sure that the functions in these examples give real roots. The discriminant b^2-4ac can, of course, be tested before QUAD1 and QUAD2 are used.

As we said before, the arguments in a function's definition are place holders. They do not conflict with actual values in the same program having the same names. Thus, QUAD1 and QUAD2 could be used this way:

```
G=QUAD1(B,C,A)
H=QUAD2(B,C,A)
```

The actual values represented here by the arguments B, C, and A do not conflict with the dummy definition arguments A, B, and C. When used, the actual argument B will be associated with the dummy argument A; the actual argument C will be associated with the dummy argument B; and the actual argument A will be associated with the dummy argument C.

FUNCTION SUBPROGRAMS

A function subprogram is a complete program in much the same way that a subroutine subprogram is a complete program.

The subprogram may use as many FORTRAN statements as are needed to accomplish a given task. There must be at least one RETURN statement in a function subprogram. An example is given in Figure 19-2.

STATEMENT NUMBER (1–5)	CONT (6)	STATEMENT (7–72)	IDENT (73–80)
		FUNCTIØN ALPHA (G,H,D)	
		IF (G.GT.D) GØ TØ 565	
		ALPHA = H ** 3	
		RETURN	
565		ALPHA = H ** 2	
		RETURN	
		END	

Figure 19-2

The function uses all three values G, H, and D in the argument list to compute a single value. Unlike subroutine subprograms which may employ both input and output arguments, functions use only input arguments. The value calculated by the function is assigned to the function's name. Note that in the above example, either the value H^3 or H^2 is assigned to ALPHA. ALPHA is the name of the function subprogram.

A function subprogram is brought into use in the same way that an arithmetic statement function or a built-in function is brought into use. That is, the function's name is mentioned in an expression. Example:

```
RSP=SQRT(D)+TAN(R)-ALPHA(P,DL,F)
```

In this example, the argument D is the actual argument for the built-in function SQRT; the argument R is the actual argument for the arithmetic statement function TAN; and the arguments P, DL, and F are the actual arguments for the function subprogram ALPHA, the one defined in the example given earlier.

When giving arguments for a function subprogram, the arguments may be real or integer but actual and dummy arguments must match by mode: real for real and integer for integer.

You may employ as many arguments as you need. In main programs, they may be variable names, actual numeric values, and/or expressions. Variable names may be subscripted; variable names may represent arrays. The dummy arguments in function subprograms must always be unsubscripted variable names.

For example, a function may be defined this way:

```
FUNCTION GRAPH (A, D, I, F, K)
```

and it may be used in a main program this way:

```
RL=T-GRAPH(V(3),W,3,7.8,K/L-2)
```

If W is the name of an array in the main program, then D must have a DIMENSION statement in the subprogram.

The name of a function subprogram defines the mode of the value given by the function. Thus, functions ALPHA and GRAPH, given as examples above, both yield one real result each. If a function's name is an integer name, the function yields an integer result. Suppose we have this statement in a main program:

```
M=(L-K)/2 + ITEM(MM,3,X)
```

The function subprogram ITEM yields a single integer value.

In timesharing, function subprograms follow main programs just as subroutine subprograms do. Each program has its own END statement; the line numbers continue from program to program without a break. In timesharing FORTRAN, we might have a series of programs as defined by this skeleton outline:

```
010  -                          )
020  -                          )
030  CALL KIM (D,J,K,A,B,C)     )
     -                          )   Main
     -                          )   Program
080  E = BETA (X,Y,Z)           )
     -                          )
     -                          )
130  END                        )
140  FUNCTION BETA (D,E,F)      )
150  -                          )
160  -                          )   Function
     -                          )   Subprogram
     -                          )   BETA
     -                          )
340  RETURN                     )
350  END                        )
```

```
360  SUBROUTINE KIM (H,I,N,P,Q,T)
370  -
     -
     -
     -
     -
530  RETURN
540  END
```

Subroutine Subprogram KIM

If there are a number of function and/or subroutine subprograms, it does not matter in what sequence they are given following the main program.

EXERCISES AND PROBLEMS

1. Give the names of the two types of functions that are available in FORTRAN.
2. What is an arithmetic statement function?
3. What is a function subprogram? Give some ways that it differs from an ASF.
4. Give some ways that a function subprogram differs from a subroutine subprogram.
5. What are the three forms that arguments given in a function's parameter list may take?
6. Study the following ASF definition:

   ```
   TABS (X,Y) = SQRT (X) / ALOG (Y)
   ```

   What type value (real or integer) does the function give when it is called into use.
7. Refer to Question 6. Give some examples of how the TABS function may be used in a main program.
8. Tell how a main program calls for the use of a function subprogram.
9. Study the following function subprogram definition:

   ```
   FUNCTION JODY (K,X,P,N)
   ```

   What type value (real or integer) does the function give when it is called into use? How many statements might you expect to find in the subprogram?

CHAPTER 20

COMMON

The COMMON statement is a statement that a programmer may place in a main program and also in one or more subprograms to help provide communications between main programs and subprograms. It looks like this:

```
COMMON DA,DX,K,PD,GAMMA,W,AG
```

This statement, placed in a main program and in one or more subprograms (subroutine subprograms or function subprograms), enables all the programs to use the *same* memory cells for the variables named. That is, both programs can access DA, DX, K, etc., for use in computations, for use in IF statements, WRITE statements, etc.

As an example, if a main program reads a value from a DATA card into GAMMA, the subprogram knows about the value at the same time and can use the value when the subprogram is called into use.

Another example, if a subprogram computes a value and assigns it to W, the main program knows about the assignment at the same time and can use W when control returns to the main program.

The COMMON statement can be used to reduce the number of parameters given in the argument list within calls to subroutines or functions. For example, if a subroutine call looks like this:

```
CALL CALC (M,D,AFT,GAMMA,PD)
```

the call can be simplified by placing one or more of the

variable names in a COMMON statement. If the COMMON statement shown on the previous page is used, the call can be simplified to

```
      CALL CALC (M,D,AFT)
```

There's no reason why all the parameters in an argument list can't be placed in a COMMON statement. Normally, programmers use the parameter list for variable names that are used in a main program and a *single* subprogram; and use the COMMON statement for variable names that are used in a main program and *several* subprograms. Individual preferences, too, help determine when a person uses the parameter list, the COMMON statement, or both.

The COMMON statement can be continued or, optionally, a programmer may use more than one COMMON statement in a program.

An example is shown in Figure 20-1.

STATEMENT NUMBER 1–5	CONT 6	STATEMENT 7–72	IDENT 73–80
		CØMMØN AA, XX, MM, PP	
		CØMMØN T, V, M, N, F, P, W, L, LL, K, LX,	
	1	RAD, EE, Z	

Figure 20-1

The COMMON statements could have been written as shown in Figure 20-2.

STATEMENT NUMBER 1–5	CONT 6	STATEMENT 7–72	IDENT 73–80
		CØMMØN AA, XX, MM, PP	
		CØMMØN T, V, M, N, F, P, W, L, LL, K, LX	
		CØMMØN RAD, EE, Z	

Figure 20-2

Corresponding COMMON statements in main and subprograms do not have to use identical variable names. Suppose, for example, that a main program has these two COMMON statements

```
      COMMON  Q,DD,M,W,AX,PF
      COMMON  RT,FL,TD,KRT
```

and a subprogram has these two COMMON statements

```
COMMON  F,TL,J,Y,S,T
COMMON  U,W
```

The names for the same memory cells will be paired as follows:

```
 Q and F
DD and TL
 M and J
 W and Y
AX and S
PF and T
RT and U
FL and W
```

Whatever happens to Q in a main program also happens to F in the subprogram. Whatever happens to T in the subprogram also happens to PF in the main program, etc.

Observe that names must match: real for real, integer for integer. Observe, also, that it is all right for one list of COMMON variables to be larger than the other. The matching of variable names ends when one list is exhausted.

Suppose, a main program has these COMMON statements:

```
COMMON  Q,DD,M,W,AX,PF
COMMON  RT,FL,TD,KRT
```

and a subprogram needs to use only M and TD from these statements calling them N and XPP, respectively. The COMMON statement of the subprogram could be written this way:

```
COMMON  D,D,N,D,D,D,D,D,XPP
```

The arbitrarily-chosen variable name D was inserted merely to skip across unwanted names. In this example, D respresents any variable name that a programmer wishes to ignore. D does not actually have to be used in the subprogram.

The COMMON statements may give dimension information. Example:

```
COMMON  F,G,X(50),L
```

This statement in a main program defines the array X. A DIMENSION statement must not be given for a defined array if the array is defined in a COMMON statement.

Given a choice whether to use a DIMENSION statement or a COMMON statement to define an array, the programmer should always choose the COMMON statement.

BLANK AND LABELED COMMON

The form of the COMMON statement discussed to this point is termed "blank" COMMON. A second form of COMMON is available, the labeled COMMON. The purpose of labeled COMMON is to enable a subprogram to select only a portion of a COMMON statement given in the main program. Suppose the main program gives this COMMON statement:

```
COMMON  /X/A,B,C,D/Y/E,F,G/Z/P,Q
```

A subprogram can give this COMMON statement:

```
COMMON  /X/A,B,C,D
```

The variables that are known to both main and subprogram are those that follow the label "/X/"; that is A, B, C, and D.

In another subprogram, the COMMON statement could be written this way:

```
COMMON  /Y/E,F,G
```

The variables that are known to both main and subprograms are E, F, and G. Observe that those names follow the label "/Y/".

Still another subprogram could employ this COMMON:

```
COMMON  /X/A,B,C,D/Z/P,Q
```

The variables listed under the labels "/X/" and "/Z/" are made COMMON in both main and subprogram.

Labeled COMMON statements may be more complex. For example, if a main program gives this COMMON statement

```
COMMON  T,U,V/D/F,G,H/E/P,Q,R
```

the variable names T, U, and V are considered blank COMMON.

The others (F, G, H, and P, Q, R) are associated with the label names "/D/" and "/F/".

One final example:

```
COMMON  AA,BB,CC/KK/PP,QQ,RR
COMMON  XX,YY,ZZ/LL/TT,UU,VV/MM/DD,EE
```

The variable names AA, BB, CC, XX, YY, and ZZ are defined as blank COMMON while all the other variable names are associated with the labels "/KK/", "/LL/", and "/MM/".

The two statements could have been written this way:

```
COMMON  AA,BB,CC,XX,YY,ZZ
COMMON  /KK/PP,QQ,RR/LL/TT,UU,VV/MM/DD,EE
```

TIMESHARING

In timesharing FORTRAN, the COMMON statement is used in exactly the same way as it is in batch FORTRAN.

EXERCISES AND PROBLEMS

1. Why can the COMMON statement be effectively used in a FORTRAN program that uses one or more subprograms?
2. Define blank COMMON. Contrast blank COMMON with labeled COMMON.
3. Must the variable names given in the COMMON statements within two or more associated programs be identical? Explain.
4. Study these two COMMON statements:

   ```
   COMMON  F,K,D,X,D,B
   COMMON  W,J,P,Z,E
   ```

   Assume these two COMMON statements are in two different programs. What value is D, in one program, common with in the other program?
5. Refer to Question 4. What value is B, in one program, common with in the other program?

6. Study these two COMMON statements:

```
COMMON  A,D,F,K,L,W,Z,T
COMMON  Q,Q,G,Q,Q,H
```

Assume these two COMMON statements are in two different programs. Why are there so many Q's in the second COMMON statement?

7. May a COMMON statement show dimension information? Under what circumstances would you give dimension information in a COMMON statement in preference to the DIMENSION statement?

8. Study this COMMON statement that appears in a main program:

```
COMMON  /A/X,Y,Z/B/P,Q,R,S/C/F,G
```

Write a COMMON statement that might be used in a subroutine. The subroutine needs F and G as values common with those having the same names in the main program.

9. Study these two COMMON statements:

```
COMMON  F,G,K/A/P,Q,R,S
COMMON  J,W,B,L/B/V,U,X
```

Tell which of the names shown above are blank COMMON values and which are labeled COMMON values.

10. Refer to Question 9. Rewrite the two COMMON's in such a way that one COMMON statement gives only the blank COMMON names and the other COMMON statement gives the labeled COMMON names.

CHAPTER 21

TYPE Statements

EXECUTABLE STATEMENTS

Certain FORTRAN statements are termed "executable". This means the statements *do something* - there is an element of action involved. Some executable statements are READ, WRITE, IF, GO TO, STOP. Assignment statements (X=P+Q) are also executable statements.

NON-EXECUTABLE STATEMENTS

Non-executable statements are those that *give information*. The element of action does not exist. Some non-executable statements are FORMAT, DIMENSION, COMMON, DATA, NAMELIST. The END statement is a special statement. It is neither executable nor non-executable. We'll discuss NAMELIST and DATA in detail later.

TYPE STATEMENTS

Six non-executable statements are the "type" statements. The six type statements are:

```
REAL
INTEGER
COMPLEX
LOGICAL
DOUBLE PRECISION
CHARACTER
```

These statements declare the modes of the variable names used in the current program. For example, a list of variable names following the word REAL declares all the names in the list to be real. Example:

```
REAL X,P,R,K,AB,MT,J,XMT
```

In the current program, the names X, P, R, K, AB, MT, J, and XMT are real. There is no absolute necessity to declare X, P, R, AB, and XMT to be real because the names themselves implicitly declare the variables. (Declaring variables as real or integer when it is not necessary to do so is not wrong. Programmers often do so for documentation.) The names K, MT, and J are real in this program even though they begin with letters that would otherwise indicate the variables to be integers.

Another example:

```
INTEGER DM,LL,Q,R,MM
```

The names DM, LL, Q, R, and MM are all integers despite the fact that DM, Q, and R begin with letters that would otherwise indicate the variables to be real. The names LL and MM do not need to be declared as integers because the first letters of the names implicitly define the variables as integers. It's all right to declare them as integers anyway for the purpose of documentation.

Up to this point, the only variable types that you have seen have been REAL and INTEGER. There are four additional types of variables that are used in FORTRAN. They are COMPLEX, LOGICAL, DOUBLE PRECISION, and CHARACTER. These variable types must *always* be declared.

Suppose we wish to declare HHH, III, PPP, and RRR as complex names. The required type statement is:

```
COMPLEX HHH,III,PPP,RRR
```

(We will discuss complex variables and constants in Chapter 23.)

Suppose we wish to declare QQ, QR, QS, and QT to be logical variables. We can declare them with this statement:

```
LOGICAL QQ,QR,QS,QT
```

(We will discuss logical variables and constants in

Chapter 24.)

Suppose we wish to declare EA, FA, JA, and VA to be double precision variables. We can accomplish the task this way:

```
DOUBLE PRECISION EA,FA,JA,VA
```

(We will discuss double precision variables and constants in Chapter 22.)

Finally, suppose we wish to declare TF and NK to be character variables. We can declare them with this statement:

```
CHARACTER TF*10,NK*18
```

TF is a character variable having a length of 10 character positions and NK is a character variable having a length of 18 character positions. (We will discuss character variables and constants in Chapter 25.)

Now, putting all these type statements together in a program, we have this:

```
REAL X,P,R,K,AB,MT,J,XMT
INTEGER DM,LL,Q,R,MM
COMPLEX HHH,III,PPP,RRR
LOGICAL QQ,QR,QS,QT
DOUBLE PRECISION EA,FA,JA,VA
CHARACTER TF*10,NK*18
```

Variable names must be declared to be real, integer, complex, logical, double precision, and/or character before they are first used. Recall, though, that real and integer values may be implicitly declared by virtue of their very names. Once typed, variable names may not be given a different type within any given program. (The same variable name may not be given in more than one type statement.)

MAXIMUMS

The maximum values of integers used in FORTRAN vary from system to system. Nine digits is common. Such integer values as "496384581" and "-146394734" can be used in most systems. Some FORTRAN's accept numbers with ten or more digits.

The maximum values of real numbers also vary. Normally,

a number can be expressed to seven or eight digits of significance but its *magnitude* can be far greater. For example, a real number may be stored in the computer's memory as $.4936897 \times 10^{30}$. It is a very large number but only the first seven digits are known. In engineering work, this degree of accuracy is usually sufficient.

The minimum sizes of real and integer numbers are virtually the same as the maximums except with leading negative signs.

Integer values are read and written using the letter "I" in FORMAT's. Example:

```
      READ (5,17) JIM,MIKE
   17 FORMAT (2I15)
        .
        .
        .
        .
        .
      WRITE (6,20) JIM,MIKE
   20 FORMAT (1X,I12,I20)
```

Real values are read and written using the letters "F" and/or "E" in FORMAT's. Here is an example using "F".

```
      READ (5,25) X,R
   25 FORMAT (2F10.0)
        .
        .
        .
        .
        .
      WRITE (6,35) X,R
   35 FORMAT (1X,F12.3,F8.1)
```

If your recollection concerning how the above two examples actually work is uncertain, refer back in the text where the reading and printing of integer and real values were covered.

Here is an example using "E".

```
      READ (5,85) A,F
   85 FORMAT (E15.0,E10.0)
        .
        .
        .
        .
        .
      WRITE (6,86) A,F
   86 FORMAT (1X,E12.3,E15.5)
```

The values of A and F would be punched as shown in Figure 21-1.

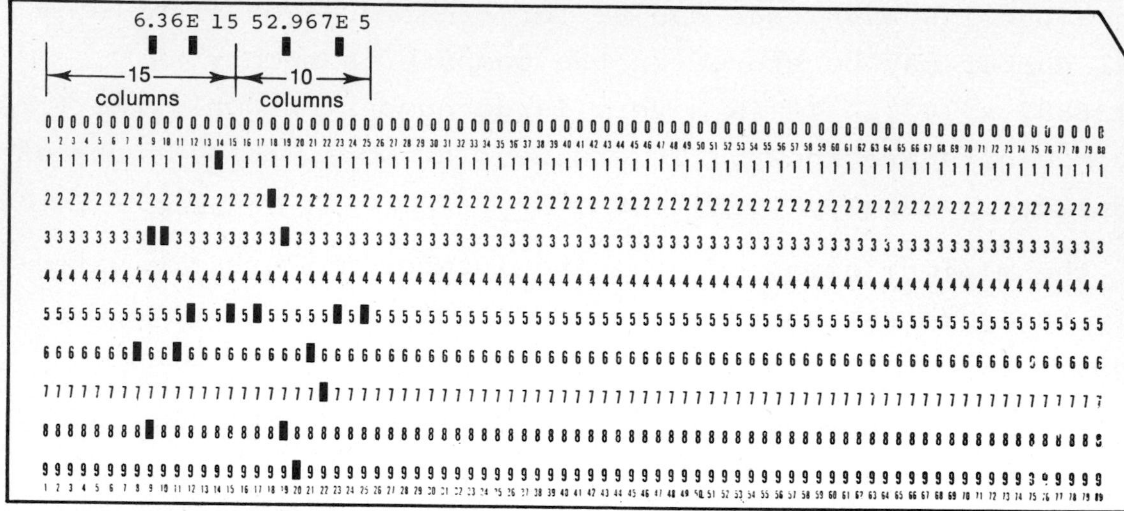

Figure 21-1

Values punched in "E" formats must be right adjusted in the fields allowed. In the example, "6.36×10^{15}" will be assigned to A and "52.967×10^{5}" will be assigned to F. The actual decimal points punched in the numbers determine the values to be assigned. The "0." entries in the FORMAT will be overridden by the system because *actual* decimal points are punched.

If the numbers punched do not have decimal points, then the FORMAT's associated with READ statements tell where the decimal points are assumed to be. For example, the value in

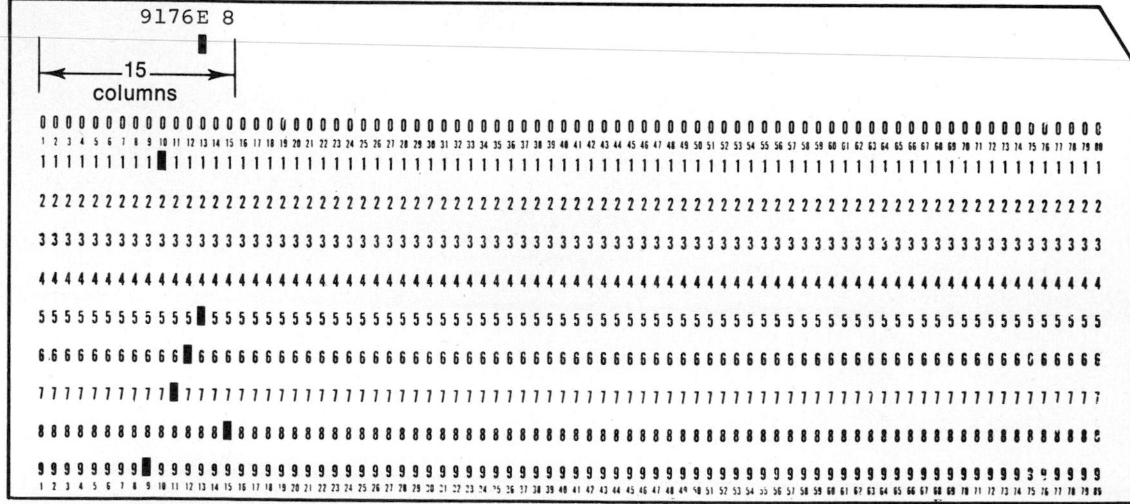

Figure 21-2

Figure 21-1 could be read with these statements:

```
      READ (5,14) G
14    FORMAT (E15.3)
```

The value assigned to G is "9.176x10^{8}". Observe that the ".3" portion of the FORMAT tells where the decimal point is assumed to be located.

In "E" output, the computer gives a fixed output. Like this:

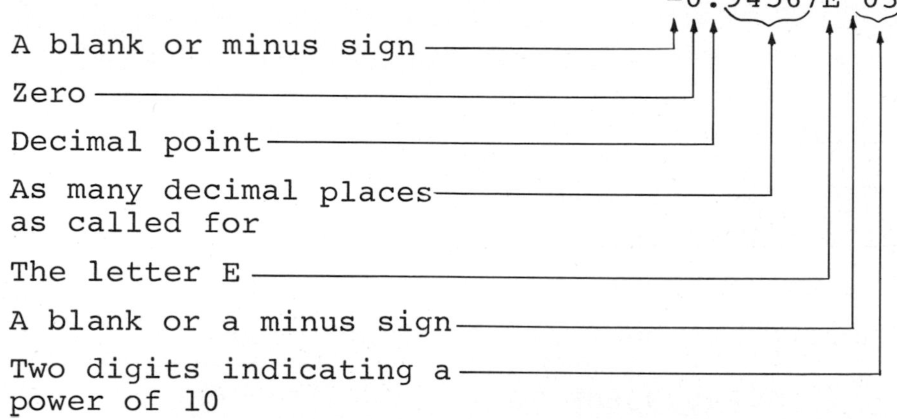

The number being printed will be interpretted as meaning "-0.94567x10^{3}" or "-945.67".

In the program example given above, the statements

```
      WRITE (6,86) A,F
86    FORMAT (1X,E12.3,E15.5)
```

cause the printout that is shown in Figure 21-3.

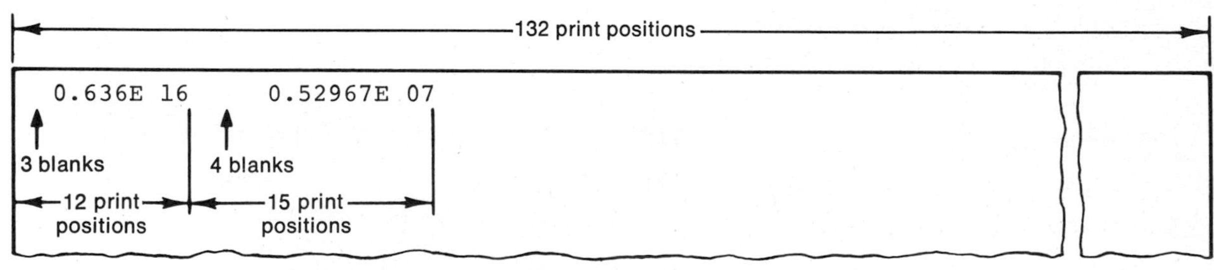

Figure 21-3

Real values may be assigned in "E" notation. For example,

```
      G=92.7
```

may also be written:

```
      G=92.7E 0
```

or

```
      G=.927E 2
```

or

```
G=9.27E 01
```

or

```
G=927.E-01
```

or in many other ways. This next statement shows that "E" notation can also be used in expressions:

```
H=(5.6 + 7.6E05) / (2.33E20 - 5.8)
```

or

```
H=(5.6 + 7.6E5) / (2.33E 20 - 5.8)
```

SCALE FACTORS

Programmers may wish to show one or more non-zero digits ahead of a value expressed in exponential ("E") notation. If the value to be printed is "674.67936", for example, it may be desired to have the value print as

```
6.74679360E 02
```

rather than the standard

```
0.67467936E 03
```

Or, it may be desired to express the value in any of these forms:

```
67.467936E 01
674.67936E 00
6746.7936E-01
67467.936E-02
```

etc.

The digits ahead of the decimal point (the scale factors) can be obtained by placing 1P, 2P, 3P, etc., ahead of the "E" in the FORMAT. Example:

```
      A=3.2568902
      B=456.23498
      C=6923.1235
      WRITE (6,9) A,B,C
    9 FORMAT (1X,3(1PE23.8))
      STOP
      END
```

The output will appear as shown in Figure 21-4.

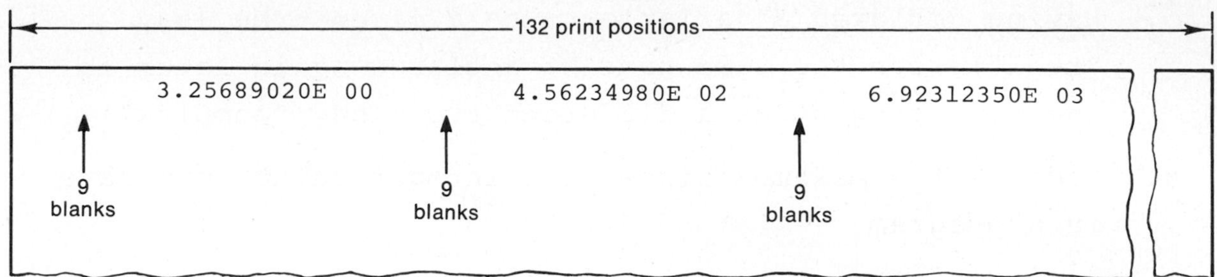

Figure 21-4

The scale factor can be from one through eight digits. If a scale factor greater than 8 is requested, the system will give 8 only.

The REAL and INTEGER type statements may give dimension information. Examples:

```
REAL PLM(20),JCX(200),RTL,MDE
INTEGER TXX(300),LAL(80),VR
```

Four arrays have been defined: PLM, JCX, TXX, and LAL. Two are real arrays and two are integer arrays.

When type statements give dimension information, the same variable names must *not* be shown in DIMENSION statements. When there is a choice, the dimension information *must* be given in a type statement, *not* in a DIMENSION statement.

In the next four chapters, we discuss double precision, complex, logical, and character values.

EXERCISES AND PROBLEMS

1. Define "executable" statement. Contrast an executable statement with a "non-executable" statement.
2. Define the term "type statement". Give the names of the six type statements and tell what each does.
3. If your program needs only real and integer values, can you avoid using type statements? Explain.
4. May a given variable name be given in more than one type statement in any given program?

5. Having declared a variable to be a given type (say "real"), can the same name be declared again later in the same program as a different type (say "complex")?

6. Discuss the maximum sizes that integer values may have in a program.

7. Discuss the maximum sizes that real values may have in a program.

8. In FORMAT's what is the alphabetic code character that is associated with integer values? What are the code characters that are associated with real values?

9. When punched on a card, where in a defined field must a number, expressed in "E" notation appear?

10. Tell how the computer will print the real number "-946.5687" according to the FORMAT "E16.5".

11. Tell what a scale factor is and how it can be used when printing real values in "E" notation.

12. Give several ways that you might give this next assignment statement in "E" notation:

```
R=84.746
```

13. It is possible to define complex, double precision, logical, and character arrays. Give an example of how a complex array space might be defined.

14. If a type statement gives dimension information for a variable, may you also use a DIMENSION statement for the same variable?

CHAPTER 22

Double Precision Values

Double precision values are essentially the same as real values but with more precision. Depending upon the system being used, only about seven or eight significant digits are available with real values. With double precision values, as many as sixteen, seventeen, or eighteen significant digits are available. Double precision values are basically ordinary real values but, since more computer memory is used for the number, more precision is available.

Double precision variable names are declared with the DOUBLE PRECISION type statement. Like this:

```
DOUBLE PRECISION A,GAMMA,T,LX,V8,GR,FT
```

The variable names A, GAMMA, T, LX, V8, GR, and FT are double precision variable names. The names may be used only for the assignment of double precision values. The DOUBLE PRECISION type statement must be given in a program before the defined variable names are used. Once declared as double precision, a variable name may not be declared differently later in the program.

Assignments to double precision names may be made this way:

```
T =7321.6728436835
A =39.6574296757D15
GR=435.8686914D6
LX=2.998D20
```

Observe the letter "D" in some of the values being assigned. "D" designates a power of 10 just as "E" does with real values. The value assigned to A is "39.6574296757 x 10^{15}". The value assigned to GR is "435.8686914 x 10^{6}", and the value assigned to LX is "2.998 x 10^{20}". The value assigned to T is self-explanatory.

The value of LX is stored in memory as a double precision value despite the fact that the full power of double precision is not being used. The value "2.998 x 10^{20}" could have been assigned to a real variable name and at a somewhat lower cost.

Double precision calculations are performed in a program where the greatest accuracy is needed. All calculations in a program can be performed in double precision, or only those calculations in a program that actually require greater accuracy need be done in double precision. Here is a calculation being performed in double precision. Assume all variable names have been declared as double precision.

```
FT=(GAMMA/1.57832569D7) + (V8/158.832181D5)
```

When read from cards, double precision values are processed in much the same way that real values are processed in "E" notation. Figure 22-1 shows an example of a card that is to be read:

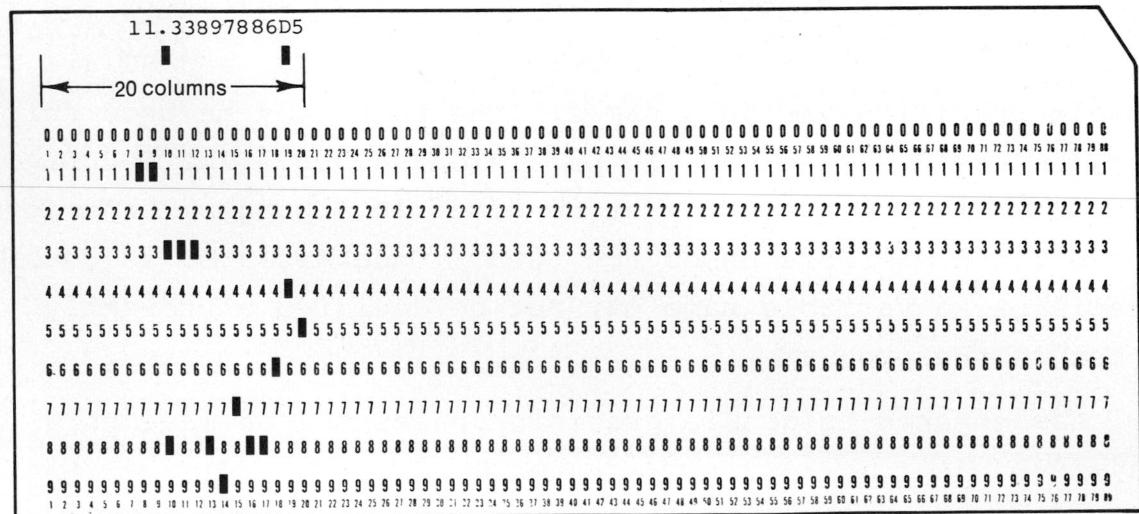

Figure 22-1

The number is right adjusted within the leftmost twenty columns of the card. Right justification is needed, otherwise, the computer will insert extra zeroes, probably unwanted, to the right of the "5" in the punched value.

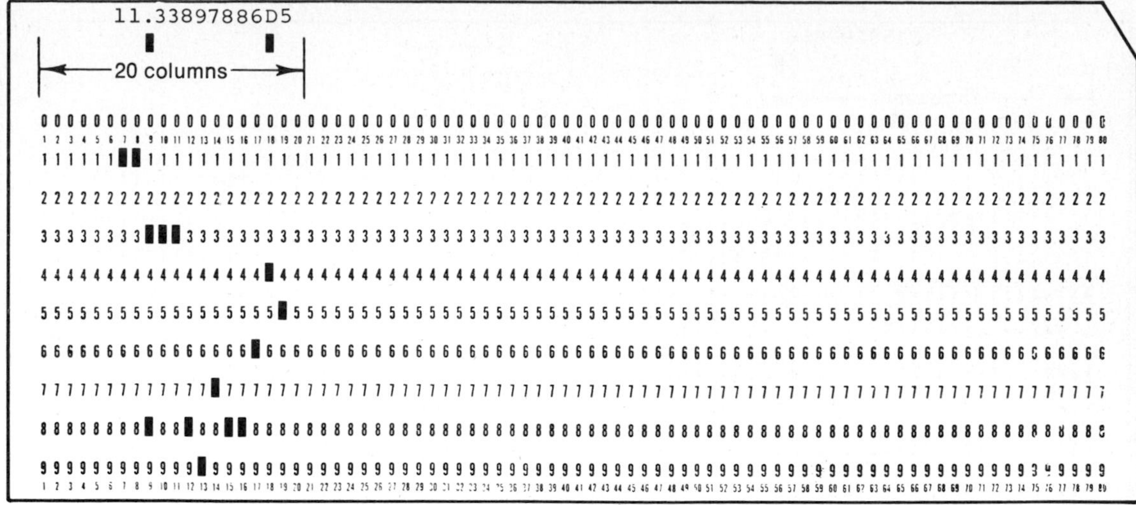

Figure 22-2

If the number is punched as shown in Figure 22-2 for example, the program will read and assign "11.33897886 x 10^{50}" instead of "11.33897886 x 10^{5}". The system assumes the programmer intended to punch a zero in column 20.

To read a punched double precision data value, a READ statement like this one may be used:

```
      READ (5,25) GAMMA
   25 FORMAT (D20.0)
```

In the FORMAT, "D" indicates that a double precision value is to be read. (We assume that GAMMA has been declared as double precision in a DOUBLE PRECISION type statement.)

The "20" in the FORMAT indicates that 20 column positions have been reserved for the value of GAMMA on the punched card. If the punched value includes a decimal point, then the remainder of the FORMAT needs only ".0". The *actual* number punched is the value that is read and assigned.

When a decimal point is not punched, the FORMAT tells how many decimal places are assumed. See Figure 22-3 on the following page.

Assume these are the READ and FORMAT statements given to read the value shown in Figure 22-3: (Assume V8 has been declared to be a double precision variable.)

```
      READ (5,30) V8
   30 FORMAT (D25.10)
```

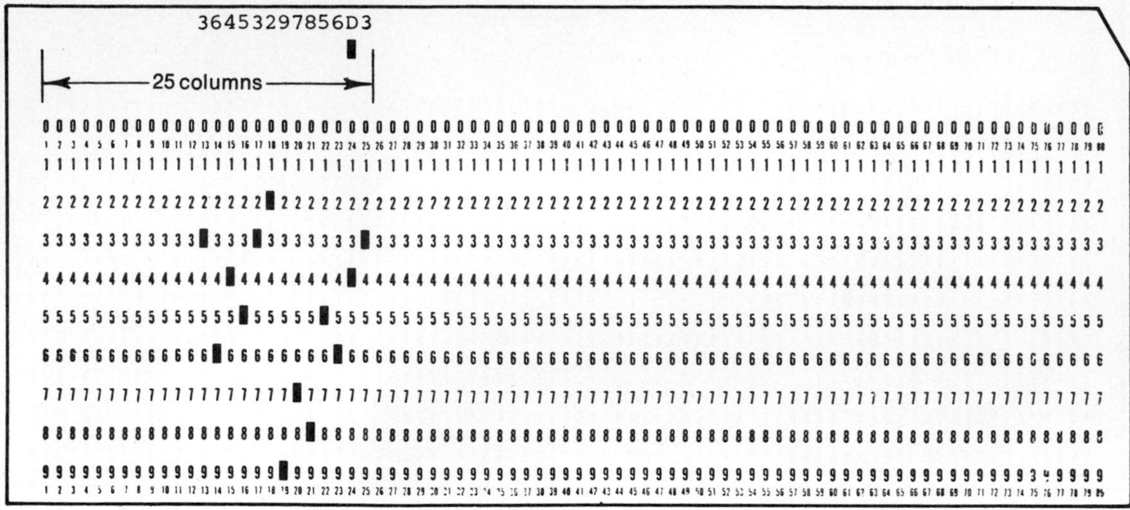

Figure 22-3

The FORMAT indicates that ten decimal places are to be assumed since the punched value does not include a decimal point. The value assigned, therefore, to V8 is "3.6453297856 x 10^3".

In printing double precision values, the code "D" is again used in the associated FORMAT's. Consider,

```
      WRITE (6,2) T,A
    2 FORMAT (1X,2D25.12)
```

Both values, T and A, have been declared as double precision variables and are to be printed in double precision form. Twenty-five print positions will be allowed for each value. See Figure 22-4.

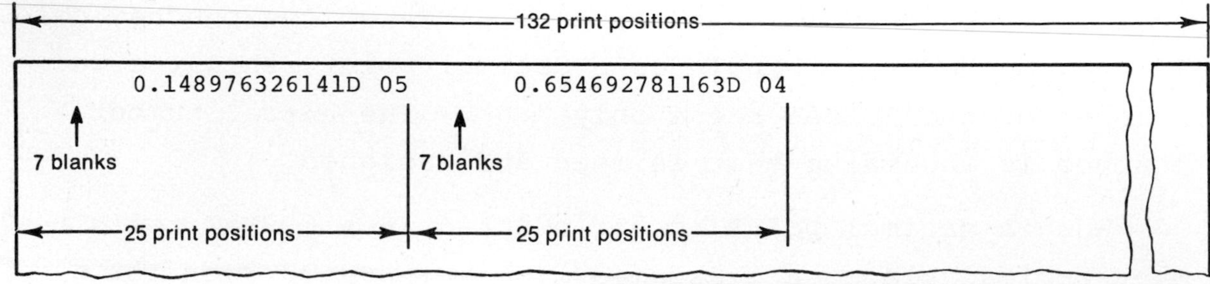

Figure 22-4

The value printed for T is "0.148976326141 x 10^5" and the value printed for A is "0.654692781163 x 10^4". Each number has a *fixed* form that looks like this:

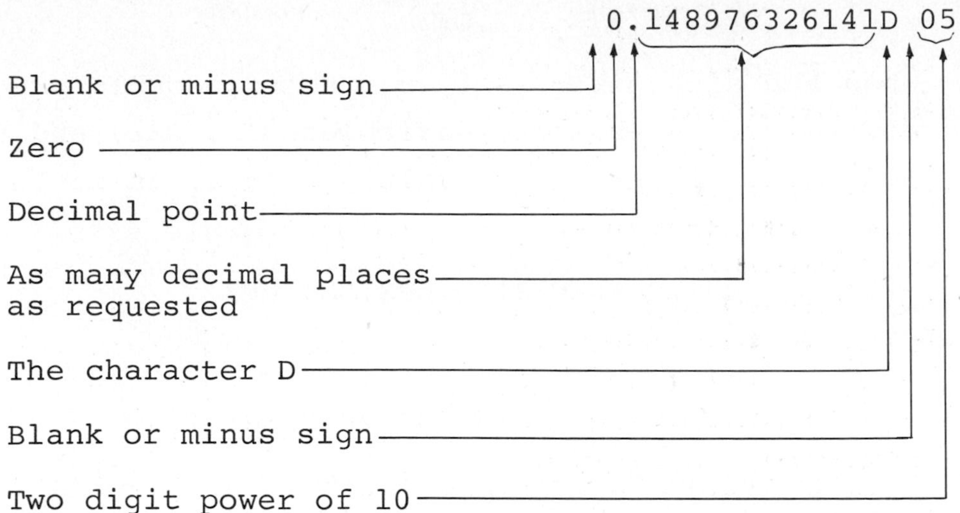

Scale factors can be defined with double precision values, as with real values, using "1P", "2P", etc., in FORMAT's.

Double precision values have the same magnitude limits as real values. In some systems, values *may* be as large or as small as $\pm 10^{\pm 38}$; in some systems, $\pm 10^{\pm 75}$, etc. Both real and double precision values can be expressed to the *same* maximum and minimum extents. It should be remembered, though, that real values may be expressed with a precision of only seven or eight digits; double precision values may be expressed with a precision of 16, 17, or 18 digits.

The DOUBLE PRECISION statement may give dimension information. Example:

```
DOUBLE PRECISION AGN,ALR(50),BLT
```

A double precision array, ALR, has been defined.

When an array is defined in a type statement, a DIMENSION statement must not be used for the same variable name. When there is a choice, the type statement must be used in preference to the DIMENSION statement.

NOTE

Some systems do not have a DOUBLE PRECISION type statement. To indicate that double precision is required, the user gives "size" information when declaring real variables. Like this:

```
REAL*8 BTX,LMZ,DF3
```

When the size given is 8 or greater, double precision is assumed. In this example, variables BTX, LMZ, and DF3 are defined as double precision values. It is as if the statement had been coded

```
DOUBLE PRECISION BTX,LMZ,DF3
```

EXERCISES AND PROBLEMS

1. What is a double precision value? How do double precision values differ from real values?

2. Discuss the maximum and minimum sizes that double precision values may have in FORTRAN programs. Contrast these limits with the maximum and minimum limits that real values may have.

3. In FORMAT's what is the alphabetic code character that is associated with double precision values?

4. When punched on a card, where in a defined field must a number, expressed in "D" notation, appear?

5. Tell how the computer will print the double precision number "-49614.963846" according to the FORMAT "D20.10". Also how the number would be printed if the FORMAT were "D20.12".

6. May scale factors be used with double precision numbers? Give some examples.

7. Give several ways that you might give the next assignment statement in "D" notation:

   ```
   G =8439.46389247
   ```

   Assume that G has been declared to be a double precision variable name.

8. Show how a double precision array space could be defined.

9. If a type statement gives dimension information for a

double precision variable, may you also use a DIMENSION statement for the same variable?

10. May a variable declared as double precision be changed later in a program and declared to be real or complex?

CHAPTER 23

Complex Values

Selected variable names may be declared COMPLEX by use of the COMPLEX type statement. This way:

```
COMPLEX Q,L,N,T,W,TX,NW,X,Y,Z
COMPLEX R,RR,RRR
```

The named variables will now be able to hold complex values - values having the form "a + bi". In a numeric value having that form, "a" represents the "real" part of the value and "bi" represents the imaginary part. The COMPLEX type statements must be placed ahead of the first use of the defined complex variables.

To assign a complex value to Q, one would use an assignment statement like this:

```
Q=(9.6,3.7)
```

Here, "9.6" is the real part of the complex value assigned to Q, and "3.7" is the imaginary part. Q represents the value "9.6 + 3.7i". The letter "i" is not actually stored within Q. The system *assumes* its presence.

In this next example

```
L=(-7.2,-5.8)
```

the value "-7.2" is the real part of the complex value assigned to L, and "-5.8" is the imaginary part. L represents the value "-7.2,-5.8i".

Complex values may be added, subtracted, multiplied, divided, and raised to powers. It is not within our scope here to delve deeply in arithmetic operations involving complex values. The subject of complex arithmetic is covered in many excellent math texts. The discussion that follows here is intended for persons who already understand complex arithmetic.

When one adds two complex values, the result is stored in complex mode. That is, if the statement

```
T=Q+L
```

is given, the computer adds the complex values and stores the result in T. The value, T, will have a real part and an imaginary part. (We assume that T, Q, and L have been declared as complex variables.)

Similarly, complex values are subtracted, multiplied, divided, and raised to powers. This way:

```
 W=Q-L
TX=Q*L
NW=Q/L
 N=Q**5
```

The operations are performed and the values stored in complex mode. (We assume all variable names have been declared to be complex.)

Students who have multiplied, divided, and raised complex values to powers manually, will realize how much effort the computer saves when it performs these calculations at electronic speeds.

In the memory of the computer, complex values are stored in real forms. There are two real numbers for each complex value.

Complex values may be read from cards or printed. Since both parts of complex values are internally stored as real values, the codes "F" and/or "E" are used in FORMAT's to read complex values and to print them.

Suppose we have the data card shown in Figure 23-1

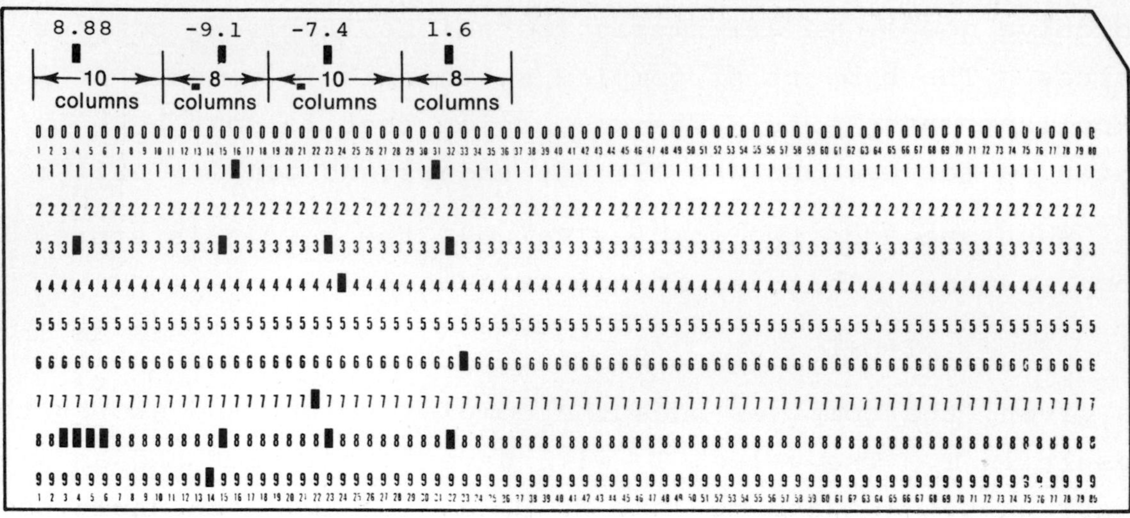

Figure 23-1

and we wish to read the four values assigning them to the two complex variables X and Y. The values could be read like this:

```
      READ (5,33) X,Y
   33 FORMAT (2(F10.0,F8.0))
```

When the card is read, the values "8.88" and "-9.1" are assigned to X. The value of X effectively becomes "8.88 - 9.1i". The values "-7.4" and "1.6" are assigned to Y. The value of Y effectively becomes "-7.4 + 1.6i".

The multiplier, "2", in the FORMAT doubles the "F10.0" and "F8.0" portions. The FORMAT could have been written this way:

```
   33 FORMAT (F10.0,F8.0,F10.0,F8.0)
```

In printing complex values, statements like this may be employed:

```
      WRITE (6,35) Q,L,T
   35 FORMAT (1X,6F10.2)
```

Since complex values are stored in memory as real values, the codes "F" and/or "E" are used within FORMAT's. Each value being printed must, of course, define two fields, one for the real part of the number and one for the imaginary part.

In response to the above two statements, we might see the output shown in Figure 23-2.

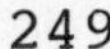

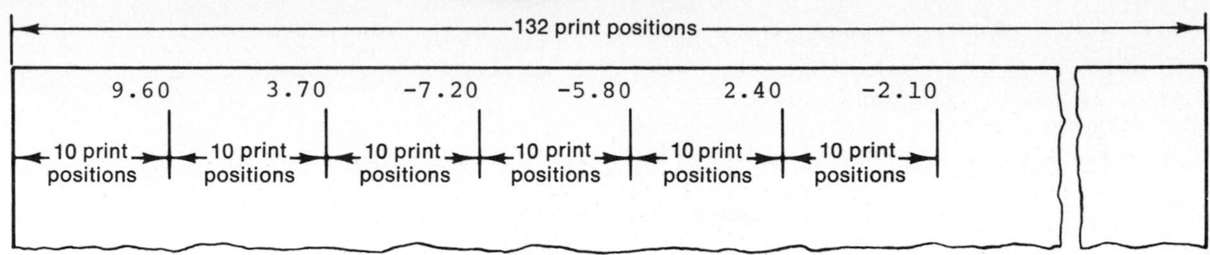

Figure 23-2

The printed numbers look like real values. There is nothing to identify them as complex. A programmer could, of course, identify the various values with column headings. See Figure 23-3.

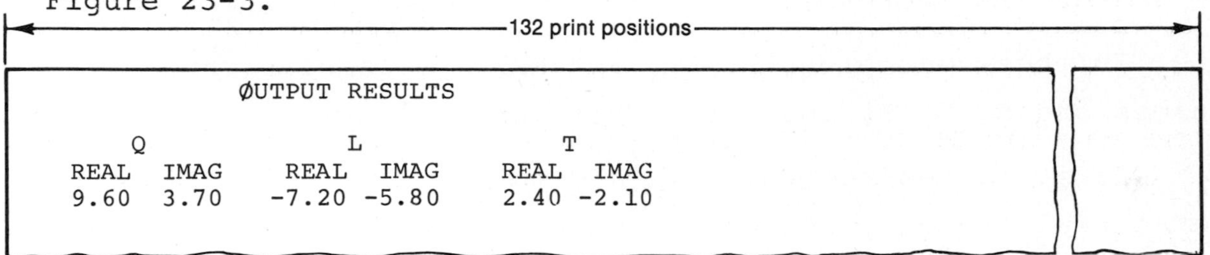

Figure 23-3

FORTRAN offers built-in functions especially designed to deal with complex values. These are

```
REAL
AIMAG
CONJG
CMPLX
```

The REAL function is used to extract the real part of a complex value and assign it to a real variable name. Example:

```
ACD=REAL (T)
```

The real part of the complex value, T, is assigned to the real variable, ACD.

The AIMAG function is used to extract the imaginary part of a complex value and assign it to a real name. Example:

```
PDY=AIMAG (T)
```

The imaginary part of the complex value, T, is assigned to the real variable, PDY.

The CONJG function is used to obtain the conjugate of a complex value and assign it to a complex variable name.

Example:

```
Z=CONJG (Q)
```

If Q's value is "9.6 + 3.7i", Z's value becomes "9.6 - 3.7i". (We assume that Z has been declared to be a complex variable.)

The CMPLX function is used to build a complex value from two real variable names or from one real variable name and one literal real number. Examples:

```
  R=CMPLX (F,G)
 RR=CMPLX (H,3.5)
RRR=CMPLX (1.2,V)
```

In these examples, R, RR, and RRR are complex variable names and F, G, H, and V are real variable names.

If it is desired to build a complex value using two literal real numbers, the CMPLX built-in function does not need to be used (though it could be). We could assign two literal real numbers to L this way:

```
L=(-7.2,-5.8)
```

or this way:

```
L=CMPLX (-7.2,-5.8)
```

If either of the two real values is represented by a variable name, the CMPLX function must be used.

The COMPLEX type statement may be used to give dimension information. Example:

```
COMPLEX JSA(100),RVT,WWV
```

A complex array space has been defined, JSA.

When an array space is defined using a type statement, the same variable name must not be given in a DIMENSION statement. When there is a choice, the type statement must be selected in preference to the DIMENSION statement.

EXERCISES AND PROBLEMS

1. What is a complex number? Give only a very general

description.

2. Show how a complex value, consisting of two actual numeric values, are assigned to a complex variable.

3. What does the CMPLX function accomplish? Give some examples.

4. What do the REAL and AIMAG functions accomplish? Give some examples of each.

5. What does the CONJG function do? Give an example.

6. In what form are the two parts of a complex value stored in the memory of a computer? Is the letter "i" stored?

7. What are the code alphabetic characters, used in FORMAT's, associated with complex values?

8. What arithmetic operations may be performed when using complex values?

9. Give some examples of how complex values could be read from punched data processing cards.

10. Give some examples of how complex values could be printed. How does a person determine which part of a printed value is the real part and which the imaginary?

11. Discuss how complex array spaces can be defined. Tell what role, if any, the DIMENSION statement plays in such a definition.

12. If a variable name has been declared as complex, may it be declared real or double precision later in the same program?

CHAPTER 24

Logical Values

Programmer-selected variable names may be declared to be logical variable names with LOGIGAL type statements. This way:

```
LOGICAL  I,P,RX,TF,VM,ZV,KMT,RLD,HMH
```

The usefulness of logical expressions can best be appreciated by persons who design electronic circuits. As with complex values, we cannot delve too deeply into the design of circuits in this text. Many excellent texts cover these subjects thoroughly.

Logical values are values selected from the two possibilities: "true" and "false". That is, the value "true" or the value "false" may be assigned to logical variables. Nothing else may be assigned.

Assignments to logical variables are made like this:

```
 I = .TRUE.
 P = .FALSE.
RX = .TRUE.
```

Observe the periods ahead of and behind the logical values. They *are* required.

Logical expressions may be coded where the logical values are connected by the words: ".AND.", ".OR.", and ".NOT.". Example:

```
TF=I.AND.P
```

The name, IF will take on the value "false". In order for TF to be "true", *both* the values I and P must be "true". If either or both of those values is "false", then TF's assigned value will be "false".

Now consider this statement:

```
VM=P.OR.RX
```

The value assigned to VM will be "true". In order for VM's assigned value to be "true", *either* P's or RX's value must be "true". If both values in the expression are "false", then VM's value will be "false". This next table shows what logical value will be assigned when two logical values in an expression have various values:

LOGICAL ASSIGNMENTS TABLE			
FIRST LOGICAL VALUE	CONNECTOR	SECOND LOGICAL VALUE	LOGICAL VALUE ASSIGNED
true	.AND.	true	true
true	.AND.	false	false
false	.AND.	true	false
false	.AND.	false	false
true	.OR.	true	true
true	.OR.	false	true
false	.OR.	true	true
false	.OR.	false	false

In logical expressions, the periods given on both sides of the words AND and OR *are* required.

The word .NOT. may also be given in logical expressions. When placed ahead of a logical value, it temporarily reverses that value. That is, if the value is currently "false", the value temporarily becomes "true"; if the value is currently "true", it temporarily becomes "false". Example:

```
 I = .TRUE.
 P = .FALSE.
RX = .TRUE.
ZV = I.AND..NOT.P
```

ZV's value is set "true". I's value is "true". P's value is initially "false", but ".NOT." temporarily changes it to "true". Now, the two values in the expression are "true" and ZV will be set "true".

P's value is not permanently changed. In the statement where P next appears, its value will be "false".

Logical expressions may be much more complex than the ones given here. You may see a statement like this, for example:

```
KMT=(I.OR.P).AND.(RX.OR..NOT.TF).OR.VM
```

The value KMT may be set "true" under a variety of conditions. For example, KMT will be "true" if I is "true" *and* RX is "true". KMT will also be set "true" if P is "true" *and* TF is "false". And, KMT will be set "true" if VM is "true".

Logical values can be read from cards or printed. Suppose we have the card shown in Figure 24-1 and we need to read the three values punched upon it.

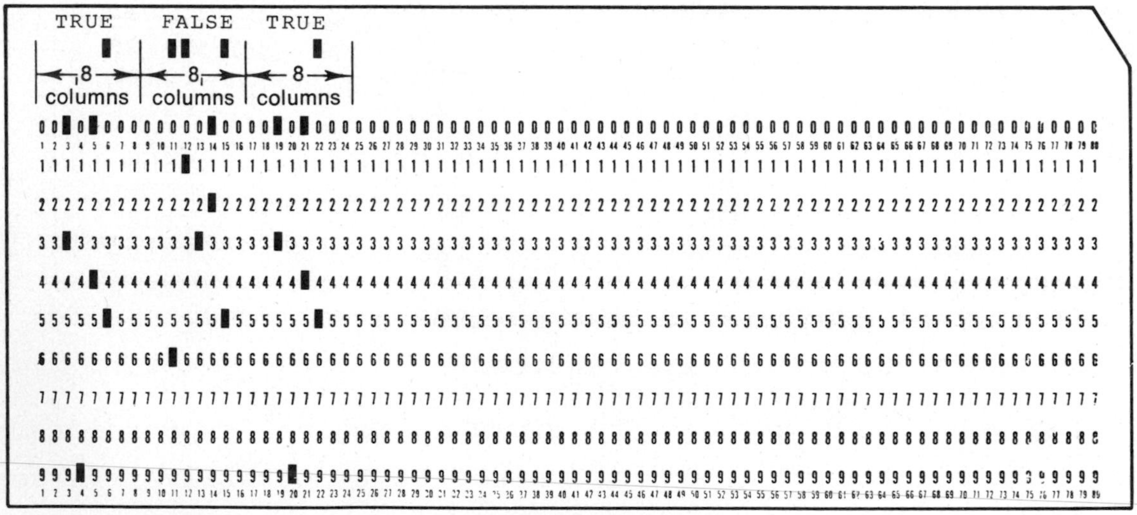

Figure 24-1

The logical values can be read and assigned to I, P, and RX this way:

```
      READ (5,45) I,P,RX
   45 FORMAT (3L8)
```

The code character in FORMAT's associated with logical values is "L". The FORMAT shown above defines three fields, each field having eight character positions. The logical values TRUE or FALSE, positioned anywhere within the defined fields, give the values to be assigned. Those values need not be completely spelled out. The letters "T" and "F" are sufficient to give the "true" and "false" values.

When printing logical values, the computer will print only the first letter of each value, "T" or "F". Example:

```
      WRITE (6,52) ZV,KMT
   52 FORMAT (1X,2L4)
```

Assuming that ZV's value is "true" and KMT's is "false", the program will give the output shown in Figure 24-2.

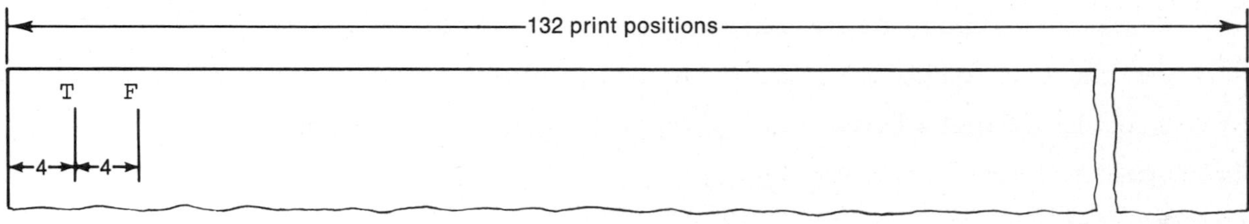

Figure 24-2

<u>LOGICAL IF</u>

We can now return to the logical IF statement to obtain a fuller understanding of how it works. Consider this IF statement:

```
      IF (SF.GT.AF) GO TO 95
```

The variable names SF and AF represent real values. If SF's value *is* greater than AF's value, then the condition being tested is "true". The program jumps to statement 95. If the condition gives a "false" result, the program goes to the next statement in sequence.

Here is a more complicated IF.

```
      IF (DG.GT.HM.AND.ELP.EQ.PLK) GO TO 800
```

The variable names DG, HM, ELP, and PLK represent real values. The program jumps to statement 800 if both conditions are "true". That is, if DG's value *is* greater than HM's value *and* if ELP's value *equals* PLK's value, the program jumps to statement 800. Otherwise, the program goes to the next statement in sequence.

The connector ".OR." and ".NOT." may also be used in

logical IF statements. Example:

```
IF (AX,LT.QQ.OR.BX.EQ.QQ) GO TO 400
```

The variable names AX, QQ, and BX represent real values. The program jumps to statement 400 if AX's value is less than QQ's value or if BX's value equals QQ's value. Otherwise, the program goes to the next statement in sequence. Consider this next example:

```
IF (BX.NOT..GT.63.5) GO TO 338
```

The variable name BX represents a real value. If BX's value is not greater than "63.5", the program jumps to statement 338; otherwise, the program goes to the next statement in sequence.

The above IF statement could have been written

```
IF (BX.LE.63.5) GO TO 338
```

Again, if BX's value is not greater than "63.5" (if it is less than or equal to "63.5"), the program jumps to statement 338. Otherwise, the program goes to the next statement in sequence.

The conditions in logical IF's may be much more complex than the ones shown here. You should give sufficient sets of parentheses within the conditions to be tested in order to define clearly their meanings. Example:

```
IF ((BX.GT.3.5.OR.TX.EQ.0.).AND.TDX.LT..52) GO TO 8
```

The variable names BX, TX, and TDX represent real values. The program jumps to statement 8 if TDX's value is less than ".52" *and* if BX is greater than "3.5" or if TX is equal to zero. Otherwise the program goes to the next statement in sequence.

A logical value may be assigned in one part of a program and tested in another. For example:

```
      READ (5,2) RLD
    2 FORMAT (L5)
      IF (RLD) GO TO 300
```

Assume that the variable name RLD has been declared to be

logical. If RLD's value is "true", the program jumps to statement 300; otherwise, the program goes to the next statement in sequence.

Another example:

```
      :
      :
HMH=SIG.EQ.ALP.OR.ZET.LT.3.3
      :
      :
IF (HMH) GO TO 396
```

The variable names SIG, ALP, and ZET represent real values. The program jumps to statement 396 if SIG's value is equal to ALP's value *or* if ZET's value is less than "3.3".

The LOGICAL statement may give dimension information. Example:

```
LOGICAL NR,TND(40),FL,RMS(100)
```

Two logical arrays have been defined, TND and RMS.

When dimension information is given in a type statement, the same variable names must not be shown in a DIMENSION statement. When there is a choice, the type statement must be used in preference to the DIMENSION statement.

EXERCISES AND PROBLEMS

1. What is a logical value?

2. What are the only two values that can ever be assigned to real variable names?

3. What is the code alphabetic character in FORMAT's that is associated with logical values?

4. Study the following program segment:

```
LOGICAL A,B,C
A = .TRUE.
B = .FALSE.
C = A.AND.B
```

What value is assigned to C?

5. Refer to Question 4. If the symbol ".AND." were changed to ".OR.", what value would be assigned to C?

6. Refer to Question 4. If the symbol ".AND." were changed to ".AND..NOT.", what value would be assigned to C?

7. Refer to Question 4. If the symbol ".AND." were changed to ".OR..NOT.", what value would be assigned to C?

8. Describe how logical values are punched upon data processing cards. Tell how logical values are printed.

9. Show some examples of the READ and FORMAT statements needed to read logical values from data cards.

10. Show some examples of the WRITE and FORMAT statements needed to print logical values on output paper.

11. Why is the word "logical" used in the term "logical IF statement"?

12. Study the statement:

```
D = X.GT.Y
```

How is the value of D determined? (Assume that D has been declared to be a logical variable name and that X and Y are real variable names.)

13. Study the statement:

```
IF (P.EQ.Q.AND.(R.LT.T.OR.A.EQ.B)) GO TO 6
```

Under what conditions will the program jump to statement 6? Assume that all variable names given are real.

14. Discuss how a logical array space could be defined. Tell what role a DIMENSION statement has, if any, in this definition.

15. If a variable name has been declared to be logical, can the same name be declared as real or integer later in the same program?

CHAPTER 25

Alphanumeric Processing and the CHARACTER TYPE Statement

The CHARACTER type statement is used when it is necessary to assign alphanumeric characters to variable names. As an example, if the variable QQ has been defined in a CHARACTER type statement like this

```
CHARACTER QQ
```

then the word, "DATA", may be assigned to QQ:

```
QQ = 'DATA'
```

The string of characters, "DATA", have been assigned to QQ. Now, QQ can be printed or used in a number of other ways.

The CHARACTER type statement must be given before any defined CHARACTER variables are used for the first time.

Numeric values can be assigned to variables that have been typed as CHARACTER, but those values may not be used for calculations. Example:

```
CHARACTER QQ,B
  :
C = 5.8
  :
B = '36.34'
  :
  :
F = B+C
```

The statement F = B+C is illegal. B cannot be used in calculations.

One of the uses of values assigned to character variables

is for the printing of messages. Here is an example:

```
      CHARACTER QQ,B,H*38
          .
          .
          .
      H = 'DATA APPEARS TO BE INCORRECT. RECHECK.'
```

The length of H has been defined to be 38 characters. (See "H*38" above.) (Where no size is given, the computer assumes a maximum of 8 characters in most FORTRAN systems.) The message,

DATA APPEARS TO BE INCORRECT. RECHECK.

has been assigned to H. Now, if the message needs to be printed in various places of the current program, it can be printed this way:

```
      WRITE (6,95) H
   95 FORMAT (1X,A38)
```

The code letter "A" is associated with variables holding character data. The computer will give the printed line shown in Figure 25-1.

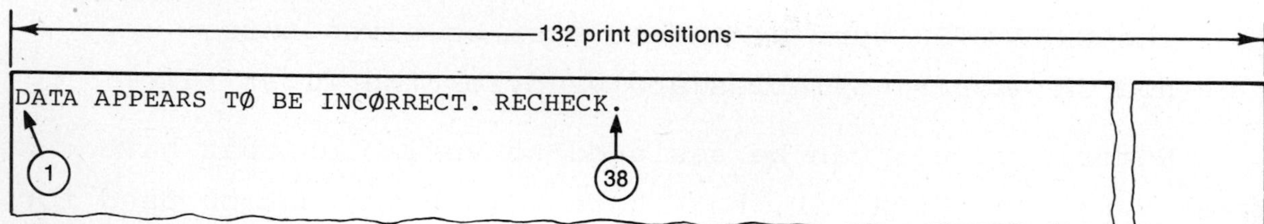

Figure 25-1

The message could, of course, be moved further to the right by defining blank characters in the FORMAT statement. Example:

```
   95 FORMAT (1X,20X,A38)
```

The message will begin at print position 21 on the output paper.

Character information may be read from punched cards. Suppose, we have this card shown in Figure 25-2, for example:

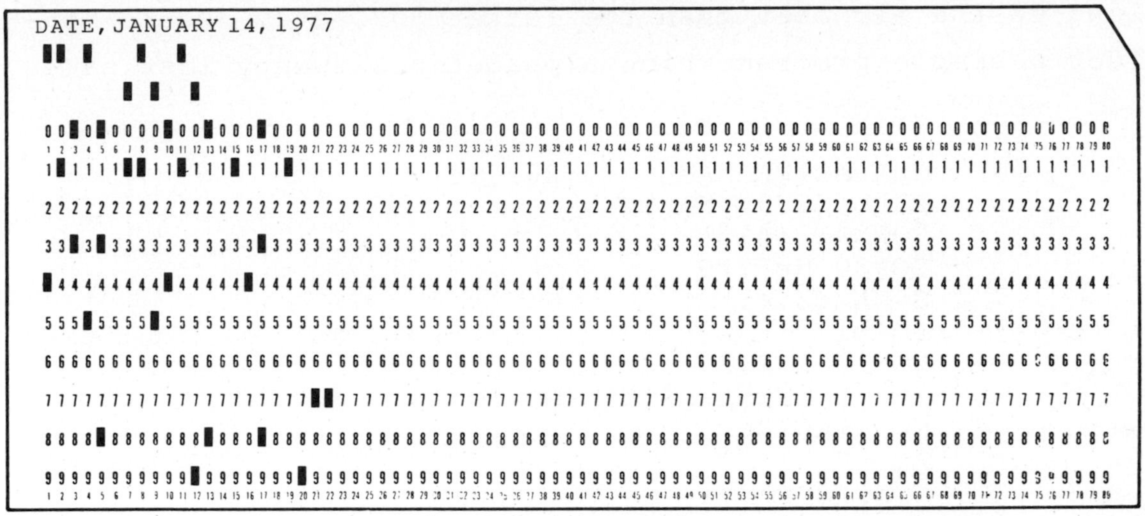

DATE,JANUARY 14,1977

Figure 25-2

The data on the card may be read this way:

```
          CHARACTER QQ,B,H*38,MSG*22
              .
              .
              .
              .
              .
          READ (5,8) MSG
        8 FORMAT (A22)
```

Now, MSG may be printed as needed in the program.

The size of an alphanumeric item may be up to 511 characters in length. Therefore, the entire content of a punched card can easily be read at one time. For example,

```
          CHARACTER QQ,B,H*38,MSG*22,CINFO*80
              .
              .
              .
              .
              .
          READ (5,8) CINFO
        8 FORMAT (A80)
```

causes all 80 characters punched on a data processing card to be stored in CINFO.

Since the internal representations of character data "increase" as the values of numeric digits increase, character information may be alphabetized. The name "SMITH", for example, is "larger" than the name "JONES"; the name "JOHNSON" is "larger" than the name "JOHNS". The letter "S" is further along in the alphabet than the letter "J", etc. Let's consider a simple program which alphabetizes twenty last names read from data cards.

```
      CHARACTER NAMES*15(20),S*15
      READ (5,9) NAMES
    9 FORMAT (A15)
      DO 30 N=1,20
      S=NAMES (1)
      LOC=1
      DO 10 K=2,20
      IF (S.LE.NAMES(K)) GO TO 10
      S=NAMES(K)
      LOC=K
   10 CONTINUE
      WRITE (6,20) S
   20 FORMAT (1X,10X,A15)
      NAMES (LOC)='ZZZZZZZZZZZZZZZ'
   30 CONTINUE
      STOP
      END
```

This program reads 20 punched cards into an array, NAMES. The array has been created to contain last names. Including trailing blanks, each last name has a length of 15 characters. See Figure 25-3.

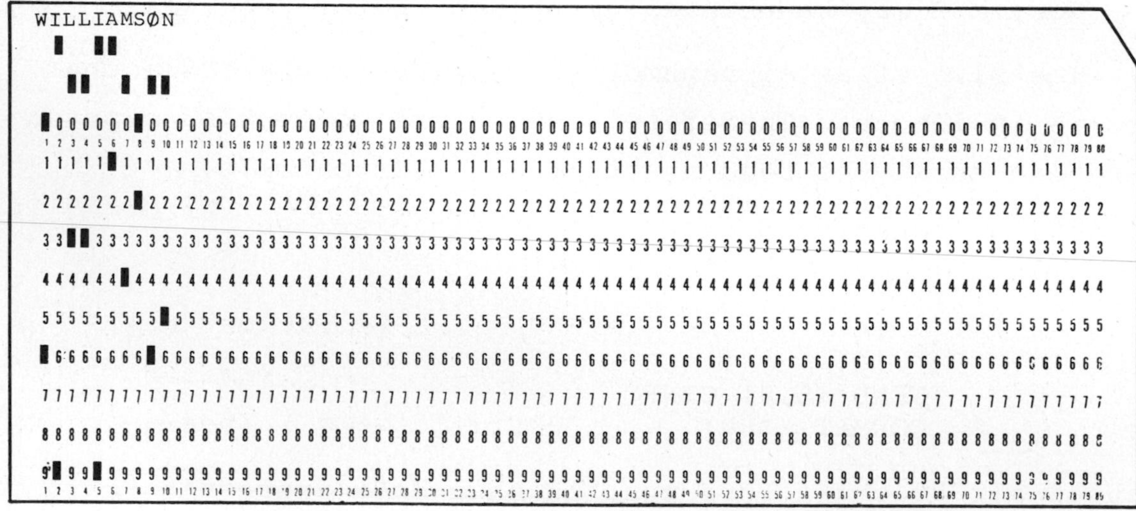

Figure 25-3

Next, the program initiates an "outer" loop to print the twenty values. The loop is controlled by the index, N.

An "inner" loop is executed to find the smallest of the twenty names. This loop is controlled by the index K. To accomplish the task, the first name within the NAMES array is assigned to S(1). Also, the numeric value "1" is assigned to LOC. The inner loop attempts to find name values that are smaller than S. Whenever that happens, S's value is replaced by the smaller name (the one lower in the alphabet), and LOC's value is changed to reflect the *position* in the NAMES array where the smaller name was found.

When the inner loop has been executed completely, S contains the smallest last name (the one lowest in the alphabet). It is printed. Then, that value within the NAMES array is changed to a large value, "ZZZZZZZZZZZZZZ". (LOC tells where the smallest value was found.) This new value is so large that all other last names in the NAMES array will subsequently be found to be smaller.

The second time the inner loop is processed, the next smallest name is found and printed. That name, too, will be changed to "ZZZZZZZZZZZZZZ".

In this fashion, all the last names will be printed. The last time that the outer loop is executed, the name found will be the only one *not* stored as "ZZZZZZZZZZZZZZ". That name will be the largest of the names originally placed in the NAMES array. Since all other names were changed to "ZZZZZZZZZZZZZZ", they now appear to be larger. The original largest name will now be found to be smallest. After it is printed, the program terminates.

As you have seen, the CHARACTER statement may give DIMENSION information. When it does so, a DIMENSION statement must not be used for the same variable name. When a choice is possible, the CHARACTER type statement must be used in preference to the DIMENSION statement.

EXERCISES AND PROBLEMS

1. What is a character variable? How is a character variable declared?

2. How does one indicate the size that a character variable must have? If no size is given, what does the system assume as a size?

3. What kinds of characters may one store in a character variable?

4. Show how the assignment statement may be used to assign characters to character variables.

5. Show how the READ statement may be used to load values into character variables.

6. What code character (letter of the alphabet) does one use in FORMAT's in association with character variables?

7. Show how one may use the WRITE statement to print character values on output paper.

8. May character variables be compared in logical IF statements? What is meant by the fact that one character value may be larger than another - or smaller?

9. Which character value is larger: "AMSTERDAM" or "AMPERE"? Also "BENSON" or "BENJAMIN"? Also "FW3" or "FW33A"? Explain your answer.

10. Study the statements that follow:

```
      CHARACTER WORD*20
      WORD = 'AMSTERDAM'
```

What are the 20 characters assigned to WORD?

11. Study the statements that follow:

```
      CHARACTER CARD*80
      READ (5,6) CARD
    6 FORMAT (A80)
```

Tell what has been assigned to the character variable, CARD.

12. Study the following statements:

```
      CHARACTER N*4
      N = '2467'
      I = N+5
```

Tell what is wrong with the computation of I.

13. May character array spaces be defined? Show how this is done. Tell what is the role of the DIMENSION statement in this definition.

14. Explain the difference between these two program segments:

```
      CHARACTER T*80
      READ (5,77) T
   77 FORMAT (A80)

      CHARACTER V*1(80)
      READ (5,78) V
   78 FORMAT (80A1)
```

15. Once a character variable has been defined in a program, may the same variable name be used in the same program, as an integer or real variable?

16. Write a program that reads all 80 characters punched on an 80-column data processing card. Then have the program test the character that was punched in column 25. If that character was a dollar sign ($), have the program print a message giving this fact. If the character was not a dollar sign, have the program print that fact.

CHAPTER 26

Combining Types in Statements

Various variable and constant types may be combined in expressions. These next examples show the most common kinds of combinations:

```
REAL A,B,C,D,E
COMPLEX F,G,H,O,P
DOUBLE PRECISION Q,R,S,T
LOGICAL V,W,X,Y
INTEGER I,J,K,L,M
CHARACTER U*4,Z*10,N*10/'NEW STREET'/
  :
  :  }     other statements not shown
  :
A = B+C
I = B+C
D = E+J
F = G+H
P = B+O
Q = R+S
R = T+A
N = I+J
V = W.AND.X
Z = N
```

These are the meanings of the ten assignment statements:

```
A = B+C
```

B and C are real values. Their combination yields a real result. The result is assigned to a real name.

```
I = B+C
```

B and C are real values. Their combination yields a real result. The result is truncated and assigned to an integer name.

```
D = E+J
```

E is a real value; J is an integer value. Their combination yields a real result. The result is assigned to a real name. (Some FORTRAN systems do not permit the mixture of real and integer values in expressions.)

```
F = G+H
```

G and H are complex values. Their combination yields a complex result. The result is assigned to a complex name. If F had been E, a real name, only the real part of "G+H" would have been assigned to E. The imaginary part would have been lost.

```
P = B+O
```

B is a real value; O is a complex value. Their combination yields a complex result. The result is assigned to a complex name.

```
Q = R+S
```

R and S are double precision values. Their combination yields a double precision result. The result is assigned to a double precision name. If Q had been E, a real name, the result would have been assigned to E but a portion of the significant digits in "R+S" might have been lost.

```
R = T+A
```

T is a double precision value. A is a real value. Their combination yields a double precision result. The result is assigned to a double precision name.

```
N = I+J
```

I and J are integer values. Their combination yields an integer result. The result is assigned to an integer name.

```
V = W.AND.X
```

W and X are logical values. Their combination yields a logical result. The result is assigned to a logical name. (Logical values may be assigned only to logical names.)

Z = N

N is a character variable that has been assigned the alphanumeric string of characters, "NEW STREET". That value is assigned to Z. It is not possible to combine character variables with arithmetic operators (+, -, *, /, **) or logical operators (.AND., .OR., and .NOT.).

The table in Figure 26-1 shows how four variable types, REAL, INTEGER, DOUBLE PRECISION, and COMPLEX can be combined with the five arithmetic operators shown above.

COMBINATIONS OF TYPES
IN EXPRESSIONS

	R	I	D	C
R	R	R	D	C
I	R	I	D	C
D	D	D	D	C
C	C	C	C	C

R = REAL
I = INTEGER
D = DOUBLE IMPRESSION
C = COMPLEX

Figure 26-1

The table shows that if a real value is combined with an integer value, the value is real. (The code "R" appears at the intersection of the row labeled "R" and the column labeled "I".) The table also shows that if a double precision value is combined with a complex value, the result is complex. (The code at the intersection of "D" and "C" is "C".)

To evaluate an expression having several variable types, a programmer may pair off the values and check the results, then pair off those results, if necessary, etc. Consider this example:

A = B + F + Q + I

The values of B and F are real and complex, respectively. The combinations table indicates that the result is complex. The values of Q and I are double precision and integer, respectively. The table indicates that the result is double precision. The two results - complex and double precision - yield the final result, complex. That result is assigned to the real name A.

When pairing off values to check them in the table, it does not matter which values are paired with which. The final result is always the same.

The table does not show logical and character variables because those types of variables cannot be combined with arithmetic operators.

Another consideration involving expressions has to do with what types of names may appear at the lefthand side of an equals sign. Real values may, of course, be assigned to real names; integer values to real names; etc. But, other assignments are also possible.

Real, integer, double precision, and complex values may be assigned to real, integer, double precision, and complex names in any combination. You should be aware of the fact, however, that part of a value may sometimes be lost. For example, a double precision value assigned to a real name may cause some of the precision to be lost. (A real variable name cannot always hold *all* the precision that a double precision variable name is capable of holding.) A real variable name can hold only the real part of a complex value. An integer name can hold only the integer portion of a real or double precision value.

The table in Figure 26-2 shows how certain values may be raised to various powers and what the results of those combinations are.

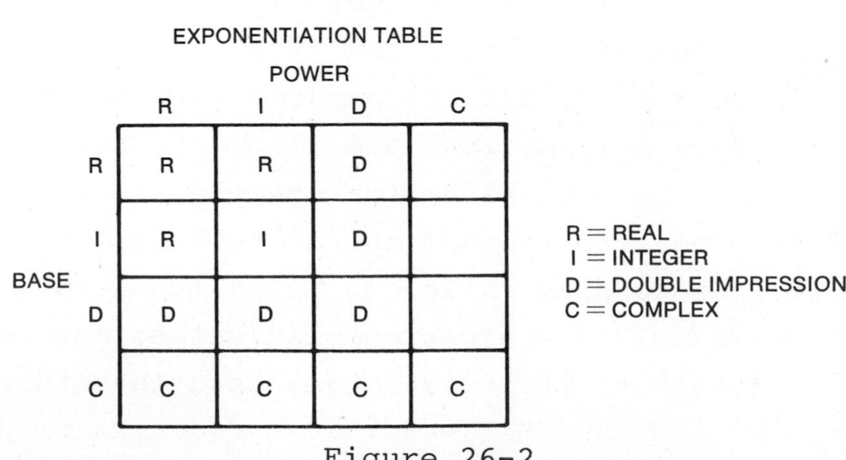

EXPONENTIATION TABLE

BASE \ POWER	R	I	D	C
R	R	R	D	
I	R	I	D	
D	D	D	D	
C	C	C	C	C

R = REAL
I = INTEGER
D = DOUBLE IMPRESSION
C = COMPLEX

Figure 26-2

The table shows that an integer value raised to a double precision power gives a double precision result; that a complex value raised to an integer power gives a complex result; etc.

Three combinations are illegal: real, integer, and double precision values raised to complex powers.

COMBINATIONS OF TYPES IN LOGICAL IF STATEMENTS

In logical IF statements, real values may be tested against other real values using the six relational symbols .GT., .GE., .LT., .LE., .EQ., and .NE. Integer values can also be compared with each other or with real values. Other combinations of variable types are permissible. The table in Figure 26-3 shows the valid combinations:

COMBINATIONS IN LOGICAL IFs

	R	I	D	C	L	CH
R	OK	OK	OK			
I	OK	OK	OK			
D	OK	OK	OK			
C				.EQ. .NE.		
L						
CH						OK

R = REAL
I = INTEGER
D = DOUBLE IMPRESSION
C = COMPLEX
L = LOGICAL
CH = CHARACTER

Figure 26-3

The table shows that an integer value can be compared with a double precision value using any of the logical operators. Also, a character value can be compared with another character value; etc. Some combinations are illegal: real, logical; and complex, double precision; for example. Some combinations are valid only for the logical operators ".EQ." and ".NE.". For example, one complex value can be examined to determine whether it is equal to another complex value, but it cannot be examined to determine if it is larger than the other.

IMPLICIT

The IMPLICIT statement may be used to designate the beginning letter of the alphabet for certain variable types. Example:

```
IMPLICIT DOUBLE PRECISION (R,T,V)
```

All variable names beginning with the letters R, T, and V are DOUBLE PRECISION in the current program. Thus, RL, TARE, VM, if used, are double precision variables.

The IMPLICIT statement may give a range of letters. Like this:

```
IMPLICIT COMPLEX (G-K,Z)
```

All variable names beginning with G, H, I, J, and K are complex variables in the current program. Also, *all* names beginning with Z.

The IMPLICIT statement does not affect the standard implicit typing of real and integer variables if those variable names are not mentioned in the IMPLICIT statement. For example, assume these statements are included in a program:

```
IMPLICIT REAL (R-T), INTEGER (A)
IMPLICIT DOUBLE PRECISION (V-Z), LOGICAL (F)
IMPLICIT COMPLEX (H)
```

If used, the variable names RS, SL, and TEMP are real; the names ALPHA, AMT, and AB are integer; the names VAL, W, XTRA, Y5, and ZETA are double precision; FT, FI, and F67 are logical; and HM is complex. Also, the variables GR, Q5, and ULTRA are real because the names begin with real letters that have not been redefined by the IMPLICIT statement. And, JR, KIM, and N are integer variables because the names begin with integer letters. Those letters have not been redefined by the IMPLICIT statement.

BUILT-IN FUNCTIONS

In addition to the functions already mentioned, built into the FORTRAN language: SIN, COS, SQRT, ALOG, etc., there are over 50 other functions that the student should be aware of.

Because of space limitations, we won't go into detail here concerning what these functions do. The student can do some independent research in this area if he or she wishes. A table showing the built-in functions follows:

BUILT-IN FUNCTIONS				
FUNCTION NAME	NUMBER OF ARGS.	TYPE OF		WHAT THE FUNCTION DOES
		ARGUMENT	FUNCTION	
ABS	1	Real	Real	Obtain absolute value
IABS	1	Integer	Integer	
DABS	1	Double	Double	
CABS	1	Complex	Complex	
AINT	1	Real	Real	Obtain integer value
INT	1	Real	Integer	
IDINT	1	Double	Integer	
AMOD	2	Real	Real	Obtain modulo value (first argument modulo second)
MOD	2	Integer	Integer	
DMOD	2	Double	Double	
AMAX0	≥ 2	Integer	Real	Find largest value amongst arguments
AMAX1	≥ 2	Real	Real	
MAX0	≥ 2	Integer	Integer	
MAX1	≥ 2	Real	Integer	
DMAX1	≥ 2	Double	Double	
MAX	≥ 2	Note 1	Note 1	
AMIN0	≥ 2	Integer	Real	Find smallest value amongst arguments
AMIN1	≥ 2	Real	Real	
MIN0	≥ 2	Integer	Integer	
MIN1	≥ 2	Real	Integer	
DMIN1	≥ 2	Double	Double	
MIN	≥ 2	Note 1	Note 1	
FLOAT	1	Integer	Real	Convert integer to real
IFIX	1	Real	Integer	Convert real to integer
SIGN	2	Real	Real	Transfer sign
ISIGN	2	Integer	Integer	
DSIGN	2	Double	Double	
DIM	2	Real	Real	Obtain positive difference
IDIM	2	Integer	Integer	
DDIM	2	Double	Double	
SNGL	1	Double	Real	Assign double to real
REAL	1	Complex	Real	Assign real to real
AIMAG	1	Complex	Real	Assign imaginary to real
DBLE	1	Real	Double	Convert to double
CMPLX	2	Real	Complex	Create complex value
CONJG	1	Complex	Complex	Obtain conjugate

BUILT-IN FUNCTIONS (Continued)				
FUNCTION NAME	NUMBER OF ARGS.	TYPE OF ARGUMENT	TYPE OF FUNCTION	WHAT THE FUNCTION DOES
EXP	1	Real	Real	Exponential
DEXP	1	Double	Double	
CEXP	1	Complex	Complex	
ALOG	1	Real	Real	Natural logarithm
DLOG	1	Double	Double	
CLOG	1	Complex	Complex	
ALOG10	1	Real	Real	Common logarithm
DLOG10	1	Double	Double	
COS	1	Real	Real	Trigonometric cosine
DCOS	1	Double	Double	
CCOS	1	Complex	Complex	
SIN	1	Real	Real	Trigonometric sine
DSIN	1	Double	Double	
CSIN	1	Complex	Complex	
TANH	1	Real	Real	Hyperbolic tangent
ATAN	1	Real	Real	Arctangent
DATAN	1	Double	Double	
ATAN2	2	Real	Real	Arctangent
DATAN2	2	Double	Double	Divide Argument 1
SQRT	1	Real	Real	Obtain square root
DSQRT	1	Double	Double	
CSQRT	1	Complex	Complex	
ARCSIN	1	Real	Real	Arcsine
ARCCOS	1	Real	Real	Arccos

Note 1: Argument may be real, integer, double precision. The value of the function matches the argument type.

In addition to the functions above, FORTRAN makes available a number of built-in subroutines that may be called as freely as a programmer's own subroutines. These are:

SUBROUTINE NAME	EXAMPLE OF CALL	WHAT THE SUBROUTINE DOES
EXIT	CALL EXIT	Same as STOP
SLITE	CALL SLITE (ZERO)	Turn all sense lights OFF
SLITE	CALL SLITE (I)	Turn ON sense light i
SLITET	CALL SLITET (I,J)	Test and turn OFF sense light i
SSWTCH	CALL SSWTCH (I,J)	Test sense switch i
OVERFL	CALL OVERFL (J)	Test exponent overflow
DVCHK	CALL DVCHK (J)	Divide check

PROBLEMS AND EXERCISES

1. Is it possible to add a real value to a double precision value in an expression? If so, what type result does the calculation give?

2. Is it possible to add a double precision value and a complex value in an expression? If so, what type result does the calculation give?

3. Is it possible to add a character value to a real value in an expression? If so, what type result does the calculation give?

4. Study this statement:

   ```
   X = R + C + D + I
   ```

   What type value does the computer obtain in the expression? Assume that R is a real variable name; C is a complex name; D is a double precision; and I is an integer.

5. Study the expression in Question 4. What would be the type of the result assigned to X if the statement were

   ```
   X = D + R + I + C
   ```

6. May a program compare two logical values in a logical IF statement? If so, give some details of which comparisons are valid and which are not.

7. May character values be compared in a program with a logical statement? If so, give details of which

comparisons are valid and which are not.

8. What does the IMPLICIT statement accomplish?

9. Study the following program segment:

```
IMPLICIT COMPLEX (G-K)
IMPLICIT DOUBLE PRECISION V-Z
IMPLICIT LOGICAL (F,T)
A = L + 3
```

What are the types of the variable names A and L? Explain your answer.

10. Write six IMPLICIT statements that divides the letters of the alphabet among the six variable types available in FORTRAN.

CHAPTER 27

The DATA Statement

The DATA statement, a non-executable statement, is used to assign initial values to variable names in programs. The values may be real, integer, double precision, complex, logical, and character. Example:

```
LOGICAL A,B,C
DOUBLE PRECISION D,E,F
COMPLEX G,H,I
REAL J,K,L
INTEGER M,N,P
DATA J,K,L/6.5,9.2,7.8/
DATA D,G,A/15.89275843D7,(2.5,9.7),.TRUE./
DATA M,N/8,4/,P,H/16,(9.2,-6.3)/
```

In this program, the initial values assigned to J, K, and L are "6.5", "9.2", and "7.8", respectively. Observe that the variable names have been defined as real.

The initial value assigned to double precision, D, is "15.89275843 x 10^7"; to complex G, "2.5 + 9.7i"; to logical A, ".TRUE.".

The initial value assigned to integers M and N are "8" and "4", respectively; to integer P, "16"; and to complex H, "9.2 - 6.3i".

Observe that a program may contain several DATA statements. Each of the statements may contain a mixture of the six value types already mentioned. The form of the statement is:

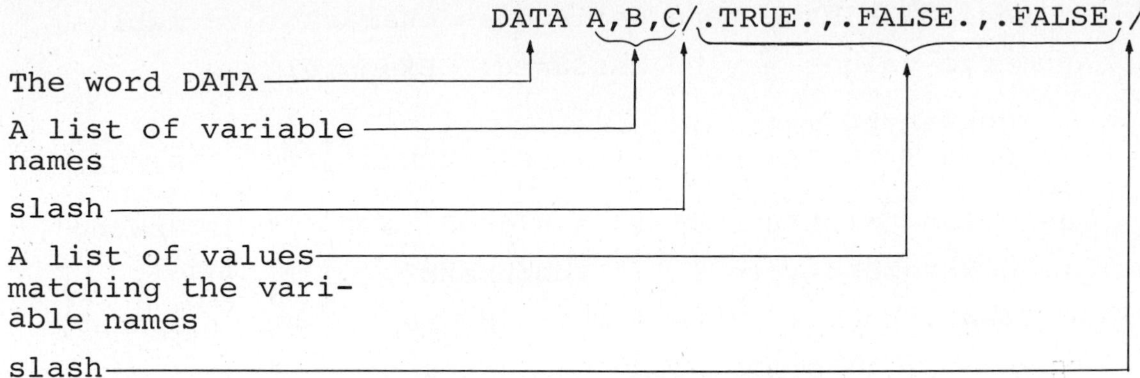

The same DATA statement shown above could have been written:

```
DATA A/.TRUE./,B/.FALSE./,C/.FALSE./
```

Observe carefully the placement of the commas in the statement.

If a variable has been dimensioned, all values may be assigned at the same time. Example:

```
DIMENSION KR(8)
DATA KR/4,8,5,3,9,12,15,6/
```

KR has been given a dimension of eight memory cells. If KR's name is mentioned in the DATA statement without a subscript, *all* values of the defined array must be supplied. The eight integer values are given between the slashes. These values are assigned as follows:

```
KR (1) = 4
KR (2) = 8
KR (3) = 5
KR (4) = 3
KR (5) = 9
KR (6) = 12
KR (7) = 15
KR (8) = 6
```

If subscripts are used, only the referenced array elements are assigned values. Example:

```
DIMENSION R(10)
DATA R(5),R(7),R(2)/5.6,9.1,2.3/
```

The value "5.6" is assigned to R_5; the value "9.1", to R_7; and the value "2.3", to R_2.

If variables have been defined as character variables, alphanumeric values may be assigned. Example:

```
CHARACTER T*10(5)
DATA T/'WILLIAMSON','SMITH','JONES','TY','PRINGLE'/
```

The value "WILLIAMSON" is assigned to T_1; "SMITHbbbbb", to T_2; "JONESbbbbb", to T_3; "TYbbbbbbbb", to T_4 and "PRINGLEbbb", to T_5. (The symbol, b, represents a space.) Each element within the array has a capacity of ten character positions. When the values are stored in T_1 through T_5, ten characters are stored in each location. As shown, some of the trailing characters may be spaces.

To print alphanumeric values, the "A" FORMAT is used. Suppose, for example, that we wish to print the contents of T_1 and T_3. The task could be accomplished this way:

```
      WRITE (6,18) T(1),T(3)
   18 FORMAT (1X,2A10)
```

The program will give the output shown in Figure 27-1.

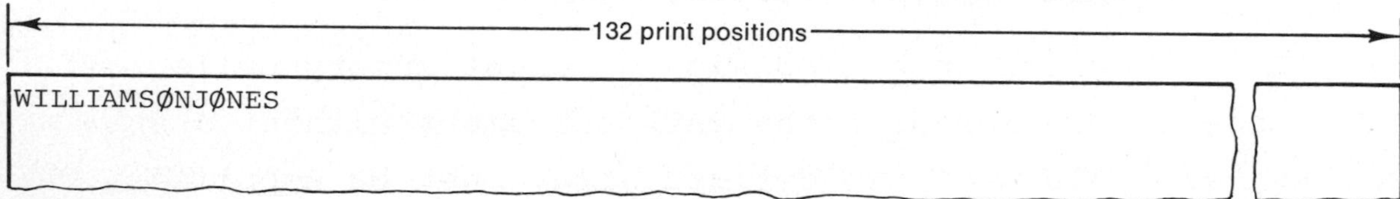

Figure 27-1

The value "WILLIAMSON" is printed within columns 1 and 10; the value "JONES", within columns 11 through 20. (The rightmost 5 print positions of T_3 are blanks.)

Below, a program is shown that uses the DATA statement to assign initial values. Note the use of the asterisk in two of the DATA statements. The asterisk acts as a multiplier. In the statement

```
      DATA Z/1.2,9*7.8/
```

the value "1.2" is assigned to Z_1, and the value "7.8" is assigned to the remaining nine elements of the Z array.

```
      DIMENSION Z(10),B(10)
      DATA X,Y/5.6,5.6/
      WRITE (6,3) X,Y
    3 FORMAT (' ',2F5.1)
      DATA Z/1.2,9*7.8/
```

```
      WRITE (6,4) Z
    4 FORMAT (' ',10F5.1)
      DATA A,B,C/9.1,2.3,8*3.4,4.5,7.8/
      WRITE (6,5) A,B,C
    5 FORMAT (' ',12F5.1)
      STOP
      END
```

When a request to execute the program is given, the output obtained is shown in Figure 27-2.

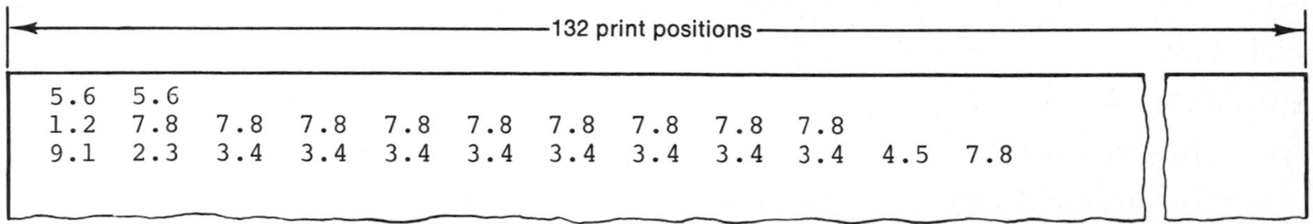

Figure 27-2

ASSIGNING INITIAL VALUES IN TYPE STATEMENTS

Initial values may be optionally assigned in type statements as well as in DATA statements. Example:

```
INTEGER I/6/,J(3)/8,7,2/,K/9/
REAL P/2.3/,R/7.9/
```

The value "6" is assigned to I. The values "8", "7", and "2" are assigned to J_1, J_2, and J_3. The value "9" is assigned to K.

The value "2.3" is assigned to P and "7.9" is assigned to R.

The punctuation is important in this type of statement. Observe where the commas are placed following various slashes. Also observe that each variable is assigned values before the next variable name is given.

The above INTEGER type statement could *not* be written like this, for instance:

```
INTEGER I,J(3),K/6,8,7,2,9/
```

BLOCK DATA SUBPROGRAM

The BLOCK DATA subprogram permits COMMON data to be entered

into labeled COMMON areas so that the data can be used by main programs and subroutines. (COMMON data may only be entered into labeled COMMON, not plain (blank) COMMON.)

A sample BLOCK DATA subprogram is shown below:

```
      BLOCK DATA
      DIMENSION B(4)
      COMMON /NN/C,A,B/RR/I,J
      DATA B/2.4,4.8,1.3,9.7/
      DATA I,J/33,24/
      END
```

The subprogram assigns values to the B array and to I and J. The variable names C and A are in the BLOCK DATA subprogram because they are members of the labeled COMMON area named NN. This labeled COMMON area is shown in the main and subroutine subprograms. Assume that this is the main program,

```
      DIMENSION B(4)
      COMMON /NN/C,A,B/RR/I,J
      COMMON W
      A=7.4
      C=4.8
      W=5.5
      CALL SUBDAT (SUM,ISUM)
      WRITE (6,19) SUM,ISUM
   19 FORMAT (' ',F8.1,I8)
      STOP
      END
```

and this is the subroutine:

```
      SUBROUTINE SUBDAT (SUM,ISUM)
      DIMENSION B(4)
      COMMON /NN/C,A,B/RR/I,J
      COMMON W
      SUM=A+C+W
      DO 50 K=1,4
      SUM=SUM+B(K)
   50 CONTINUE
      ISUM=I+J
      RETURN
      END
```

The main program calls subroutine, SUBDAT, and computes SUM. SUM is made up of the values A plus C plus W (those values are obtained from the main program) and plus the four values of B (those values obtained from the BLOCK DATA subprogram). The subroutine also sums I and J giving ISUM. The values of I and J are obtained from the BLOCK DATA subprogram.

The output from the program is shown in Figure 27-3.

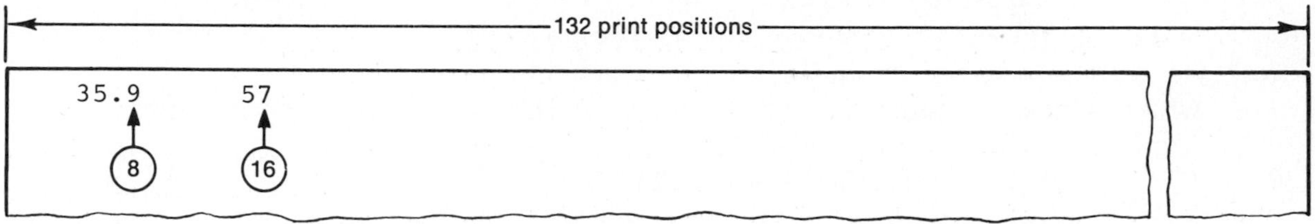

Figure 27-3

Since the BLOCK DATA subprogram's primary purpose is to give data, there must be no executable statements in the program. The subprogram must not be "called" in any way. It is automatically present when you take the trouble to prepare one and place it with the other cards of your job deck.

EXERCISES AND PROBLEMS

1. What does the DATA statement accomplish?
2. Show how "6.5" would be assigned to W and "-183" would be assigned to K in a DATA statement.
3. Show how all eight elements of the array, M, could be loaded with integer values.
4. Show how all five elements of the character array, WORDS, could be loaded with values. Each element in the array has a size of 3.
5. Show how a type statement can be used to declare R to be complex, and also how the same type statement can give R an initial value of "9.4 + 7.2i".
6. Tell why the DATA statement need never be used in a program. Give two alternate ways that initial values can be assigned in a program.
7. What is a BLOCK DATA subprogram? What does it accomplish?

8. Study this program segment:

```
LOGICAL A,B,C
REAL J,K,L
INTEGER N(15)
DATA N/4,7,3,6,4,3,7,8,4,7,1/
```

What do you see in the segment that's not correct?

9. Study this program segment:

```
LOGICAL A,B,C
REAL J,K,L
INTEGER N(15)
```

Give the DATA statement that will assign the integer values "7", "3", "4", and "5" to N_8 through N_{11}.

10. Give the type statement that will declare the name, LDX, to be a real array name for an array having 6 elements. Also have the type statement for LDX give those elements the values: "8.3", "-4.7", "-9.1", "7.3", "5.8", and "2.6".

CHAPTER 28

The NAMELIST Statement

The NAMELIST statement is one that has an appearance similar to DATA but is used for a different purpose. It is a non-executable statement and looks like this:

```
NAMELIST /X/A,D,C,I,L
```

In the current program, the variables A, D, C, I, and L have been assigned to a special name, in this example, "X". The name "X" is a special name called a NAMELIST name. A NAMELIST name may be any FORTRAN name the user selects. Ordinary variable names are associated with NAMELIST names. The variable names assigned to NAMELIST names may be real, integer, double precision, logical, complex, and character. Any of the names may be dimensioned.

A program may now read values from data cards without FORMAT's. Like this:

```
READ (5,X)
```

Observe that the READ statement references file 5 in the usual way, but instead of giving a FORMAT reference, the READ statement gives the NAMELIST name. There is *no* list of variables following the set of parentheses in the READ statement.

This program reads cards. Those cards have been punched and arranged as shown in Figure 28-1 on the following page.

There is a dollar sign punched in column 2 of the data card. Then, the NAMELIST name follows. A comma is given next. Then, FORMAT-free assignments are made to the various variable names shown in the NAMELIST statements. The assignments do not have to be made in any particular order and not all values need be assigned. Any values not assigned cause the corresponding variable names to retain the values assigned to them at an earlier time.

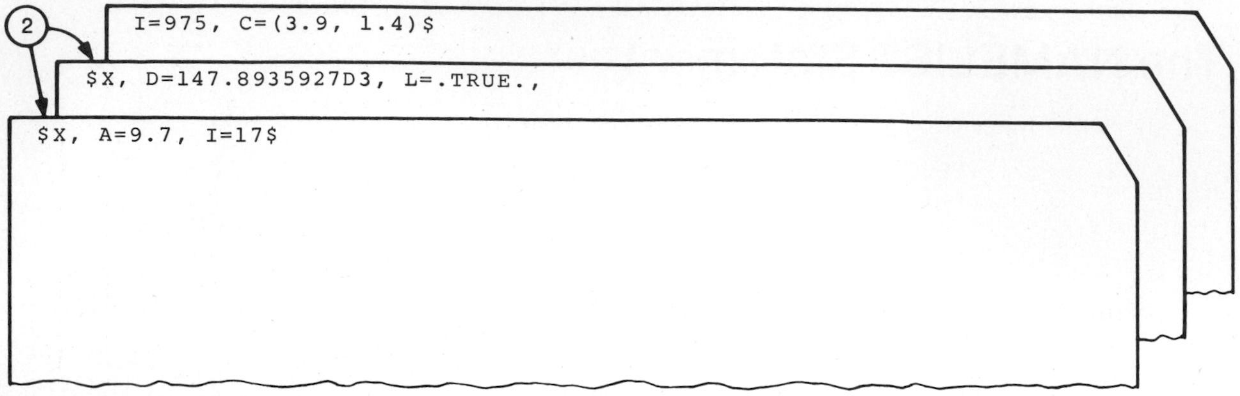

Figure 28-1

The assignments continue until a second dollar sign is detected. The assignments are separated by commas. (Blanks may be given following commas, if desired.)

In this example, the values "9.7" and "17" are assigned to A and I, respectively. The program then continues. When the program cycles back to the same READ statement (or one like it), the program assigns values again from dollar sign to dollar sign in the data cards.

Observe that the next READ statement causes values to be assigned to D, L, I, and C. Note the comma following the assignment to L. We have seen that variables A and I are real and integer, respectively. Variables D, L, and C are double precision, logical, and complex, respectively. These variable names must be declared in type statements preceding the NAMELIST statement. Like this:

```
DOUBLE PRECISION D
COMPLEX C
LOGICAL L
NAMELIST /X/A,D,C,I,L
```

(Variables A and I are assumed real and integer because those variable names are not declared in any type statements and are, therefore, implicitly declared.)

If a variable is dimensioned, some or all of the values

may be assigned at one time. Example:

```
DIMENSION J(10),R(5)
NAMELIST /F/J,R,T,W
READ (5,F)
```

The cards may be punched as shown in Figure 28-2.

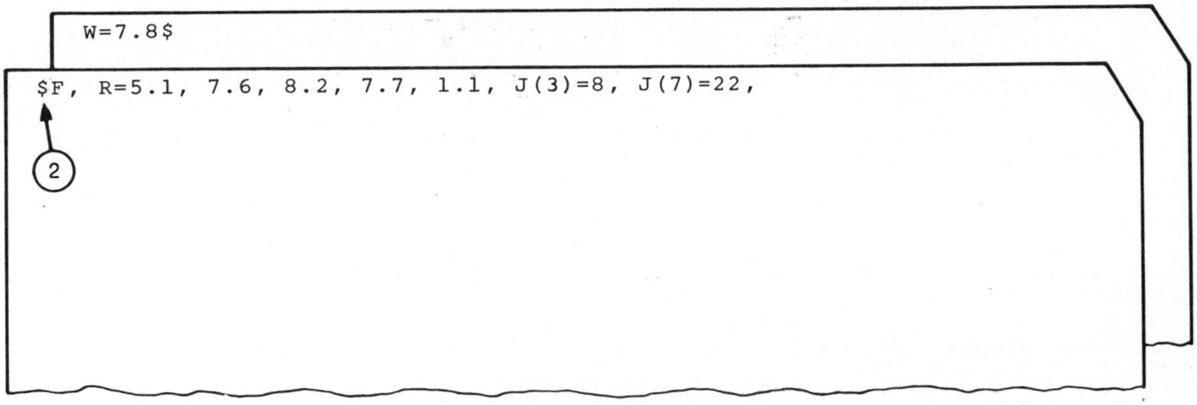

```
W=7.8$
$F, R=5.1, 7.6, 8.2, 7.7, 1.1, J(3)=8, J(7)=22,
```
(2)

Figure 28-2

The values "5.1", "7.6", "8.2", "7.7", and "1.1" are assigned to R_1, R_2, R_3, R_4, and R_5, respectively. The values "8" and "22" are assigned to J_3 and J_7, respectively. The value "7.8" is assigned to W.

Character information may also be read using NAMELIST. Example:

```
DIMENSION M*10(3)
NAMELIST /Q/M,JL,TD
READ (5,Q)
```

Study Figure 28-3.

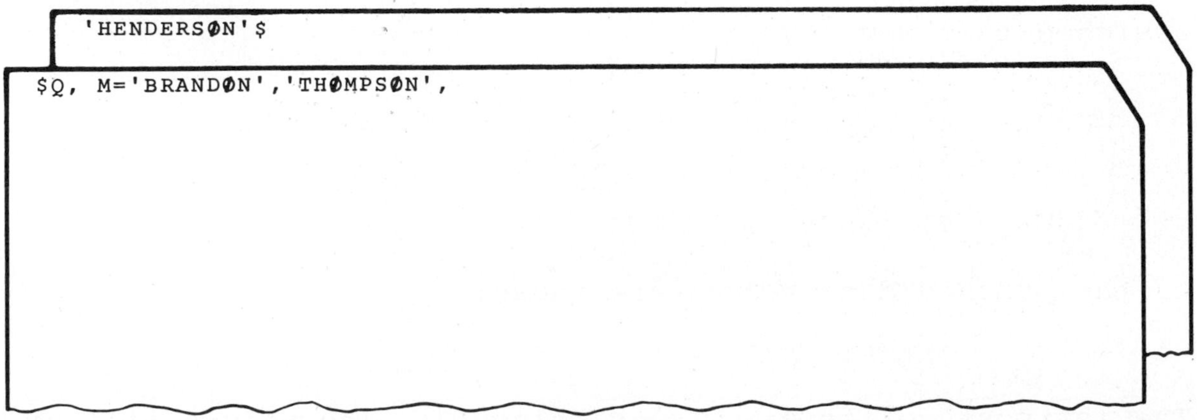

```
'HENDERSØN'$
$Q, M='BRANDØN','THØMPSØN',
```

Figure 28-3

The values "BRANDON", "THOMPSON", and "HENDERSON" are assigned to M_1, M_2, and M_3, respectively. (The size of each character value is 10.) No values are assigned to JL and TD during this READ. Later in the same program, the READ statement might be executed again. If so, the data card might appear as shown in Figure 28-4.

```
$Q,M(2)='ADAMS', JL=4, TD=9.1$
```

Figure 28-4

This time, the value "ADAMS" is assigned to M_2, the value "4" is assigned to JL and the value "9.1" is assigned to TD. To assign values to arrays, we've seen that a programmer may first set up a NAMELIST list this way

```
DIMENSION J(5)
NAMELIST /XLIST/J
READ (5,XLIST)
  .
  .
  .
```

then punch the data values this way:

```
$XLIST, J = 23,61,45,83,71$
```

The leftmost dollar sign is in column 2. The values will be assigned this way:

23 to J_1
61 to J_2
45 to J_3
83 to J_4
71 to J_5

If the punched data values are these:

```
$XLIST, J(2) = 61,45,83$
```

The leftmost dollar sign is in column 2. The values will be assigned this way:

61 to J_2
45 to J_3
83 to J_4

Since J_1 and J_5 are not affected by this input, those two variables will retain the values they had before the READ statement was executed.

NAMELIST can also be used for output. In this next program,

```
      NAMELIST /OUTLST/A,F,K,W,L
      READ (5,3) A,F,K,W,L
    3 FORMAT (2F10.0,I5,F5.0,I5)
      WRITE (6,OUTLST)
      STOP
      END
```

the program will read values for A, F, K, W, and L, then print them when the WRITE command is given. The output will give the name of the list (OUTLST) and the five values properly identified. The output could look like this:

```
$OUTLST
A = 0.45000000E 01  F = 0.98000000E 02
K =      237
W = 0.12345678E 03
L =      -34
```

EXERCISES AND PROBLEMS

1. What is the NAMELIST statement and what does it accomplish?
2. Is it possible for a numeric value to be assigned to a NAMELIST name?
3. Is it permissible for a variable name to be associated with more than one NAMELIST name?
4. What are the advantages of NAMELIST when used for reading values from punched cards?
5. What are the advantages of NAMELIST when used for writing output values?
6. Can NAMELIST be used with a variety of variable types? Give an example.
7. Can NAMELIST be used to load array spaces or portions of array spaces? Give an example.

CHAPTER 29

The DECODE and ENCODE Statement

In order to understand completely how the DECODE and ENCODE statements work, a person should have an in-depth knowledge of how information is stored in the memory of a computer. Space does not permit us to discuss internal representation of data exhaustively, but we can introduce the two statements mentioned above and give some ideas of what can be done with them.

DECODE

Suppose we have a deck of data cards. Let us suppose that each of the cards may have one of three formats. Figure 29-1 shows the first (Model 1 card).

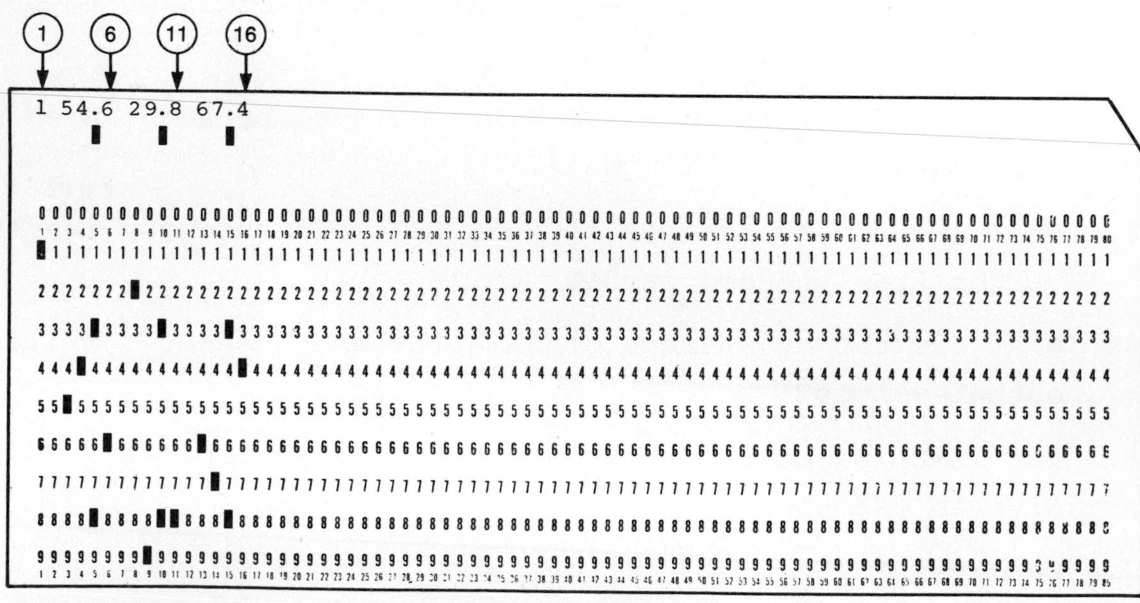

Figure 29-1

Figure 29-2 shows the second (Model 2 card).

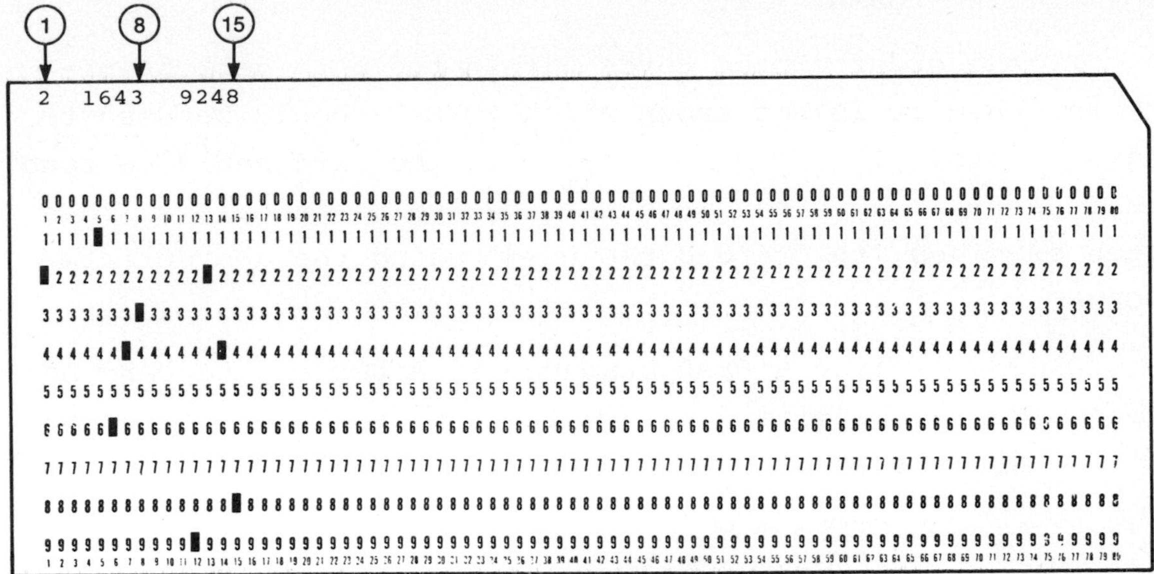

Figure 29-2

Figure 29-3 shows the third (Model 3 card).

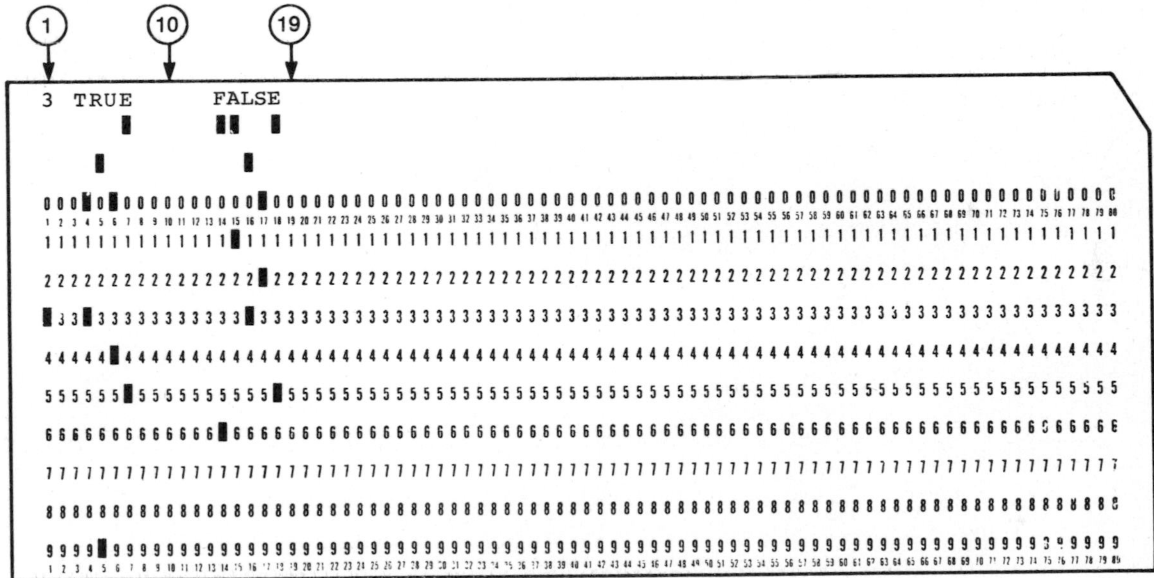

Figure 29-3

The numbers within circles show where various characters on each of the three cards are located. The first card should be read with a FORMAT like,

```
      8  FORMAT (I1,3F5.0)
```

The second card should be read with a FORMAT like,

```
      9  FORMAT (I1,2I7)
```

The third card should be read with a FORMAT like,

```
      10  FORMAT (I1,2L9)
```

If the order of the cards within the data deck is unknown, then it is not known which FORMAT should be used to read a card. It would be helpful if the card could be read in a *general way*, then when the code value in column 1 has been examined, to "reread the card" using the appropriate FORMAT.

DECODE is like a READ statement. After a data card has been read, it permits a card's image to be "read" a second time. Study this program segment:

```
          LOGICAL T,V
          CHARACTER X*18
      2   READ (5,3,END=500) KODE,X
      3   FORMAT (I1,A18)
          GO TO (100,200,300), KODE
    100   DECODE (X,108) A,B,C
    108   FORMAT (3F5.0)
             .
             .
             .
          GO TO 2
    200   DECODE (X,209) J,L
    209   FORMAT (2I7)
             .
             .
             .
          GO TO 2
    300   DECODE (X,310) T,V
    310   FORMAT (2L9)
             .
             .
             .
          GO TO 2
    500   STOP
          END
```

The program reads a card. The data on the card is assigned to KODE and to X. Observe that KODE is a one-digit integer and that X is an 18-position CHARACTER variable. Regardless of whether the card is a Model 1, Model 2, or Model 3 card, the characters found on the card between character positions 2 and 19, inclusive, are stored in the character variable, X. A value for KODE (1, 2, or 3) is always found in position 1 of each data card.

KODE directs the program to proceed to statement 100, 200, or 300. If KODE is 1, the program jumps to statement 100 and the data found on the card is "reread" in a different way (using a different FORMAT). If KODE is 2, the program proceeds to statement 200 for the same purpose; and, if the KODE is 3, the program goes to statement 300. (The GO TO statement, used in this example, is called a COMPUTED GO TO. See Chapter 34 for a complete discussion of the COMPUTED GO TO statement.)

To "reread" a card, the DECODE statement, *not* the READ statement, is used. DECODE gives the name of the character variable that holds the data to be reread. In the example, the data to be reread is stored in X.

If the program jumps to statement 100, the 18 characters stored in X are "reread" according to "FORMAT 3F5.0". The values found there are assigned to real variables A, B, and C. If the program jumps to statement 200, the 18 characters are "reread" according to "FORMAT 2I7". The values are assigned to integer variables J and L. If the program jumps to statement 300, the 18 characters are "reread" according to "FORMAT 2L9". The values are assigned to logical variables T and V.

After the information on each card has been processed, the program goes back to the READ statement to read another card. At end-of-file time, the program jumps to statement 500 and stops.

DECODE permits the examination and restructuring of any value that has been stored as a *character* value. Pictorially, DECODE permits a string of characters to be broken into a series of characters in the real, integer, complex, logical, double precision and/or character types. Figure 29-4 shows what DECODE can do.

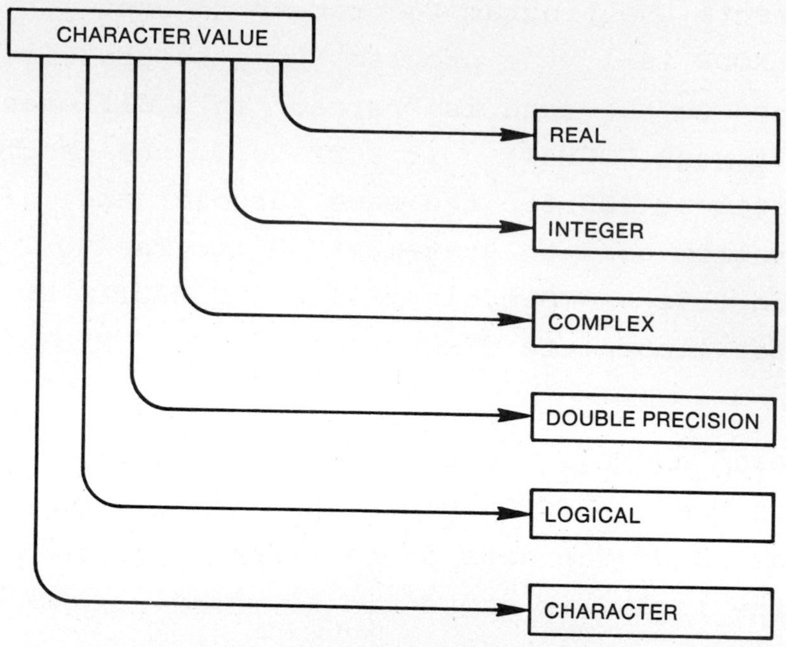

Figure 29-4

Consider this next example where 18 characters assigned to the CHARACTER variable W are "read" and restructured to form values of F, K, and Z:

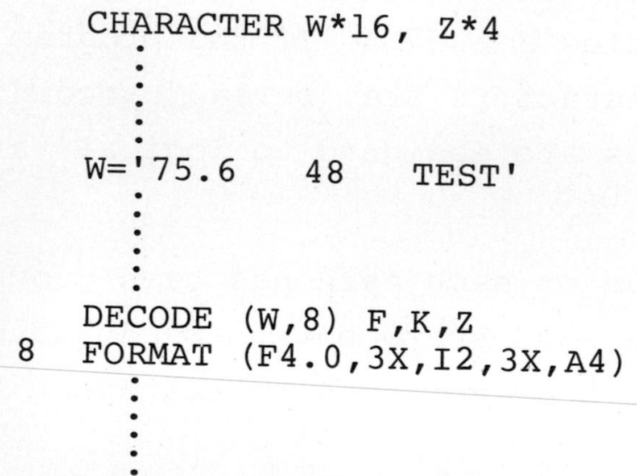

```
      CHARACTER W*16, Z*4
          .
          .
          .
      W='75.6   48   TEST'
          .
          .
          .
      DECODE (W,8) F,K,Z
    8 FORMAT (F4.0,3X,I2,3X,A4)
          .
          .
          .
```

The value "75.6" is assigned to F; the value "48" is assigned to K; and the value "TEST" is assigned to Z.

Another example:

```
      CHARACTER G*1(14),H*14
          .
          .
          .
      H='TEN FIFTY-FIVE'
          .
          .
          .
```

```
         DECODE (H,30) G
      30 FORMAT (14A1)
              .
              .
              .
```

The string of 14 characters "TEN FIFTY-FIVE" is broken in one-character elements and assigned to the array G. The values assigned are:

T to G_1
E to G_2
N to G_3
blank to G_4
etc.

Now, each of the characters that were stored in H can be examined or otherwise processed individually.

ENCODE

ENCODE permits various values in the real, integer, complex, double precision, logical, and/or character forms to be structured to build character variables. Figure 29-5 shows what ENCODE does.

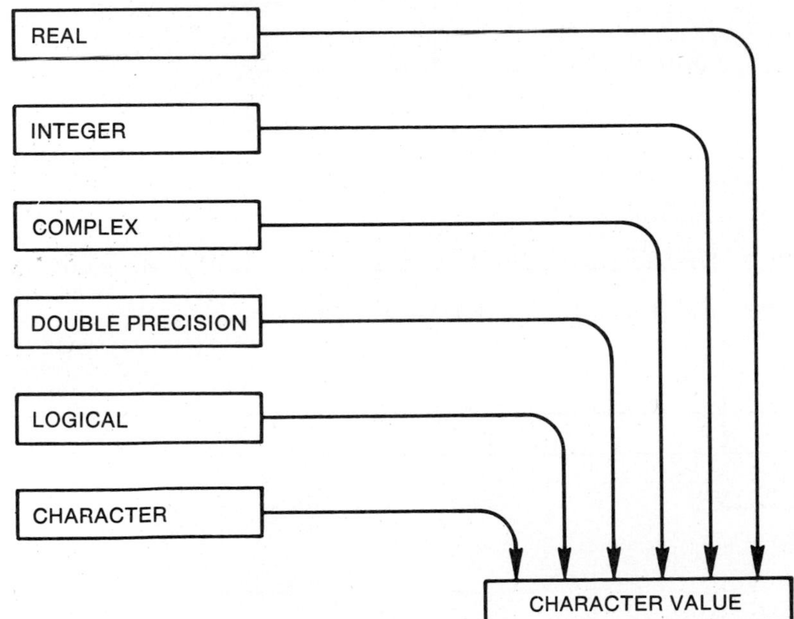

Figure 29-5

Example:

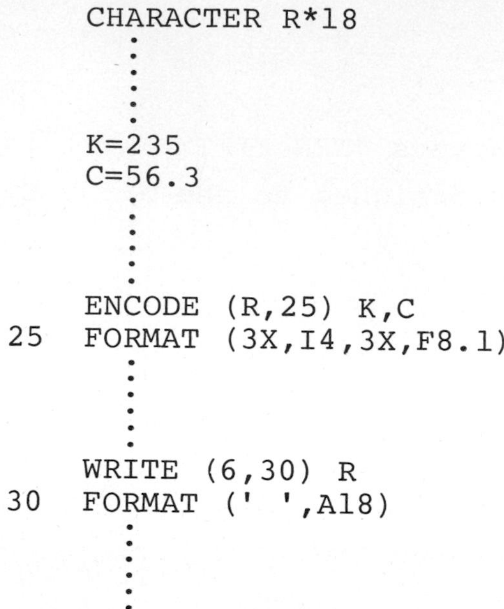

```
         CHARACTER R*18
             .
             .
             .
         K=235
         C=56.3
             .
             .
             .
         ENCODE (R,25) K,C
    25   FORMAT (3X,I4,3X,F8.1)
             .
             .
             .
         WRITE (6,30) R
    30   FORMAT (' ',A18)
             .
             .
             .
```

The integer value "235" and the real value "56.3" are installed as some of the characters of R according to FORMAT statement 25. Blanks are also placed in R. After the ENCODE statement has been executed, R appears as shown in Figure 29-6.

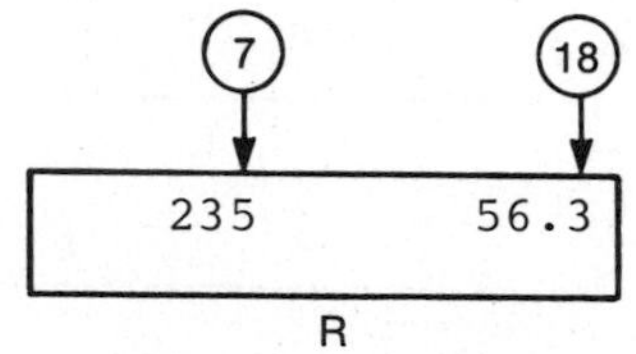

Figure 29-6

When the WRITE statement is executed, a line prints. The line appears as shown in Figure 29-7.

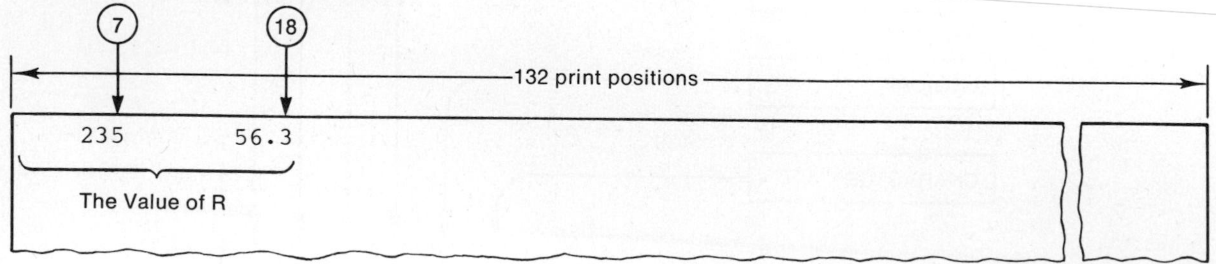

Figure 29-7

The next example gives another idea of what ENCODE can be used for.

```
      CHARACTER X*1(50)
      CHARACTER W*50
      DO 50 I=1,50
      X(I)=' '
   50 CONTINUE
      X(4)='5'
      X(5)='6'
      X(6)='7'
      X(7)='.'
      X(8)='8'
      ENCODE (W,60) X
   60 FORMAT (50A1)
      DECODE (W,80) Q
   80 FORMAT (F10.0)
      WRITE (6,90) Q
   90 FORMAT (' ',F20.1)
      STOP
      END
```

This program first establishes a character array, X, having 50 elements. Each element is capable of holding one character. The DO loop that follows places a space in each of the 50 character locations. Then, the individual characters "5", "6", "7", ".", and "8", are placed at X_4, X_5, X_6, X_7, and X_8, replacing the spaces there.

The ENCODE statement, given next, changes the 50 characters of X to a single character variable, W. The size of W is 50 character positions. In memory, W then appears as shown in Figure 29-8.

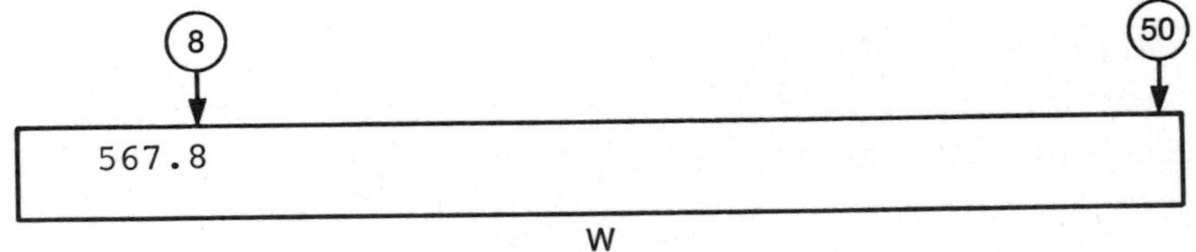

Figure 29-8

W begins with three blanks, and is then followed by the five characters, "567.8". These characters are followed by 42 blanks.

The ENCODE command has created a 50-character value, W, from individually placed characters into an array (in this example, X).

Using DECODE, the value W can now be "read" with the statements,

```
      DECODE (W,80) Q
   80 FORMAT (F10.0)
```

A real value is found within the first ten character positions of W. This value is assigned to Q, then printed.

VARIABLE FORMAT's

FORMAT's to be associated with READ and WRITE statements may be defined in a variety of ways during the execution of a program.

A FORMAT can be assigned to a CHARACTER variable, for example. Like this:

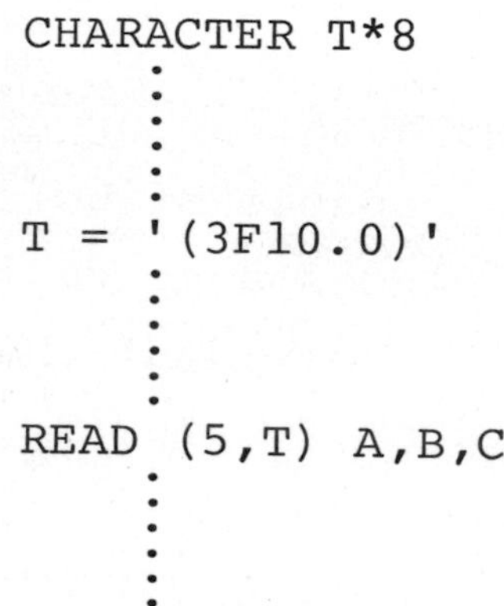

```
      CHARACTER T*8
          .
          .
      T = '(3F10.0)'
          .
          .
      READ (5,T) A,B,C
          .
          .
```

T, a character variable, is assigned the characters "(3F10.0)". This variable can be used in a READ statement to supply the FORMAT. The READ statement,

```
      READ (5,T) A,B,C
```

acts the same as if these statements had been coded:

```
      READ (5,7) A,B,C
    7 FORMAT (3F10.0)
```

A FORMAT configuration containing quotes may employ an alternate set of quote marks. Thus, T can be assigned this way:

```
      T = '("1",3F10.2)'
```

or

```
      T = "('1',3F10.2)"
```

T must be defined as a character variable having a size of 12. Like this:

```
      CHARACTER T*12
```

FORMAT's can be read from cards. Example:

```
      CHARACTER V*5
         .
         .
         .
      READ (5,20) V
   20 FORMAT (A5)
         .
         .
         .
      READ (5,V) M,N
         .
         .
         .
```

If a card has been punched as shown in Figure 29-9,

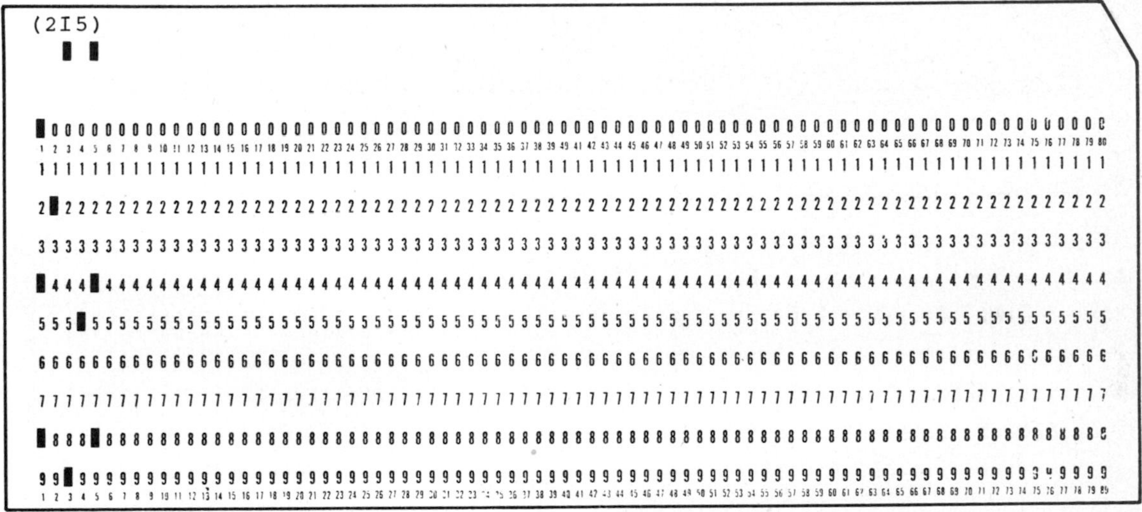

Figure 29-9

then the READ statement would function as if it had been written

```
      READ (5,30) M,N
   30 FORMAT (2I5)
```

A FORMAT may be defined in a DATA statement. Like this:

```
      CHARACTER G*18
      DATA G/'("0","END OF RUN")'/
```

then used like this:

```
      WRITE (6,G)
```

The WRITE statement functions as if it had been written

```
      WRITE (6,80) G
   80 FORMAT ("0","END OF RUN")
```

Finally, a FORMAT may be obtained from a punched card under NAMELIST control. Like this:

```
      INTEGER Y
      CHARACTER H*8
      NAMELIST /D/A,F,N,H,Y
          :
      READ (5,D)
          :
      READ (5,H) ALPHA, BETA, GAMMA
          :
```

If a data card has been punched as shown in Figure 29-10,

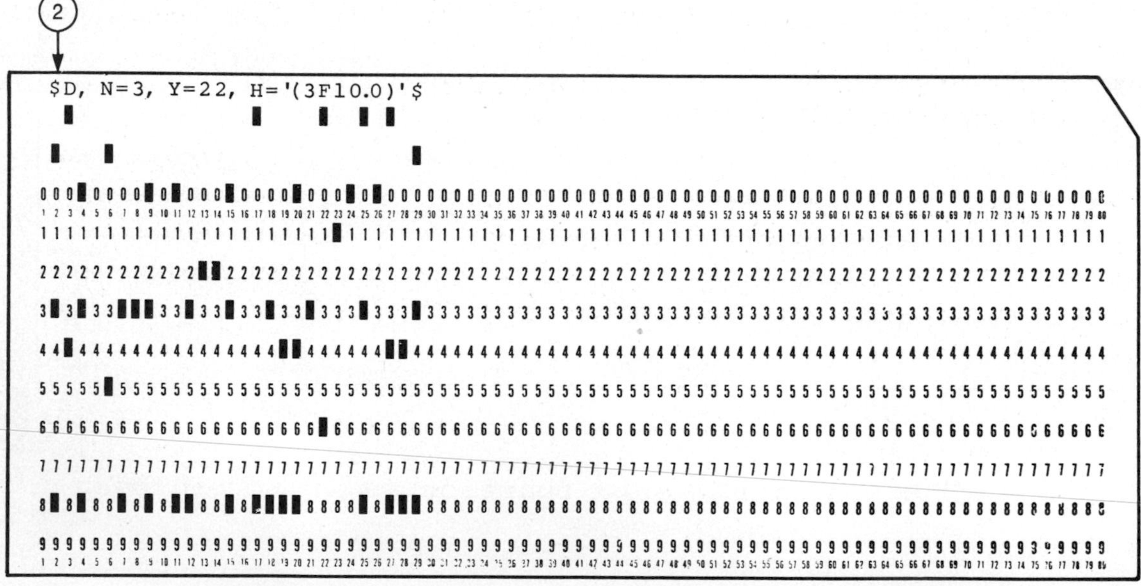

Figure 29-10

then the second READ statement functions as if these statements had been coded:

```
      READ (5,88) ALPHA, BETA, GAMMA
   88 FORMAT (3F10.0)
```

EXERCISES AND PROBLEMS

1. What is the DECODE statement? How can it be used?

2. What variable type holds the values that must be "read" using DECODE? How are those values assigned? Give some examples.

3. Show how a character variable having a size of 5 and containing a value like "31.88" can have the value transformed so that it can be used in an arithmetic expression.

4. Show how character values can be read from punched cards, then decoded in various ways. Show, for example, how the integer value "4678445804" can be read from a punched card and assigned to various integer names in various ways.

5. What does it mean to "reread" a data card? Why might it sometimes be necessary to read a card, check a code upon the card, then reread the values found upon the card?

6. What is the ENCODE statement? How can it be used? How would you compare the usefulness of the ENCODE statement versus the DECODE statement?

7. What is a variable FORMAT? How can variable FORMAT's be assigned to character variable names, then used?

8. Show how a variable FORMAT can be read under NAMELIST control.

CHAPTER 30

File Operations

A number of FORTRAN statements are oriented toward "file" operations. A file is an organized collection of "records" and a record is a set of related data items concerning some person or thing.

Consider a personnel file. It may exist on magnetic tape and as shown in Figure 30-1.

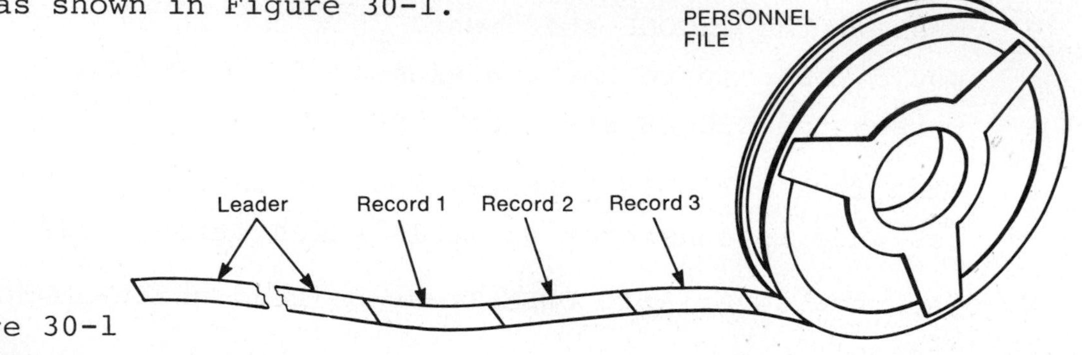

Figure 30-1

Record 1 is Bill Walker's record; Record 2 is Lucy Miller's record; Record 3 is Ann Macy's record; etc. The records are recorded in increasing sequence by social security number. Bill's social security number is 030-14-3697; Lucy's is 030-14-3709; Ann's is 030-15-2605; etc.

Each record contains social security number, pay rate, year-to-date earnings, and many other data values.

Files may be stored on magnetic tape, magnetic disks, punch cards and other media. When files are on cards, the entire deck is considered a file and each card is considered a record.

We have seen that when a statement like

```
20  READ (5,8,END=20) X,Y,Z
```

is given, a card is read. File 5 is reserved for cards. When a statement like

```
WRITE (6,9) D,A,B,C
```

is given, a line is printed upon the high-speed printer. File 6 is reserved for the on-line printer.

If a file is on magnetic tape or magnetic disk, a READ statement may contain a file number other than 5. We might see this, for example:

```
30  READ (8,10,END=80) F,P,N
```

File 8 is to be read. That file may be on a reel of magnetic tape or on disk. With the use of a JCL card, the file number is associated with an input device. Example:

```
$  TAPE    08
```

or

```
$  DISK    08
```

Similarly, an output file may be on tape or disk. A WRITE command might look like this:

```
WRITE (20,15) T,H,N,A
```

As with input files, file 15 may be associated with tape or disk by the use of JCL cards.

When reading from tape or disk, the organization of each record must be clearly known so that the FORMAT associated with the READ can correctly match the recorded data items. The size of an input record may contain any reasonable number of characters. Records may contain as few as two characters or as many as several thousands. It simplifies programming, of course, if all *input* records are of the same size.

When writing into a file, the desired organization of individual records is determined by the FORMAT associated with the WRITE statement. When designing *output* records, it would be well to plan them so that they all have the same size.

In addition to READ and WRITE statements, files may also employ REWIND, BACKSPACE, and END FILE statements. REWIND positions a pointer to the beginning of a file; BACKSPACE backspaces a file one record; END FILE places an end-of-file mark upon a file having been created.

Suppose we have a file on magnetic tape. We may read and process input values this way:

```
10   READ (9,15,END=80) A,B,C
15   FORMAT (3F10.0)
     D = A+B+C
     WRITE (6,20) A,B,C,D
20   FORMAT (' ',4F15.1)
     WRITE (25,30) A,B,C,D
30   FORMAT (4F8.1)
     GO TO 10
80   END FILE 25
     REWIND 25
90   READ (25,30,END=200) A,B,C,D
     WRITE (6,20) A,B,C,D
     GO TO 90
200  STOP
     END
```

This program reads 30-character records from file 9. It then makes a calculation and prints a line on the high-speed printer. The program also writes a 32-character record into file 25.

When file 9 is completely processed, the program places an end-of-file mark at the end of file 25 and rewinds file 25. File 25 is then read and values found within its records are printed. When that file is completely processed, the program stops.

In many systems, file 7 is especially reserved for punching cards. A statement like

```
WRITE  (7,9) P,Q,R
```

punches data processing cards in accordance with the FORMAT given.

On some systems, cards are punched in response to the punch command. This way:

```
PUNCH  9,P,Q,R
```

The values of P, Q, and R are punched in accordance with

FORMAT 9, which could look like this:

```
9 FORMAT (3F10.2)
```

The processing of files, when they exist on media other than punched cards and high-speed printer, is not difficult to master when one thinks of each record in a file as a variable-length punched card or a variable-length print line. The FORMAT's given in association with the READ, WRITE, and PUNCH statements determine how the tape and disk files are to be processed.

TIMESHARING FILES

In timesharing FORTRAN, magnetic tapes cannot be used. When a READ statement is given, the input must be obtained from the terminal or from magnetic disk files. When output is requested, it must be given upon the terminal or written into magnetic disk files. Examples:

```
400  3 READ (5,7) P,L.T
```

The input is obtained from the terminal.

```
450  8 READ (20,7) P,L.T
```

The input is obtained from magnetic disk file "20".

```
500  WRITE (6,20) X,J,N
```

The output is given upon the terminal.

```
550  WRITE (30,20) X,J,N
```

The output is written into magnetic disk file "30".

No JCL cards are used in timesharing FORTRAN.

There is a good deal more to be learned about files and their usage, but much of the additional material requires that a person have at least some experience in writing FORTRAN programs and understand, at least to some degree, the internal representation of data.

Students who wish to do so, may refer to the computer manufacturer's FORTRAN reference manual and research the topics of reading and writing of files. The manual also contains information on how to deal with randomly organized files.

EXERCISES AND PROBLEMS

1. What is a file? Upon what media can files be stored? What is a record?

2. What are the two standard files used in FORTRAN? What are those file's file codes? (What are the file numbers associated with the two files?)

3. Give a READ statement that causes data to be read from a file other than a card file.

4. How are files, other than card files, associated with external sources? (How does one tell the system where a file is stored?)

5. Give a WRITE statement that causes the system to write upon a file that is not a printer file.

6. Give the FORTRAN statements that are specifically oriented toward magnetic tape and magnetic disk files.

7. What command may a programmer use in order to have the system punch data processing cards.

8. When writing upon magnetic tape and/or magnetic disk, why aren't printer control characters given in the corresponding FORMAT's?

CHAPTER 31

Unformatted Output

Many FORTRAN systems permit unformatted output. The appearance of this output often leaves something to be desired but, as a debugging tool, unformatted output can be a time-saver.

Consider this example:

```
      DO 80 K=1,10
      PRINT, K
   80 CONTINUE
      STOP
      END
```

The PRINT statement gives no FORMAT reference. The program will employ a *standard* FORMAT when printing the output. The output will appear as shown in Figure 31-1.

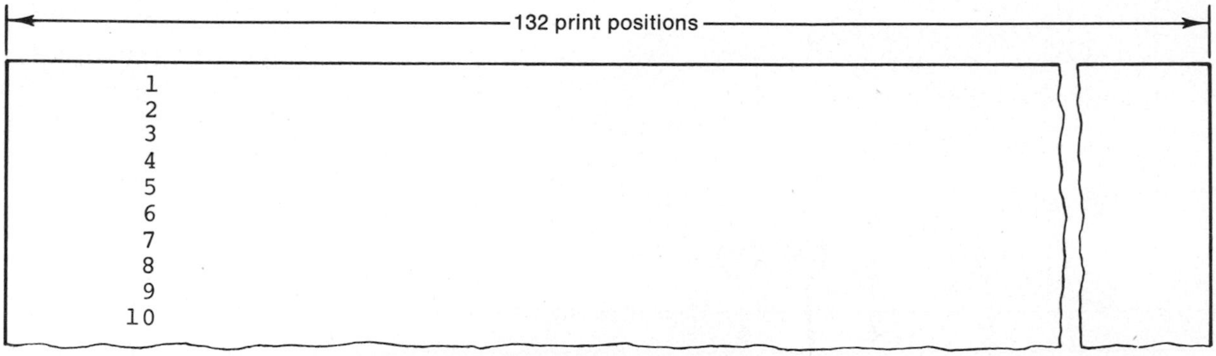

```
|<------------------------ 132 print positions ------------------------>|
       1
       2
       3
       4
       5
       6
       7
       8
       9
      10
```

Figure 31-1

Sixteen print positions are used to print each integer value. There are fifteen blanks ahead of integers "1", "2", "3", etc. There are fourteen blanks ahead of integer "10".

Real values are printed in exponential notation employing 16 print positions. Thus, in response to

```
PRINT,W
```

the program might print the line shown in Figure 31-2.

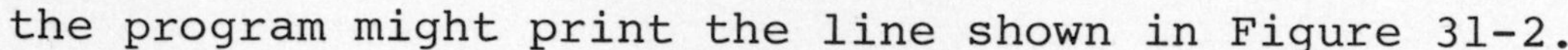

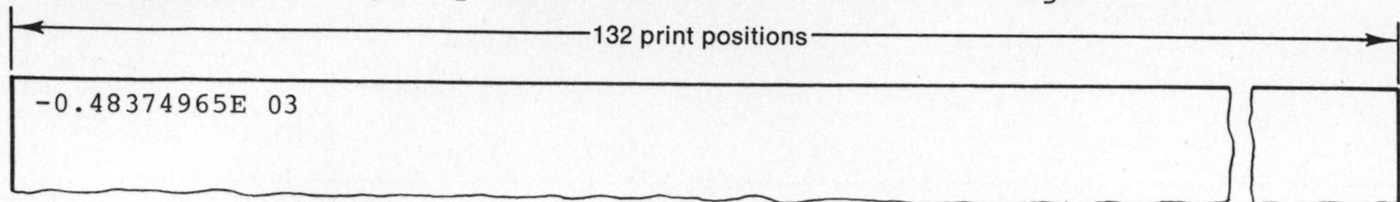

Figure 31-2

There is one blank ahead of the minus sign.

When printing values in unformatted forms, the program gives the values in accordance with the way they've been typed. If values are integer, they are printed in integer form; if real, in exponential form; if complex, in 2-part exponential form; if double precision, in double-precision exponential form; and if logical, in "T" or "F" form. Example:

```
REAL A,B,C
INTEGER J,K,L
DOUBLE PRECISION D,E,F
LOGICAL P,Q,R
COMPLEX T,U,V
A=-4.5
J=175
D=36496.3643763
P=.TRUE.
Q=.FALSE.
T=(1.5,-2.3)
PRINT, A,J
PRINT,D
PRINT,P,Q
PRINT,T
STOP
END
```

The program will print this:

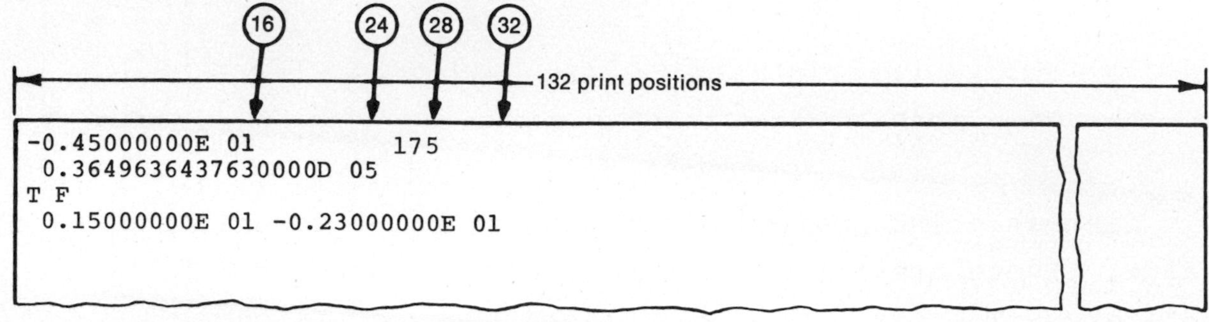

Figure 31-3

Compare the printed results with the program. Observe that double precision values require more print positions than real, integer, and logical values; but that complex values require more print positions than any other type.

Character values can be printed in unformatted form also. For example,

```
PRINT, "THIS IS A COST REPORT"
```

will appear as shown in Figure 31-4.

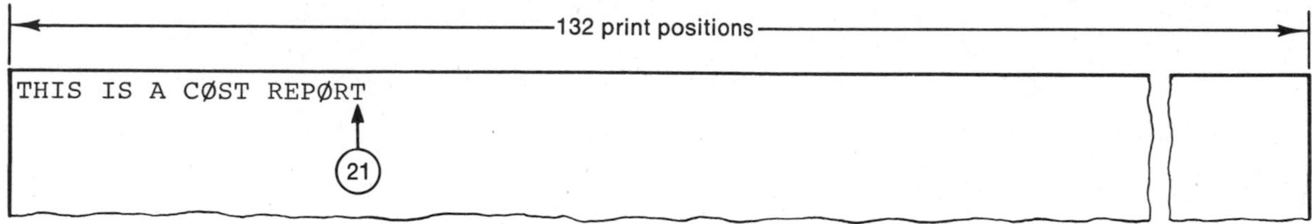

Figure 31-4

Study, also, this program:

```
CHARACTER AA*17,BB*18
AA='JANUARY 23, 1978 '
BB='YEAR-TO-DATE COSTS'
PRINT,AA,BB
STOP
END
```

The program will print the line shown in Figure 31-5.

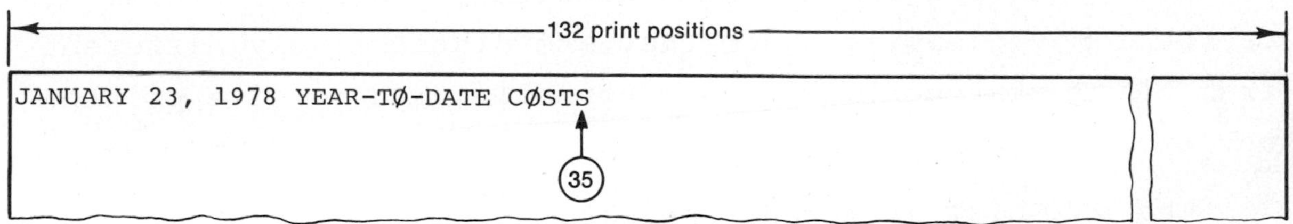

Figure 31-5

Extra blanks can be inserted between the printed values by writing the PRINT statement this way:

```
PRINT, AA,'   ',BB
```

There are three blanks defined within the quote marks.

We suggested that unformatted output can be employed as a debugging tool. If programs don't execute properly, a programmer might insert PRINT statements at carefully-selected positions in a program. This way:

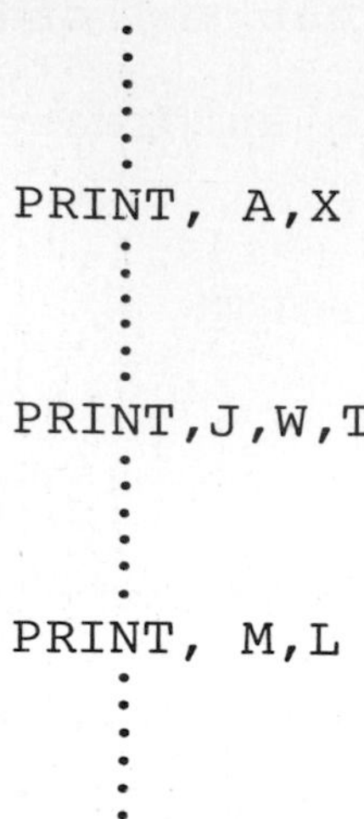

```
PRINT, A,X

PRINT,J,W,T

PRINT, M,L
```

When the program encounters these statements, it will print the current values of A, X, J, W, T, M, and L. The programmer can examine the printed output to determine why the program isn't executing properly. If the PRINT statements given in the example are within a loop, the corresponding values are printed over and over, thus, providing a "moving picture" of what is going on in the program.

After the program has been debugged, the PRINT statements can be removed easily since they are distinctively different from WRITE statements that are normally used to give printed output.

The NAMELIST statement can also be used to provide unformatted output. For example, if these NAMELIST statements have been defined in a program:

```
LOGICAL P,Q,W
DOUBLE PRECISION ZK
NAMELIST /L/X,Y,Z
NAMELIST /M/P,Q,I,ZK/N/W,X,K
```

Then these WRITE statements may be given:

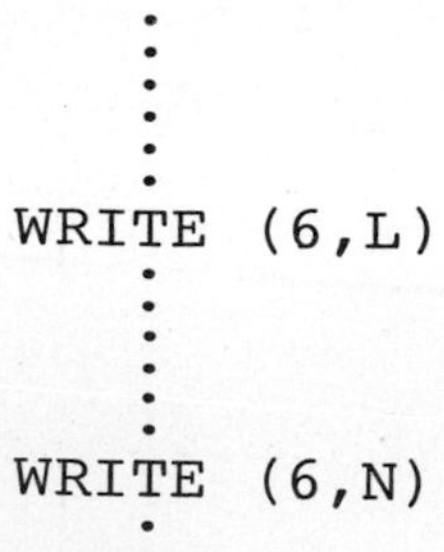

```
WRITE (6,L)

WRITE (6,N)
```

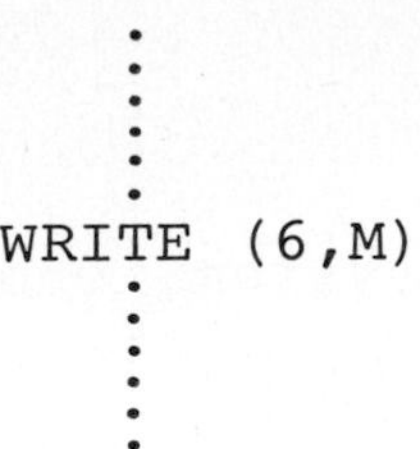

When WRITE (6,L) is encountered, the program might print lines like those shown in Figure 31-6.

132 print positions

```
X = 0.36472894E 03     Y = 0.48374030E 02
Z = 0.12000000E 04
```

Figure 31-6

When WRITE (6,M) is encountered, the program might print lines like those shown in Figure 31-7.

132 print positions

```
P = T   Q = F   I = 1272434832
ZK = 0.224943260000000D 03
```

Figure 31-7

And, when WRITE (6,N) is encountered, the program might print lines like those shown in Figure 31-8.

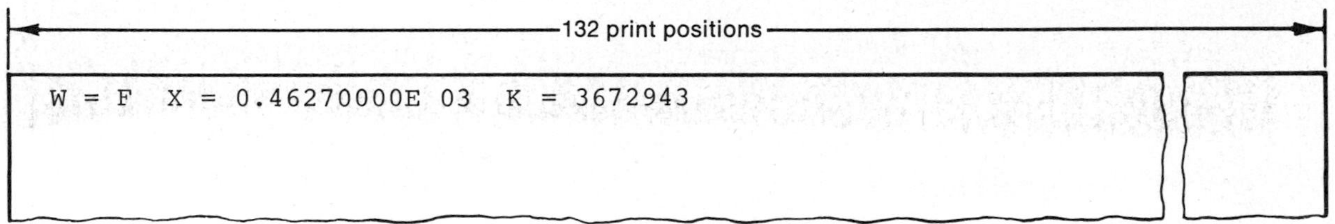

Figure 31-8

Students should be aware of the fact that unformatted output, when available, is likely to differ slightly from system to system. For example, some systems require a colon rather than a comma in PRINT statements. Example:

```
PRINT: W,K,N
```

Others require an asterisk and a comma following the word

PRINT. Like this:

```
PRINT*, M,T,X,L
```

If "PRINT," doesn't work in your system, check out "PRINT:" and "PRINT*,".

Some FORTRAN systems permit calculations to be performed and printed at the same time. Suppose, for example, we need to print the value of "22 x K" and "Y - 3.9". The PRINT statement could look like this:

```
PRINT,22*K,Y-3.9
```

The printout could then appear as shown in Figure 31-9. (Assume K's value is 6 and Y's value is 180.2.)

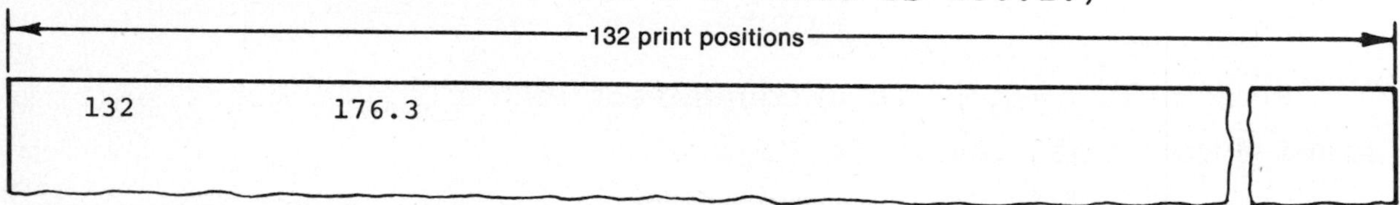

Figure 31-9

EXERCISES AND PROBLEMS

1. What is meant by the term "unformatted output"?
2. Why does unformatted output "leave something to be desired"?
3. Why is the use of unformatted output a useful debugging tool?
4. Show how messages such as "ERROR IN DATA" or "END OF JOB" can be printed without the use of a FORMAT.
5. Show how the NAMELIST statement can be used to give unformatted output.
6. Show how a PRINT statement can be used to compute and give the results of calculations.

CHAPTER 32

Random Numbers

Some FORTRAN systems provide the facility to obtain and work with "random" numbers. These numbers can be used for statistical problems. Consider this example:

```
      DO 30 K=1,5
      A=RND(X)
      WRITE (6,4) A
    4 FORMAT (' ',F10.7)
   30 CONTINUE
      STOP
      END
```

The program will print five numbers similar to these:

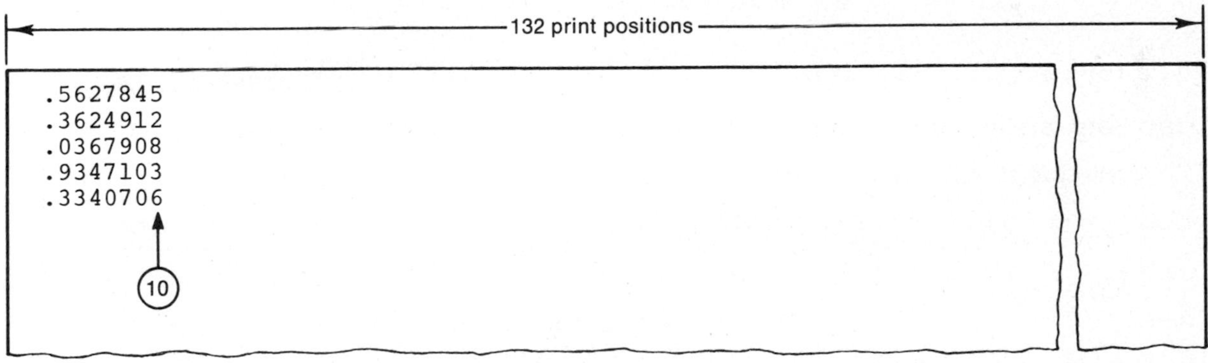

Figure 32-1

Random numbers lie between "0" and "1". (It is possible to obtain zero but not "1".) Every possible number within that range has as much chance to appear as any other.

When one is requested, the computer uses an elaborate formula to give a random number. The objective is to give a number that cannot be predicted ahead of time. The function that provides the random number is RND. The argument given in parentheses may or may not have any significance depending upon how RND has been implemented in various systems. As an example, in some systems the statement shown below may be used.

```
W = RND(X)
```

The argument, X, accomplishes nothing. It is present merely to enable the RND function to present an appearance similar to that of other functions. Whenever the program is run, the *same* sequence of random numbers is always given. This is the system's "standard" sequence of random numbers.

The statement

```
W = RND(34.8)
```

selects a *repeatable* point within the random number series, a series that contains several million numbers. Example:

```
      W=RND(34.8)
      DO 30 K=1,5
      W=RND(X)
      WRITE (6,4) W
    4 FORMAT (' ',F10.7)
   30 CONTINUE
      STOP
      END
```

This program gives five random numbers. These numbers can be repeated from time to time whenever the value "34.8" is used as the argument in the RND function. Observe that the initializing "W=RND(34.8)" statement is executed only once. Any real positive value may be placed within parentheses. The resulting series of random numbers will appear to bear no connection with the argument given.

A non-repeatable list of random numbers can be obtained if the value of the first argument is negative. Example:

```
      W=RND(-1.)
      DO 30 K=1,5
      W=RND(X)
      WRITE (6,4) W
    4 FORMAT (' ',F10.7)
   30 CONTINUE
      STOP
      END
```

Any negative number given as the RND argument will give

the non-repeatable series of random numbers. If the program is executed more than once, the program will give a *different* series of random numbers each time.

Normally, a repeatable series of random numbers is desirable during the time that a program is being debugged. The non-repeatable series is useful for production runs *after* the program has been debugged.

To illustrate in a very simple program how random numbers can be used, let's simulate the tossing of 1000 coins. We wish to know how many times heads will turn up, and how many times tails will appear.

We arbitrarily decide that all values of random numbers less than ".5" represent tails and all values of random numbers equal to or greater than ".5" represent heads. These assignments exactly divide the random number range in half. (Recall that zero can appear as a random number but that "1." cannot.)

The program to simulate the tossing of coins is this:

```
      JT=0
      R=RND(-1.)
      DO 20 N=1,1000
      R=RND(X)
      IF (R.GE..5) GO TO 20
      JT=JT+1
   20 CONTINUE
      JH=1000-JT
      WRITE (6,30) JT
   30 FORMAT (' ','TAILS=',I5)
      WRITE (6,40) JH
   40 FORMAT (' ','HEADS=',I5)
      STOP
      END
```

If your FORTRAN system does not have a random number generator, you may want to use the random number subroutine that follows. This routine gives several thousand random numbers before the series begins to repeat.

```
      SUBROUTINE RND(IR,R)
      IP1=4093
      IP2=1044479
      IZ =IR*IP1
```

```
      IR =IZ-((IZ/IP2)*IP2)
      R  =FLOAT(IR)/FLOAT(IP2)
      RETURN
      END
```

To use the random number subroutine, one should call the subroutine, giving it an *odd* integer value assigned to IR (any integer value greater than 12300 can be used.) The subroutine will generate a random number and return it with the name R. The subroutine also computes a new value of IR so no further effort will be needed on the part of the programmer to give values of IR. The next time RND is called, the subroutine will use the value that it calculated for IR the last time the subroutine was used.

Here is an example of how RND may be called to give 1000 random numbers:

```
      IR=12345
      DO 50 J=1,1000
      CALL RND (IR,R)
      WRITE (6,9) R
    9 FORMAT (' ',F20.7)
   50 CONTINUE
      STOP
      END
```

Random numbers can be made to fall into whatever integer range is needed. This next relationship can be used:

```
      INTR = AINT(R*N) + I
```

R is the random number given by RND; N is the number of numbers within the range; and I is the initial value of the range. For example, if you need random numbers within the range "21" through "36", the value of INTR could be computed this way:

```
      INTR = AINT(R*16)+21
```

There are 16 integer numbers within the range "21" through "36".

EXERCISES AND PROBLEMS

1. What is a random number? What are they used for? What FORTRAN function gives random numbers?

2. If the entire range of random numbers were to be divided exactly in half, which numbers would you expect to find in one of the halves and which in the other half? If the range were divided exactly in quarters, which numbers would you expect to find in each of the quarters?

3. How do you use RND to get the same "standard" sequence of "random" numbers over and over?

4. How do you use the RND function when it is necessary to obtain a repeatable sequence of random numbers, but not the system's standard sequence?

5. How do you use the RND function when it is necessary to obtain a sequence of random numbers that is completely unpredictable?

6. When would you want repeatable random numbers? When would you want unpredicable random numbers?

7. What formula can you give to have the system give you a series of random integers within some desired range? Explain the terms in the formula.

8. Write a FORTRAN program that computes the average of the first 1000 random numbers in the system's standard random number sequence.

CHAPTER 33

Direct Access

The subject of direct access is complex and requires a certain amount of programming maturity. In this chapter, we give some of the ideas concerning this subject and leave it to the student to do some independent research as needed.

One of the problems with the discussion of direct access is that its implementation varies from system to system. You may find that the procedures described in this chapter will not work on your system without some modifications.

Direct access is associated with magnetic disk. If an area has been reserved on disk for the storage of data, related data items (records) can be stored at scattered points on the disk. The exact location for each record is determined by applying a formula to a *key* data item within the record.

Assume we have the area on magnetic disk as shown in Figure 33-1.

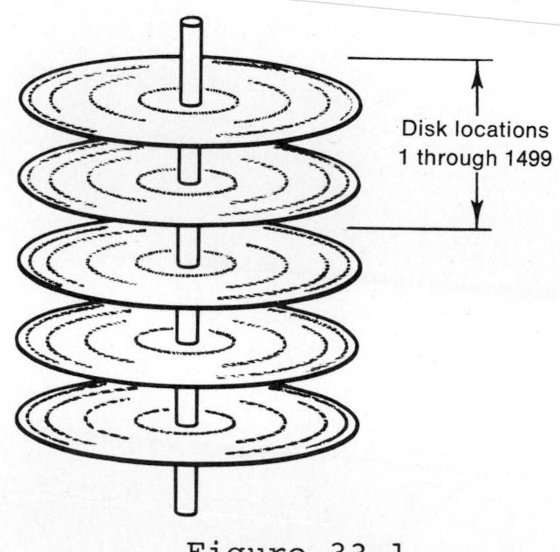

Figure 33-1

We can place a collection of related data values (a record) in locations 1, 2, 3, ..., 1499, depending upon what the associated formula indicates. That is, we can store a complete record at disk address 1, disk address 2, etc.

Let's consider a concrete example. Suppose we have the data card shown in Figure 33-2.

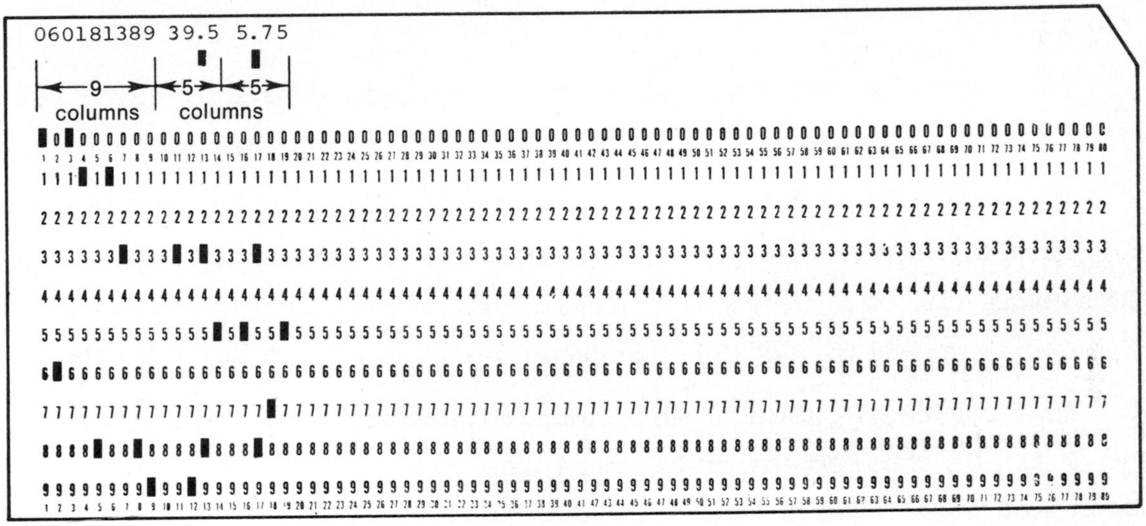

060181389 39.5 5.75

Figure 33-2

The leftmost number is a social security number, the middle value represents hours worked, and the rightmost value represents pay rate. The information on the card is called a record because the three data items are related. The social security number identifies an individual; the hours worked value tells how many hours that person worked last week; and the pay rate value tells what the person's pay rate is.

We want to read the card, then store the record upon some record location on the disk between disk locations 1 and 1500.

Let us first read the card:

```
      CHARACTER N*9
    2 READ (5,8,END=50) N,H,R
    8 FORMAT (A9,2F5.0)
```

At this point, N holds the character value "060181389", H holds the value "39.5", and R holds the value "5.75". The next step is to break up the value "060181389" into several integer values so that a formula can be applied to them. We can employ DECODE to accomplish this task:

```
      DECODE (N,88) I,J,K,L
   88 FORMAT (I3,3I2)
      M=I+J+K+L
```

At this point, I holds the value "60"; J holds the value "18"; K holds the value "13"; L holds the value "89"; and M holds the value "180" (the sum of I, J, K, and L). The value 180 is the location upon the disk where the record is to be stored.

The formula that was applied to obtain the address "180" was rather simple. In actual practice, formulas are more complex.

To store the record at location 180, we employ this WRITE command:

```
      WRITE (20'M) N,H,R
```

No FORMAT is used. The command causes the values of N, H, and R to be stored in file 20. The record is stored at disk location 180. This is the value that M has.

A corresponding job control language card such as this one

```
      $  DISK 20,1500,RANDOM
```

causes a file to be set up for the application described here.

To retrieve a record that has been stored randomly (by use of an equation applied to a key value), the *same formula* must be applied when a record needs to be retrieved.

The READ statement that reads a record from file 20 is one like this:

```
      READ (20'M) N,H,R
```

Again no FORMAT is used. Whatever was stored as a record is now retrieved as the same record. M tells where the record is.

Putting all these ideas into a complete program, we have this:

```
      CHARACTER N*9,NN*9
    2 READ (5,8,END=50) N,H,R
    8 FORMAT (A9,2F5.0)
      DECODE (N,88) I,J,K,L
   88 FORMAT (I3,3I2)
```

```
      M=I+J+K+L
      WRITE (20'M) N,H,R
      GO TO 2
   50 NN='443072346'
      DECODE (NN,88) I,J,K,L
      M=I+J+K+L
      READ (20'M) N,H,R
      WRITE (6,99) N,H,R
   99 FORMAT (' ',A9,2F10.2)
      STOP
      END
```

This program randomly stores several records on magnetic disk (file 20). Then it assigns the social security number "443072346" to NN and finds the stored record having that same social security number. The record is located at disk location 519 (M=443+7+23+46).

The retrieved record is printed.

In actual practice, there are several problems to be solved. They are:

1. How many disk locations should there be reserved for the most effective use of the disk?
2. What should the randomizing formula be?
3. What should the program do if a record tries to store itself at the same disk location that another record has already occupied? (Social Security numbers "443072346" and "336837624" attempt to randomize to the same disk location, 519, for example.)

We leave these questions for the student to resolve if he or she ever has to access records directly from randomly organized files.

EXERCISES AND PROBLEMS

1. What is meant by the term "direct access"? Discuss how records are stored upon disk and retrieved. What are some of the problems associated with direct access?

2. What are the special FORTRAN statements that allow the direct access of randomly organized files? How are random files defined?

CHAPTER 34

Additional FORTRAN Features

We have now covered the most useful features of FORTRAN. There are, however, a few more features that every programmer should be at least aware of.

ASSIGNED GO TO

The ASSIGNED GO TO statement is a statement that has this form:

```
GO TO N,(17,25,36,47,9)
```

The program jumps to statement 17, 25, 36, 47, or 9 depending upon what statement number was assigned earlier to N. The ASSIGN statement was used to give the statement number. Example:

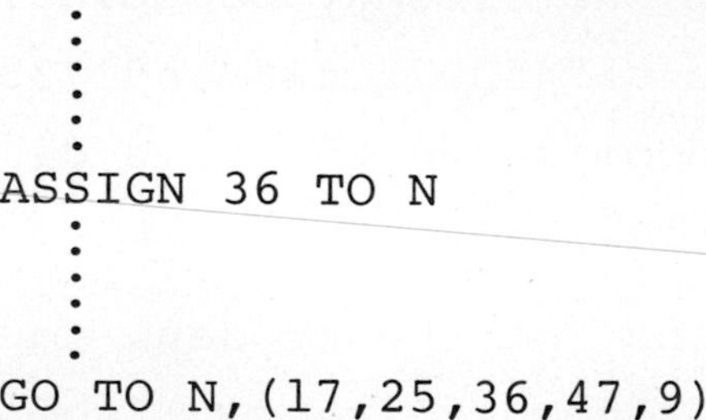

```
      .
      .
      .
ASSIGN 36 TO N
      .
      .
      .
GO TO N,(17,25,36,47,9)
```

The program jumps to statement 36. (There may be as many statement numbers within parentheses as required.)

The correct way to assign a statement number to the GO TO variable name is with the ASSIGN statement. Thus,

```
ASSIGN 36 TO N
```

is acceptable but

```
N=36
```

will not work.

The variable name given in the ASSIGNED GO TO statement must be an integer name. That name may not be used in arithmetic expressions.

Another, simpler way to use the ASSIGNED GO TO is this:

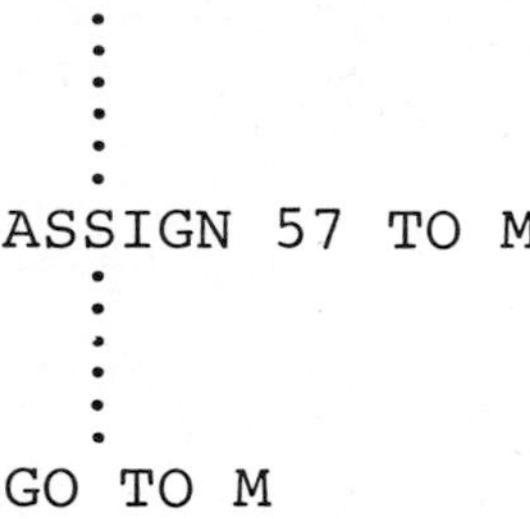

```
    .
    .
    .
ASSIGN 57 TO M
    .
    .
    .
GO TO M
```

The program jumps to statement 57. The assignment of a statement number to a variable name is, as before, made with the ASSIGN statement. The difference between the two assignments is simply the fact that one way you might get an error message during program's execution, the other, you won't. For example, if we have this:

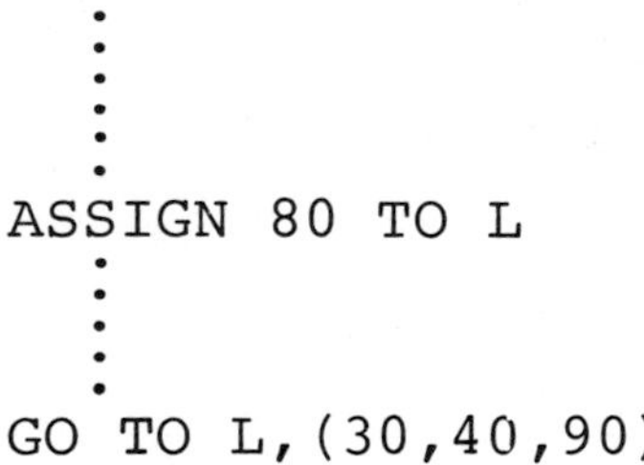

```
    .
    .
    .
ASSIGN 80 TO L
    .
    .
    .
GO TO L,(30,40,90)
```

the program will not jump to statement 80. The program will stop, giving an error message. The message will tell the user that statement 80 has been assigned to L but that the statement number is not given within parentheses in the ASSIGNED GO TO statement.

If the statements are:

```
ASSIGN 80 TO L
    .
    .
    .
GO TO L
```

the program jumps unconditionally to statement 80.

COMPUTED GO TO

The COMPUTED GO TO has this form:

```
GO TO (36,9,15,3,44),J
```

The program will jump to statement 36, 9, 15, 3, or 44 depending upon what integer value J currently holds. If a previous statement had read

```
J = 3
```

the program will jump to statement 15, the third one given in the set of parentheses. If the earlier statement had been

```
J = 5
```

the program would jump to statement 44, the fifth one within the set of parentheses.

There may be as many statement numbers within parentheses as required. The variable name given in the COMPUTED GO TO must have a value "1", "2", "3", etc. If it is "1", the program jumps to the *first* statement number given within parentheses; if "2", to the *second* statement number, etc.

The value assigned to the variable must not be outside the expected range for the COMPUTED GO TO being executed. That is, when you have this COMPUTED GO TO:

```
GO TO (3,91,7),K
```

K's value may only be "1", "2", or "3". If the value is outside this range, the program gives an error message during execution, then stops.

The controlling variable may be a real name. That value will be truncated to form an integer; the resulting integer will be used to control the action of the COMPUTED GO TO. An expression, too, may be used. Again, the expression must yield an integer value. These COMPUTED GO TO's are acceptable:

```
GO TO (9,7,14,9),(J*K)/2
GO TO (14,3,21),(P+R)*3.
```

In the first example, "(J*K)/2" must yield an integer value "1", "2", "3", or "4". In the second example, "(P+R)*3." must yield an integer value "1", "2", or "3".

Observe that the same statement number may be given more than once in the set of parentheses.

When the controlling element of a COMPUTED GO TO is a variable name, the name must be assigned a value with an arithmetic assignment statement like

```
          J = 4
```

or

```
          X = 3.
```

not with the ASSIGN statement. The ASSIGN statement is used only with ASSIGNED GO TO's.

TABULATING

The code T may be used in a FORMAT to tabulate. Example:

```
          WRITE (6,78) N,X
     78   FORMAT (' ',T30,I5,T60,F10.2)
```

The program will tabulate to print position 30, then print the value of N in accordance with the "I5" portion of the FORMAT. Then the program will tabulate to print position 60 and print the value of X according to the "F10.2" portion of the FORMAT. If N's value is "41673" and X's value is "323.72", the output will be that shown in Figure 34-1.

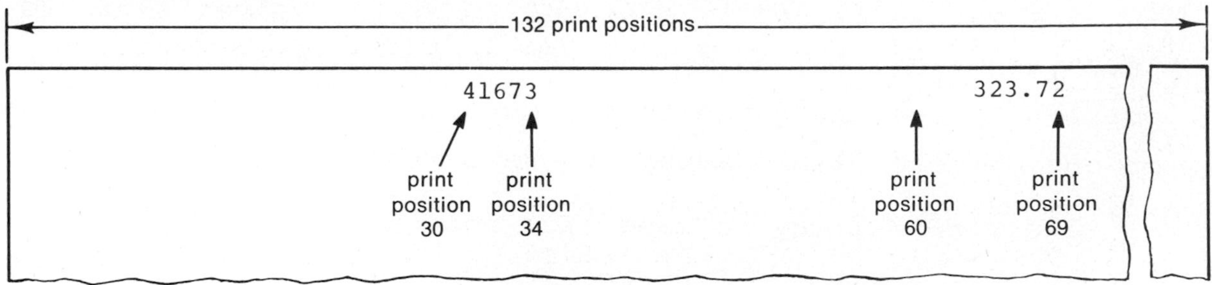

Figure 34-1

The result is the same as if the FORMAT had been written

```
     78   FORMAT (' ',29X,I5,25X,F10.2)
```

or

```
     78   FORMAT (' ',I34,F35.2)
```

Observe that the program tabulates to the print position specified and prints the first character of the required value there. If the value is shorter than the field allowed, one or more blanks is given at that point.

V FORMAT

The V format permits input values to be separated by commas or blanks on a punched card or in a timesharing file. Example:

```
      READ (5,33) W,X,Y,Z,K
   33 FORMAT (V)
```

The punched values on a card may appear as shown in Figure 34-2.

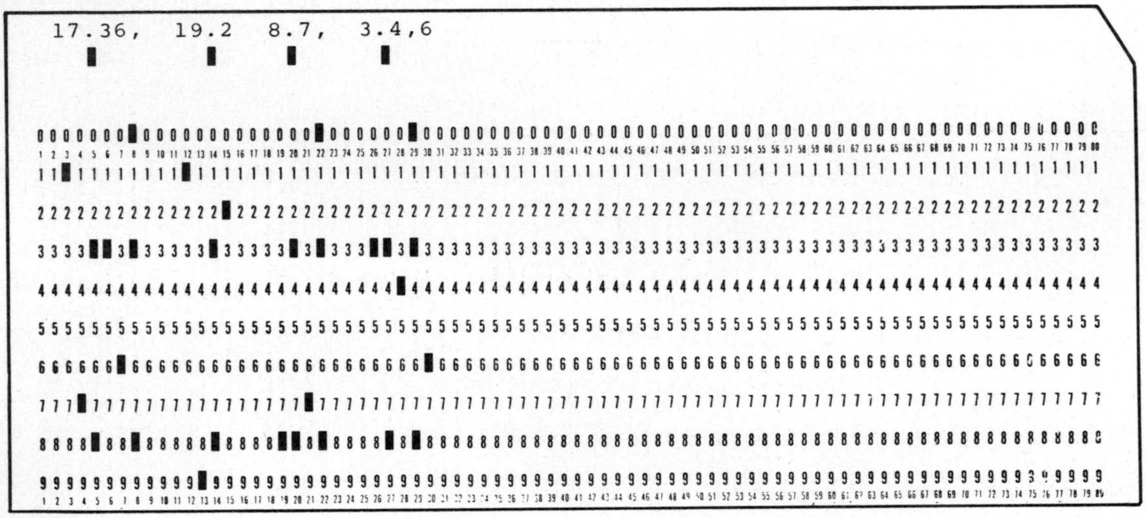

17.36, 19.2 8.7, 3.4,6

Figure 34-2

The value "17.36" is assigned to W; the value "19.2" to X; "8.7", to Y; "3.4", to Z; and "6" to K. Note that there is no particular spacing given on the card. Commas separate values, or one or more blanks separate them.

The V FORMAT may be used also for output. Example:

```
      A=3.5
      B=4.5
      C=3.9
      WRITE (6,9) A,B,C
    9 FORMAT (V)
      STOP
      END
```

The output will have the appearance shown in Figure 34-3.

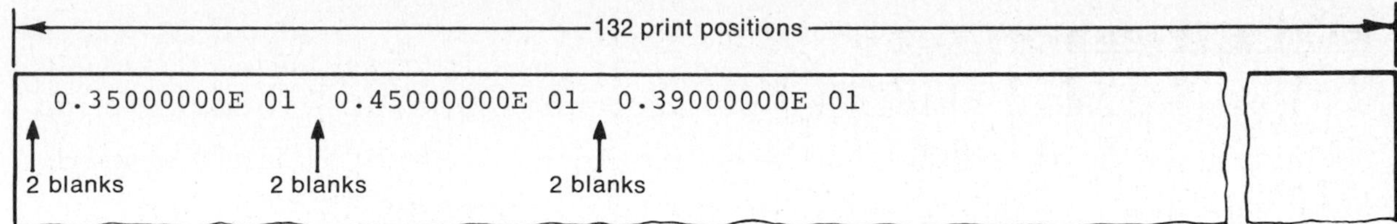

Figure 34-3

The values will be printed as if unformatted output had been requested; that is, as if the WRITE statement had been

```
        PRINT,A,B,C
```

and no FORMAT had been specified.

G FORMAT

The G FORMAT is a general-purpose FORMAT that may be used with real values. The FORMAT gives output in either "F" or "E" notation depending upon which notation is most effective. The computer decides which notation to use. Example:

```
        A=3.2568902
        B=456.23498
        C=6923.1235
        WRITE (6,9) A,B,C
      9 FORMAT (' ',3G15.3)
        STOP
        END
```

The output will be given as shown in Figure 34-4.

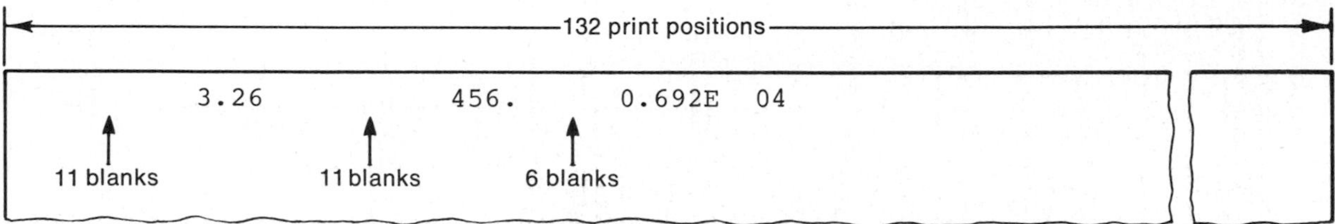

Figure 34-4

The FORMAT requires three digits to be given for each value. (That's what the "3" in "G15.3" specifies.) If the value can be given in the requested number of digits with the "F" FORMAT, then the "F" FORMAT is used; otherwise, the system uses the "E" FORMAT. Observe that the value of A can be given in rounded form in three digits. So can the value of B. But there is no way to give C's value within three digits in the "F" FORMAT; therefore, the system uses the "E" FORMAT.

EXTERNAL STATEMENT

The EXTERNAL statement permits the name of a function to be used as a parameter in a subroutine. Here is an example program that calls a subroutine named SUBTST.

```
      EXTERNAL SQRT,ALOG
      X=144.0
      Y=2.7182818
      CALL SUBTST (X,SQRT,ANS)
      WRITE (6,8) X,ANS
    8 FORMAT (' ','THE SQ. RT. OF ',F6.1,' IS',F6.1)
      CALL SUBTST (Y,ALOG,ANS)
      WRITE (6,9) Y,ANS
    9 FORMAT (' ','THE LOG OF ',F10.7,' IS',F6.1)
      STOP
      END
```

The subroutine is this:

```
      SUBROUTINE SUBTST (VAL,FUNCT,RESLT)
      RESLT = FUNCT (VAL)
      RETURN
      END
```

Since SQRT and ALOG have been named in the EXTERNAL statement, they are permitted to be used in the two CALL SUBTST statements. The subroutine first substitutes SQRT for FUNCT and obtains the square root of "144.0.". Then it substitutes ALOG for FUNCT and obtains the natural logarithm of "2.7182818".

The output from the program is shown in Figure 34-5.

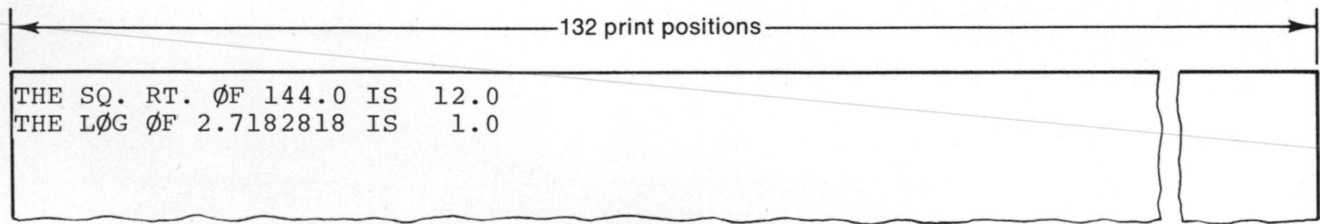

132 print positions
THE SQ. RT. ØF 144.0 IS 12.0
THE LØG ØF 2.7182818 IS   1.0

Figure 34-5

PAUSE

PAUSE is a statement that may be useful when operating in timesharing mode. It has limited utility value in the BATCH mode especially if programmers are not permitted to run their own programs.

When a program encounters PAUSE, it stops. Then if the user types RUN, it resumes executing. If the programmer types

STOP, the program terminates.

Here is a timesharing example showing PAUSE in use.

```
010     X=4.5
020     PAUSE 'IF DATA READY, TYPE RUN; ELSE, STOP'
030     WRITE (6,9) X
040 9   FORMAT (' ',F10.1)
050     STOP
060     END

READY

*RUN

   PAUSE    IF DATA READY, TYPE RUN; ELSE, STOP
??STOP

*RUN

   PAUSE    IF DATA READY, TYPE RUN; ELSE, STOP
??RUN
        4.5
```

The programmer ran the program twice. The first time, he or she typed STOP and the program terminated; the second time, the programmer typed RUN and the program continued.

EQUIVALENCE

The purpose of the EQUIVALENCE statement is to cause two or more variable names to share the same memory cell. Example:

```
EQUIVALENCE (A,W,T) (I,N)
```

The same memory locations will be referenced when anything affects either A, W, or T. Also, the same memory locations are referenced when anything affects either I or N.

Happy FORTRAN'ing!

EXERCISES AND PROBLEMS

1. What is an ASSIGNED GO TO? How is the word ASSIGN used?

2. What is the COMPUTED GO TO? How does a computed GO TO differ from an assigned GO TO?

3. What does the code "T" accomplish in FORMAT's? Give an example showing the use of "X", "I", and "F" in a FORMAT, then give the same FORMAT using "T".

4. How can the "V" FORMAT be used for the reading of input values? How can it be used for writing output?
5. How can the "G" FORMAT be used? Give some examples.
6. When would a programmer use the EXTERNAL statement?
7. Discuss the usefulness of PAUSE.
8. What does EQUIVALENCE accomplish?

Index

C

E

G

M

P

Q

R

S

T

W